CANDIDE
AND
PHILOSOPHICAL LETTERS

VOLTAIRE

CANDIDE

TRANSLATED BY RICHARD ALDINGTON

PHILOSOPHICAL

LETTERS

EDITED AND TRANSLATED BY
ERNEST DILWORTH

THE MODERN LIBRARY

NEW YORK

1992 Modern Library Edition

Biographical note copyright © 1992 by Random House, Inc.

Copyright 1956, © 1984 by Random House, Inc.

Copyright © 1985 by the Macmillan Publishing Company,
a division of Macmillan, Inc.

Copyright © 1961 by The Bobbs-Merrill, Inc.

Jacket portrait courtesy of Culver Pictures

Printed on recycled, acid-free paper.

Library of Congress Cataloging-in-Publication Data
Voltaire, 1694–1778.
  [Candide.   English.]
  Candide; and, Philosophical letters / Voltaire
     p.   cm.
  Translation of: Candide and Lettres philosophiques.
  ISBN 0-679-60003-5 (acid-free paper)
  1. Voltaire, 1694–1778—Translations into English.
2. Great Britain—Civilization—18th century.   3. Philosophy,
Modern—18th century.   4. Imaginary letters.
I. Voltaire, 1694–1778.   Lettres philosophiques.   English. 1992.
II. Title: Candide   III. Title: Philosophical letters
  PQ2075   1992
843'.5—dc20   92-50226

Manufactured in the United States of America

2 4 6 8 9 7 5 3 1

VOLTAIRE

Voltaire (François-Marie Arouet) was born in Paris in 1694, the son of a notary who later served as a tax collector for the Royal Exchequer. He studied with the Jesuits and at an early age became acquainted with the free-thinking circles of the capital, including the celebrated courtesan Ninon de l'Enclos, then in her eighties, who left him a small legacy, and the libertines and poets associated with the Society of the Temple. In 1717 he was imprisoned in the Bastille for eleven months as a result of a satirical poem with which his name had been linked. Shortly after he was released, the earliest of his verse-tragedies, *Oedipe*, was performed at the Comedie-Française. By this time he had adopted the pseudonym Voltaire, the provenance of which is uncertain. His literary reputation was further consolidated with *La Henriade*, published in Geneva in 1723 as *La Ligue*, a neoclassical epic poem about Henri IV, the first Bourbon king of France, who converted to Catholicism ("Paris is worth a mass," he remarked).

Financial speculations made Voltaire wealthy, and he was at the center of Parisian intellectual life until he was again briefly imprisoned in the Bastille (for threatening the Chevalier de Rohan-Chabot with a duel) before going into voluntary exile in England in 1726. He remained there for three years, studying English literature and institutions, and enjoying the friendship of Pope, Swift, Congreve, Berkeley, and many others. On his return to Paris he resumed his extraordinarily active literary life, turning out a string of tragedies, including *Zaire* (1732) and *The Death of Caesar* (1731), a history of the reign of Charles XII, and literary essays. *Lettres Philosophiques*, also known as *The English Letters* (1734), drawing on his observations of English life and politics, was an overt criticism of the ancien régime, and its appearance had repercussions that led Voltaire to leave Paris.

For the next ten years Voltaire took up residence at the home of his mistress, Mme. du Châtelet, at Cirey in Lorraine. After 1743 he temporarily regained favor at court and was admitted to the Académie Française in 1746. *Zadig* (1747) was the first of the philosophical tales that were to be his most enduringly popular works. Following the death of Mme. du Châtelet he accepted an invitation from Frederick the Great of Prussia to his court at Potsdam, where during a three-year stay he completed his monumental historical study *The Century of Louis XIV* (1751). A quarrel with the king led to his departure from Prussia in 1753; he now established himself in Switzerland, continuing to publish poetry and drama and contributing articles to Diderot's *Encyclopedia*. Under pressure from Swiss Calvinists he moved to

Ferney, a French town close to the Swiss frontier, where he settled for the rest of his life, maintaining a lavish estate and receiving a steady stream of international visitors, including James Boswell and Edward Gibbon.

Of the many writings produced in Voltaire's latter years, the most celebrated are *Candide* (1759), a satire on the philosophical optimism of Leibniz which has long been his most popular work, and *The Philosophical Dictionary* (1764), a compendium of his views on such topics as atheism, Christianity, idolatry, free will, miracles, and tolerance. "It is clear," he wrote, "that every individual who persecutes a man, his brother, because he does not agree with him, is a monster," and in his last years he became actively involved in righting what he regarded as miscarriages of justice and religious persecutions. He made a final return to Paris in 1778 in connection with the performance of his last tragedy, *Irène*. He died a few weeks later in a house on what is now the Quai Voltaire. He was refused a Christian burial in Paris, but thirteen years later was installed in the Pantheon, where homage was paid to him until the 1860s, when his coffin was opened and found to be empty.

CANDIDE
or Optimism

CHAPTER I

How Candide was brought up in a noble castle and how he was expelled from the same

IN the castle of Baron Thunder-ten-tronckh in Westphalia there lived a youth, endowed by Nature with the most gentle character. His face was the expression of his soul. His judgment was quite honest and he was extremely simpleminded; and this was the reason, I think, that he was named Candide. Old servants in the house suspected that he was the son of the Baron's sister and a decent honest gentleman of the neighborhood, whom this young lady would never marry because he could only prove seventy-one quarterings,[1] and the rest of his genealogical tree was lost, owing to the injuries of time. The Baron was one of the most powerful lords in Westphalia, for his castle possessed a door and windows. His Great Hall was even decorated with a piece of tapestry. The dogs in his stable-yards formed a pack of hounds when necessary; his grooms were his huntsmen; the village curate was his Grand Almoner. They all called him "My Lord," and laughed heartily at his stories. The Baroness weighed about three hundred and fifty pounds, was therefore greatly respected, and did the honors of the house with a dignity which rendered her still more respectable. Her daughter Cunegonde, aged seventeen, was rosy-cheeked, fresh, plump and tempting. The Baron's son appeared in every respect worthy of his father. The tutor Pangloss was the oracle of the house, and little Candide followed his lessons with all the candor of his age and character. Pan-

[1] A quartering of a nobility represents a generation.

gloss taught metaphysico-theologo-cosmolonigology. He proved admirably that there is no effect without a cause and that in this best of all possible worlds, My Lord the Baron's castle was the best of castles and his wife the best of all possible Baronesses. "'Tis demonstrated," said he, "that things cannot be otherwise; for, since everything is made for an end, everything is necessarily for the best end. Observe that noses were made to wear spectacles; and so we have spectacles. Legs were visibly instituted to be breeched, and we have breeches. Stones were formed to be quarried and to build castles; and My Lord has a very noble castle; the greatest Baron in the province should have the best house; and as pigs were made to be eaten, we eat pork all the year round; consequently, those who have asserted that all is well talk nonsense; they ought to have said that all is for the best." Candide listened attentively and believed innocently; for he thought Mademoiselle Cunegonde extremely beautiful, although he was never bold enough to tell her so. He decided that after the happiness of being born Baron of Thunder-ten-tronckh, the second degree of happiness was to be Mademoiselle Cunegonde; the third, to see her every day; and the fourth to listen to Doctor Pangloss, the greatest philosopher of the province and therefore of the whole world. One day when Cunegonde was walking near the castle, in a little wood which was called The Park, she observed Doctor Pangloss in the bushes, giving a lesson in experimental physics to her mother's waiting-maid, a very pretty and docile brunette. Mademoiselle Cunegonde had a great inclination for science and watched breathlessly the reiterated experiments she witnessed; she observed clearly the Doctor's sufficient reason, the effects and the causes, and returned home very much excited, pensive, filled with the desire of learning, reflecting that she might be the sufficient reason of young Candide and that he might be hers.

On her way back to the castle she met Candide and blushed; Candide also blushed. She bade him good-morning in a hesitating voice; Candide replied without knowing what he was saying. Next day, when they left the table after dinner, Cunegonde and Candide found themselves behind a screen; Cunegonde dropped her handkerchief, Candide picked it up; she innocently held his hand; the young man innocently kissed the young lady's hand with remarkable vivacity, tenderness and grace; their lips met, their eyes sparkled, their knees trembled, their hands wandered. Baron Thunder-ten-tronckh passed near the screen, and, observing this cause and effect, expelled Candide from the castle by kicking him in the backside frequently and hard. Cunegonde swooned; when she recovered her senses, the Baroness slapped her in the face; and all was in consternation in the noblest and most agreeable of all possible castles.

CHAPTER II

What happened to Candide among the Bulgarians[1]

CANDIDE, expelled from the earthly paradise, wandered for a long time without knowing where he was going, turning up his eyes to Heaven, gazing back frequently at the noblest of castles which held the most beautiful of young Baronesses; he lay down to sleep supperless between two furrows in the open fields: it snowed heavily in large flakes. The next morning the shivering Candide, penniless, dying of

[1] The Bulgarians represent the Prussians in the Seven Years War.

cold and exhaustion, dragged himself towards the neighboring town, which was called Waldberghoff-trarbk-dikdorff. He halted sadly at the door of an inn. Two men dressed in blue noticed him. "Comrade," said one, "there's a well-built young man of the right height." They went up to Candide and very civilly invited him to dinner. "Gentlemen," said Candide with charming modesty, "you do me a great honor, but I have no money to pay my share." "Ah, sir," said one of the men in blue, "persons of your figure and merit never pay anything; are you not five feet five tall?" "Yes, gentlemen," said he, bowing, "that is my height." "Ah, sir, come to table; we will not only pay your expenses, we will never allow a man like you to be short of money; men were only made to help each other." "You are in the right," said Candide, "that is what Doctor Pangloss was always telling me, and I see that everything is for the best." They begged him to accept a few crowns, he took them and wished to give them an IOU, they refused to take it and all sat down to table. "Do you not love tenderly . . ." "Oh, yes," said he. "I love Mademoiselle Cunegonde tenderly." "No," said one of the gentlemen. "We were asking if you do not tenderly love the King of the Bulgarians." "Not a bit," said he, "for I have never seen him." "What! He is the most charming of Kings, and you must drink his health." "Oh, gladly, gentlemen." And he drank. "That is sufficient," he was told. "You are now the support, the aid, the defender, the hero of the Bulgarians, your fortune is made and your glory assured." They immediately put irons on his legs and took him to a regiment. He was made to turn to the right and left, to raise the ramrod and return the ramrod, to take aim, to fire, to march double time, and he was given thirty strokes with a stick; the next day he drilled not quite so badly, and received only twenty strokes; the day after, he only had ten and was looked on as a prodigy by his comrades. Candide was completely mystified and could not make out how he was a hero. One fine spring day he thought he would take a walk, going straight ahead, in the belief that to use his legs as he pleased was a privilege of the human species as well as of animals. He had not gone two leagues when four other heroes, each six feet tall, fell upon him, bound him and dragged him back to a cell. He was asked by his judges whether he would rather be thrashed thirty-six times by the whole regiment or receive a dozen lead bullets at once in his brain. Although he protested that men's wills are free and that he wanted neither one nor the other, he had to make a choice; by virtue of that gift of God which is called *liberty*, he determined to run the gauntlet thirty-six times and actually did so twice. There were two thousand men in the regiment. That made four thousand strokes which laid bare the muscles and nerves from his neck to his backside. As they were about to proceed to a third turn, Candide, utterly exhausted, begged as a favor that they would be so kind as to smash his head; he obtained this favor; they bound his eyes and he was made to kneel down. At that moment the King of the Bulgarians came by and inquired the victim's crime, and as this King was possessed of a vast genius, he perceived from what he learned about Candide that he was a young metaphysician very ignorant in worldly matters, and therefore pardoned him with a clemency which will be praised in all newspapers and all ages. An honest surgeon healed Candide in three weeks with the ointments recommended by Dioscorides. He had already regained a little skin and could walk when the King of the Bulgarians went to war with the King of the Abares.

CHAPTER III

*How Candide escaped from the Bulgarians and what
became of him*

NOTHING could be smarter, more splendid, more brilliant, better drawn up than the two armies. Trumpets, fifes, hautboys, drums, cannons, formed a harmony such as has never been heard even in hell. The cannons first of all laid flat about six thousand men on each side; then the musketry removed from the best of worlds some nine or ten thousand blackguards who infested its surface. The bayonet also was the sufficient reason for the death of some thousands of men. The whole might amount to thirty thousand souls. Candide, who trembled like a philosopher, hid himself as well as he could during this heroic butchery. At last, while the two Kings each commanded a Te Deum in his camp, Candide decided to go elsewhere to reason about effects and causes. He clambered over heaps of dead and dying men and reached a neighboring village, which was in ashes; it was an Abare village which the Bulgarians had burned in accordance with international law. Here, old men dazed with blows watched the dying agonies of their murdered wives who clutched their children to their bleeding breasts; there, disembowelled girls who had been made to satisfy the natural appetites of heroes gasped their last sighs; others, half-burned, begged to be put to death. Brains were scattered on the ground among dismembered arms and legs. Candide fled to another village as fast as he could; it belonged to the Bulgarians, and Abarian heroes had treated it in the same way. Candide, stumbling over

quivering limbs or across ruins, at last escaped from the
theatre of war, carrying a little food in his knapsack, and
never forgetting Mademoiselle Cunegonde. His provisions
were all gone when he reached Holland; but, having heard
that everyone in that country was rich and a Christian, he
had no doubt at all but that he would be as well treated as
he had been in the Baron's castle before he had been
expelled on account of Mademoiselle Cunegonde's pretty
eyes. He asked alms of several grave persons, who all
replied that if he continued in that way he would be shut
up in a house of correction to teach him how to live. He
then addressed himself to a man who had been discoursing
on charity in a large assembly for an hour on end. This orator, glancing at him askance, said: "What are you doing
here? Are you for the good cause?" "There is no effect
without a cause," said Candide modestly. "Everything is
necessarily linked up and arranged for the best. It was necessary that I should be expelled from the company of
Mademoiselle Cunegonde, that I ran the gauntlet, and that
I beg my bread until I can earn it; all this could not have
happened differently." "My friend," said the orator, "do
you believe that the Pope is Anti-Christ?" "I had never
heard so before," said Candide, "but whether he is or isn't,
I am starving." "You don't deserve to eat," said the other.
"Hence, rascal; hence, you wretch; and never come near me
again." The orator's wife thrust her head out of the window and seeing a man who did not believe that the Pope
was Anti-Christ, she poured on his head a full . . . O
Heavens! To what excess religious zeal is carried by ladies!
A man who had not been baptized, an honest Anabaptist
named Jacques, saw the cruel and ignominious treatment
of one of his brothers, a featherless two-legged creature
with a soul; he took him home, cleaned him up, gave him
bread and beer, presented him with two florins, and even

offered to teach him to work at the manufacture of Persian stuffs which are made in Holland. Candide threw himself at the man's feet, exclaiming: "Doctor Pangloss was right in telling me that all is for the best in this world, for I am vastly more touched by your extreme generosity than by the harshness of the gentleman in the black cloak and his good lady." The next day when he walked out he met a beggar covered with sores, dull-eyed, with the end of his nose fallen away, his mouth awry, his teeth black, who talked huskily, was tormented with a violent cough and spat out a tooth at every cough.

CHAPTER IV

*How Candide met his old master in philosophy,
Doctor Pangloss, and what happened*

CANDIDE, moved even more by compassion than by horror, gave this horrible beggar the two florins he had received from the honest Anabaptist, Jacques. The phantom gazed fixedly at him, shed tears and threw its arms round his neck. Candide recoiled in terror. "Alas!" said the wretch to the other wretch, "don't you recognize your dear Pangloss?" "What do I hear? You, my dear master! You, in this horrible state! What misfortune has happened to you? Why are you no longer in the noblest of castles? What has become of Mademoiselle Cunegonde, the pearl of young ladies, the masterpiece of Nature?" "I am exhausted," said Pangloss. Candide immediately took him to the Anabaptist's stable where he gave him a little bread to eat; and when Pangloss had recovered: "Well!" said he. "Cunegonde?" "Dead," replied the other. At this word Candide swooned; his friend restored him to his senses with a little bad vinegar which happened to be in the stable. Candide opened his eyes. "Cunegonde dead! Ah! best of worlds, where are you? But what illness did she die of? Was it because she saw me kicked out of her father's noble castle?" "No," said Pangloss. "She was disembowelled by Bulgarian soldiers, after having been raped to the limit of possibility; they broke the Baron's head when he tried to defend her; the Baroness was cut to pieces; my poor pupil was treated exactly like his sister, and as to the castle, there is not one stone standing on another, not a barn, not a sheep, not a duck, not a tree; but we were well avenged, for the Abares did exactly the same to a neighboring barony which belonged to a Bulgarian Lord." At this, Candide swooned again; but, having recovered and having said all that he ought to say, he inquired the cause and effect, the sufficient reason which had reduced Pangloss to so piteous a state. "Alas!" said Pangloss, "'tis love; love, the consoler of the human race, the preserver of the universe, the soul of all tender creatures, gentle love." "Alas!" said Candide, "I am acquainted with this love, this sovereign of hearts, this soul of our soul; it has never brought me anything but one kiss and twenty kicks in the backside. How could this beautiful cause produce in you so abominable an effect?" Pangloss replied as follows: "My dear Candide! You remember Paquette, the maid-servant of our august Baroness; in her arms I enjoyed the delights of Paradise which have produced the tortures of Hell by which you see I am devoured; she was infected and perhaps is dead. Paquette received this present from a most learned monk, who had it from the source; for he received it from an old countess, who had it from a cavalry captain, who owed it to a marchioness, who derived it from a page, who had received it from a Jesuit, who, when a novice, had it in a direct line from one of the companions of Christopher Columbus. For my part, I shall not give it to anyone, for I am dying." "O Pangloss!" exclaimed Candide, "this is a strange genealogy! Wasn't the devil at the root of it?" "Not at all," replied that great man. "It was something indispensable in this best of worlds, a necessary ingredient; for, if Columbus in an island of America had not caught this disease, which poisons the source of generation, and often indeed prevents generation, we should not have chocolate and cochineal; it must also be noticed that hitherto in our continent this disease is peculiar to us, like theological disputes. The Turks, the Indians, the Persians, the Chinese, the Siamese and the Japanese are not yet familiar with it; but there is a sufficient reason why they in their turn should become familiar with it in a few centuries. Meanwhile, it has made marvelous progress among us, and especially in those large armies composed of honest, wellbred stipendiaries who decide the destiny of States; it may be asserted that when thirty thousand men fight a pitched battle against an equal number of troops, there are about twenty thousand with the pox on either side." "Admirable!" said Candide. "But you must get cured." "How can I?" said Pangloss. "I haven't a sou, my friend, and in the whole extent of this globe, you cannot be bled or receive an enema without paying or without someone paying for you." This last speech determined Candide; he went and threw himself at the feet of his charitable Anabaptist, Jacques, and drew so touching a picture of the state to which his friend was reduced that the good easy man did not hesitate to succor Pangloss; he had him cured at his own expense. In this cure Pangloss only lost one eye and one ear. He could write well and knew arithmetic perfectly. The Anabaptist made him his book-keeper. At the end of two months he was compelled to go to Lisbon on business and took his two philosophers on the boat with him. Pangloss explained to him how everything was for the best. Jacques was not of this opinion. "Men," said he, "must have corrupted nature a little, for they were not born wolves, and they have become wolves. God did not give them twenty-four-pounder cannons or bayonets, and they have made bayonets and cannons to destroy each other. I might bring bankruptcies into the account and Justice which seizes the goods of bankrupts in order to deprive the creditors of them." "It was all indispensable," replied the one-eyed doctor, "and private misfortunes make the public good, so that the more private misfortunes there are, the more everything is well." While he was reasoning, the air grew dark, the winds blew from the four quarters of the globe and the ship was attacked by the most horrible tempest in sight of the port of Lisbon.

CHAPTER V

Storm, shipwreck, earthquake, and what happened to Dr. Pangloss, to Candide and the Anabaptist Jacques

HALF the enfeebled passengers, suffering from that inconceivable anguish which the rolling of a ship causes in the nerves and in all the humours of bodies shaken in contrary directions, did not retain strength enough even to trouble about the danger. The other half screamed and prayed; the sails were torn, the masts broken, the vessel leaking. Those worked who could, no one cooperated, no one commanded.

The Anabaptist tried to help the crew a little; he was on the main-deck; a furious sailor struck him violently and stretched him on the deck; but the blow he delivered gave the sailor so violent a shock that he fell head-first out of the ship. He remained hanging and clinging to part of the broken mast. The good Jacques ran to his aid, helped him to climb back, and from the effort he made was flung into the sea in full view of the sailor, who allowed him to drown without condescending even to look at him. Candide came up, saw his benefactor reappear for a moment and then be engulfed for ever. He tried to throw himself after him into the sea; he was prevented by the philosopher Pangloss, who proved to him that the Lisbon roads had been expressly created for the Anabaptist to be drowned in them. While he was proving this *a priori*, the vessel sank, and every one perished except Pangloss, Candide and the brutal sailor who had drowned the virtuous Anabaptist; the blackguard swam successfully to the shore and Pangloss and Candide were carried there on a plank. When they had recovered a little, they walked toward Lisbon; they had a little money by the help of which they hoped to be saved from hunger after having escaped the storm. Weeping the death of their benefactor, they had scarcely set foot in the town when they felt the earth tremble under their feet; the sea rose in foaming masses in the port and smashed the ships which rode at anchor. Whirlwinds of flame and ashes covered the streets and squares; the houses collapsed, the roofs were thrown upon the foundations, and the foundations were scattered; thirty thousand inhabitants of every age and both sexes were crushed under the ruins. Whistling and swearing, the sailor said: "There'll be something to pick up here." "What can be the sufficient reason for this phenomenon?" said Pangloss. "It is the last day!" cried Candide. The sailor immediately ran among the debris, dared death to find money, found it, seized it, got drunk, and having slept off his wine, purchased the favors of the first woman of goodwill he met on the ruins of the houses and among the dead and dying. Pangloss, however, pulled him by the sleeve. "My friend," said he, "this is not well, you are disregarding universal reason, you choose the wrong time." "Blood and 'ounds!" he retorted. "I am a sailor and I was born in Batavia; four times have I stamped on the crucifix during four voyages to Japan; you have found the right man for your universal reason!" Candide had been hurt by some falling stones; he lay in the street covered with debris. He said to Pangloss: "Alas! Get me a little wine and oil; I am dying." "This earthquake is not a new thing," replied Pangloss. "The town of Lima felt the same shocks in America last year; similar causes produce similar effects; there must certainly be a train of sulphur underground from Lima to Lisbon." "Nothing is more probable," replied Candide; "but, for God's sake, a little oil and wine." "What do you mean, probable?" replied the philosopher; "I maintain that it is proved." Candide lost consciousness, and Pangloss brought him a little water from a neighboring fountain. Next day they found a little food as they wandered among the ruins and regained a little strength. Afterwards they worked like others to help the inhabitants who had escaped death. Some citizens they had assisted gave them as good a dinner as could be expected in such a disaster; true, it was a dreary meal; the hosts watered their bread with their tears, but Pangloss consoled them by assuring them that things could not be otherwise. "For," said he, "all this is for the best; for, if there is a volcano at Lisbon, it cannot be anywhere else; for it is impossible that things should not be where they are; for all is well." A little, dark man, a familiar of the Inquisition, who sat beside him, politely took up the conversation, and said: "Apparently, you do not believe in original sin; for, if everything is for the best, there was neither fall nor punishment." "I most humbly beg your excellency's pardon," replied Pangloss still more politely, "for the fall of man and the curse necessarily entered into the best of all possible worlds." "Then you do not believe in free-will?" said the familiar. "Your excellency will pardon me," said Pangloss; "free-will can exist with absolute necessity; for it was necessary that we should be free; for in short, limited will . . ." Pangloss was in the middle of his phrase when the familiar nodded to his armed attendant who was pouring out port or Oporto wine for him.

CHAPTER VI

How a splendid auto-da-fé was held to prevent earthquakes and how Candide was flogged

AFTER the earthquake which destroyed three-quarters of Lisbon, the wise men of that country could discover no more efficacious way of preventing a total ruin than by giving the people a splendid *auto-da-fé*. It was decided by the university of Coimbre that the sight of several persons being slowly burned in great ceremony is an infallible secret for preventing earthquakes. Consequently they had arrested a Biscayan convicted of having married his fellow-godmother, and two Portuguese who, when eating a chicken, had thrown away the fat; after dinner they came and bound Dr. Pangloss and his disciple Candide, one because he had spoken and the other because he had listened with an air of approbation; they were both carried separately to extremely cool apartments, where there was never any discomfort from the sun; a week afterwards each was dressed in a sanbenito and their heads were ornamented with paper mitres; Candide's mitre and sanbenito were painted with flames upside down and with devils who had neither tails nor claws; but Pangloss's devils had claws and tails, and his flames were upright. Dressed in this manner they marched in procession and listened to a most pathetic sermon, followed by lovely plain-song music. Candide was flogged in time to the music, while the singing went on; the Biscayan and the two men who had not wanted to eat fat were burned, and Pangloss was hanged, although this is not the custom. The very same day, the earth shook again with a terrible clamor. Candide, terrified, dumbfounded, bewildered, covered with blood, quivering from head to foot, said to himself: "If this is the best of all possible worlds, what are the others? Let it pass that I was flogged, for I was flogged by the Bulgarians, but, O my dear Pangloss! The greatest of philosophers! Must I see you hanged without knowing why! O my dear Anabaptist! The best of men! Was it necessary that you should be drowned in port! O Mademoiselle Cunegonde! The pearl of women! Was it necessary that your belly should be slit!" He was returning, scarcely able to support himself, preached at, flogged, absolved and blessed, when an old woman accosted him and said: "Courage, my son, follow me."

CHAPTER VII

*How an old woman took care of Candide and how
he regained that which he loved*

CANDIDE did not take courage, but he followed the old
woman to a hovel; she gave him a pot of ointment to rub
on, and left him food and drink; she pointed out a fairly
clean bed; near the bed there was a suit of clothes. "Eat,
drink, sleep," said she, "and may our Lady of Atocha, my
Lord Saint Anthony of Padua and my Lord Saint James of
Compostella take care of you; I shall come back tomorrow."
Candide, still amazed by all he had seen, by all he had suffered, and still more by the old woman's charity, tried to
kiss her hand. "'Tis not my hand you should kiss," said the
old woman, "I shall come back to-morrow. Rub on the ointment, eat and sleep." In spite of all his misfortune, Candide
ate and went to sleep. Next day the old woman brought him
breakfast, examined his back and smeared him with another
ointment; later she brought him dinner, and returned in the
evening with supper. The next day she went through the
same ceremony. "Who are you?" Candide kept asking her.
"Who has inspired you with so much kindness? How can I
thank you?" The good woman never made any reply; she
returned in the evening but without any supper. "Come
with me," said she, "and do not speak a word." She took
him by the arm and walked into the country with him for
about a quarter of a mile; they came to an isolated house,
surrounded with gardens and canals. The old woman
knocked at a little door. It was opened; she led Candide up
a back stairway into a gilded apartment, left him on a bro-

caded sofa, shut the door and went away. Candide thought
he was dreaming, and felt that his whole life was a bad
dream and the present moment an agreeable dream. The old
woman soon reappeared; she was supporting with some difficulty a trembling woman of majestic stature, glittering
with precious stones and covered with a veil. "Remove the
veil," said the old woman to Candide. The young man
advanced and lifted the veil with a timid hand. What a
moment! What a surprise! He thought he saw Mademoiselle
Cunegonde, in fact he was looking at her, it was she herself. His strength failed him, he could not utter a word and
fell at her feet. Cunegonde fell on the sofa. The old woman
dosed them with distilled waters; they recovered their senses
and began to speak: at first they uttered only broken words,
questions and answers at cross purposes, sighs, tears, excla-
mations. The old woman advised them to make less noise
and left them alone. "What! Is it you?" said Candide. "You
are alive, and I find you here in Portugal! Then you were
not raped? Your belly was not slit, as the philosopher Pangloss assured me?" "Yes, indeed," said the fair Cunegonde;
"but those two accidents are not always fatal." "But your
father and mother were killed?" "'Tis only too true," said
Cunegonde, weeping. "And your brother?" "My brother
was killed too." "And why are you in Portugal? And how
did you know I was here? And by what strange adventure
have you brought me to this house?" "I will tell you everything," replied the lady, "but first of all you must tell me
everything that has happened to you since the innocent kiss
you gave me and the kicks you received." Candide obeyed
with profound respect; and, although he was bewildered,
although his voice was weak and trembling, although his
back was still a little painful, he related in the most natural
manner all he had endured since the moment of their sepa-
ration. Cunegonde raised her eyes to heaven; she shed tears

at the death of the good Anabaptist and Pangloss, after
which she spoke as follows to Candide, who did not miss a
word and devoured her with his eyes.

CHAPTER VIII

Cunegonde's story

"I was fast asleep in bed when it pleased Heaven to send
the Bulgarians to our noble castle of Thunder-ten-tronckh;
they murdered my father and brother and cut my mother
to pieces. A large Bulgarian six feet tall, seeing that I had
swooned at the spectacle, began to rape me; this brought me
to, I recovered my senses, I screamed, I struggled, I bit, I
scratched, I tried to tear out the big Bulgarian's eyes, not
knowing that what was happening in my father's castle was
a matter of custom; the brute stabbed me with a knife in the
left side where I still have the scar." "Alas! I hope I shall
see it," said the naïve Candide. "You shall see it," said
Cunegonde, "but let me go on." "Go on," said Candide.
She took up the thread of her story as follows: "A Bulgarian
captain came in, saw me covered with blood, and the soldier
did not disturb himself. The captain was angry at the
brute's lack of respect to him, and killed him on my body.
Afterwards, he had me bandaged and took me to his billet
as a prisoner of war. I washed the few shirts he had and did
the cooking; I must admit he thought me very pretty; and
I will not deny that he was very well built and that his skin
was white and soft; otherwise he had little wit and little philosophy; it was plain that he had not been brought up by

Dr. Pangloss. At the end of three months he lost all his money and got tired of me; he sold me to a Jew named Don Issachar, who traded in Holland and Portugal and had a passion for women. This Jew devoted himself to my person but he could not triumph over it; I resisted him better than the Bulgarian soldier; a lady of honor may be raped once, but it strengthens her virtue. In order to subdue me, the Jew brought me to this country house. Up till then I believed that there was nothing on earth so splendid as the castle of Thunder-ten-tronckh; I was undeceived. One day the Grand Inquisitor noticed me at Mass; he ogled me continually and sent a message that he wished to speak to me on secret affairs. I was taken to his palace; I informed him of my birth; he pointed out how much it was beneath my rank to belong to an Israelite. A proposition was made on his behalf to Don Issachar to give me up to His Lordship. Don Issachar, who is the court banker and a man of influence, would not agree. The Inquisitor threatened him with an *auto-da-fé*. At last the Jew was frightened and made a bargain whereby the house and I belong to both in common. The Jew has Mondays, Wednesdays and the Sabbath day, and the Inquisitor has the other days of the week. This arrangement has lasted for six months. It has not been without quarrels; for it has often been debated whether the night between Saturday and Sunday belonged to the old law or the new. For my part, I have hitherto resisted them both; and I think that is the reason why they still love me. At last My Lord the Inquisitor was pleased to arrange an *auto-da-fé* to remove the scourge of earthquakes and to intimidate Don Issachar. He honored me with an invitation. I had an excellent seat; and refreshments were served to the ladies between the Mass and the execution. I was indeed horror-stricken when I saw the burning of the two Jews and the honest Biscayan who had married his fellow-godmother; but what was my surprise, my terror, my anguish, when I saw in a sanbenito and under a mitre a face which resembled Pangloss's! I rubbed my eyes, I looked carefully, I saw him hanged; and I fainted. I had scarcely recovered my senses when I saw you stripped naked; that was the height of horror, of consternation, of grief and despair. I will frankly tell you that your skin is even whiter and of a more perfect tint than that of my Bulgarian captain. This spectacle redoubled all the feelings which crushed and devoured me. I exclaimed, I tried to say: 'Stop, Barbarians!' but my voice failed and my cries would have been useless. When you had been well flogged, I said to myself: 'How does it happen that the charming Candide and the wise Pangloss are in Lisbon, the one to receive a hundred lashes, and the other to be hanged, by order of My Lord the Inquisitor, whose darling I am? Pangloss deceived me cruelly when he said that all is for the best in the world.' I was agitated, distracted, sometimes beside myself and sometimes ready to die of faintness, and my head was filled with the massacre of my father, of my mother, of my brother, the insolence of my horrid Bulgarian soldier, the gash he gave me, my slavery, my life as a kitchen-wench, my Bulgarian captain, my horrid Don Issachar, my abominable Inquisitor, the hanging of Dr. Pangloss, that long *miserere* in counterpoint during which you were flogged, and above all the kiss I gave you behind the screen that day when I saw you for the last time. I praised God for bringing you back to me through so many trials, I ordered my old woman to take care of you and to bring you here as soon as she could. She has carried out my commission very well; I have enjoyed the inexpressible pleasure of seeing you again, of listening to you, and of speaking to you. You must be very hungry; I have a good appetite; let us begin by having supper." Both sat down to supper; and after supper they returned to the handsome sofa we have already mentioned; they were still there when Signor Don Issachar, one of the masters of the house, arrived. It was the day of the Sabbath. He came to enjoy his rights and to express his tender love.

CHAPTER IX

What happened to Cunegonde, to Candide, to the Grand Inquisitor and to a Jew

THIS Issachar was the most choleric Hebrew who had been seen in Israel since the Babylonian captivity. "What!" said he. "Bitch of a Galilean, isn't it enough to have the Inquisitor? Must this scoundrel share with me too?" So saying, he drew a long dagger which he always carried and, thinking that his adversary was unarmed, threw himself upon Candide; but our good Westphalian had received an excellent sword from the old woman along with his suit of clothes. He drew his sword, and although he had a most gentle character, laid the Israelite stone-dead on the floor at the feet of the fair Cunegonde. "Holy Virgin!" she exclaimed, "what will become of us? A man killed in my house! If the police come we are lost." "If Pangloss had not been hanged," said Candide, "he would have given us good advice in this extremity, for he was a great philosopher. In default of him, let us consult the old woman." She was extremely prudent and was beginning to give her advice when another little door opened. It was an hour after midnight, and Sunday was beginning. This day belonged to My Lord the Inquisitor. He came in and saw the flogged Candide sword in hand, a corpse lying on the ground, Cunegonde in terror, and the old woman giving advice. At this moment, here is what happened in Candide's soul and the manner of his reasoning: "If this holy man calls for help, he will infallibly have me burned; he might do as much to Cunegonde; he had me pitilessly lashed; he is my rival; I am in the mood to kill, there is no room for hesitation." His reasoning was clear and swift; and, without giving the Inquisitor time to recover from his surprise, he pierced him through and through and cast him beside the Jew. "Here's another," said Cunegonde. "There is no chance of mercy; we are excommunicated, our last hour has come. How does it happen that you, who were born so mild, should kill a Jew and a prelate in two minutes?" "My dear young lady," replied Candide, "when a man is in love, jealous, and has been flogged by the Inquisition, he is beside himself." The old woman then spoke up and said: "In the stable are three Andalusian horses, with their saddles and bridles; let the brave Candide prepare them; mademoiselle has moidores and diamonds; let us mount quickly, although I can only sit on one buttock, and go to Cadiz; the weather is beautifully fine, and it is most pleasant to travel in the coolness of the night." Candide immediately saddled the three horses. Cunegonde, the old woman and he rode thirty miles without stopping. While they were riding away, the Holy Hermandad arrived at the house; My Lord was buried in a splendid church and Issachar was thrown into a sewer. Candide, Cunegonde and the old woman had already reached the little town of Avacena in the midst of the mountains of the Sierra Morena; and they talked in their inn as follows.

CHAPTER X

*How Candide, Cunegonde and the old woman arrived at
Cadiz in great distress, and how they embarked*

"WHO can have stolen my pistoles and my diamonds?"
said Cunegonde, weeping. "How shall we live? What shall
we do? Where shall we find Inquisitors and Jews to give me
others?" "Alas!" said the old woman, "I strongly suspect a
reverend Franciscan father who slept in the same inn at
Badajoz with us; Heaven forbid that I should judge rashly!
But he twice came into our room and left long before we
did." "Alas!" said Candide, "the good Pangloss often proved
to me that this world's goods are common to all men and
that every one has an equal right to them. According to
these principles the monk should have left us enough to
continue our journey. Have you nothing left then, my fair
Cunegonde?" "Not a maravedi," said she. "What are we to
do?" said Candide. "Sell one of the horses," said the old
woman. "I will ride postillion behind Mademoiselle Cunegonde, although I can only sit on one buttock, and we will
get to Cadiz." In the same hotel there was a Benedictine
friar. He bought the horse very cheap. Candide, Cunegonde
and the old woman passed through Lucena, Chillas,
Lebrixa, and at last reached Cadiz. A fleet was there being
equipped and troops were being raised to bring to reason
the reverend Jesuit fathers of Paraguay, who were accused
of causing the revolt of one of their tribes against the kings
of Spain and Portugal near the town of Sacramento. Candide, having served with the Bulgarians, went through the
Bulgarian drill before the general of the little army with so

much grace, celerity, skill, pride and agility, that he was given the command of an infantry company. He was now a captain; he embarked with Mademoiselle Cunegonde, the old woman, two servants, and the two Andalusian horses which had belonged to the Grand Inquisitor of Portugal. During the voyage they had many discussions about the philosophy of poor Pangloss. "We are going to a new world," said Candide, "and no doubt it is there that everything is for the best; for it must be admitted that one might lament a little over the physical and moral happenings in our own world." "I love you with all my heart," said Cunegonde, "but my soul is still shocked by what I have seen and undergone." "All will be well," replied Candide; "the sea in this new world already is better than the seas of our Europe; it is calmer and the winds are more constant. It is certainly the new world which is the best of all possible worlds." "God grant it!" said Cunegonde, "but I have been so horribly unhappy in mine that my heart is nearly closed to hope." "You complain," said the old woman to them. "Alas! you have not endured such misfortunes as mine." Cunegonde almost laughed and thought it most amusing of the old woman to assert that she was more unfortunate. "Alas! my dear," said she, "unless you have been raped by two Bulgarians, stabbed twice in the belly, have had two castles destroyed, two fathers and mothers murdered before your eyes, and have seen two of your lovers flogged in an *auto-da-fé*, I do not see how you can surpass me; moreover, I was born a Baroness with seventy-two quarterings and I have been a kitchen wench." "You do not know my birth," said the old woman, "and if I showed you my backside you would not talk as you do and you would suspend your judgment." This speech aroused intense curiosity in the minds of Cunegonde and Candide. And the old woman spoke as follows.

CHAPTER XI

The old woman's story

"MY eyes were not always bloodshot and red-rimmed; my nose did not always touch my chin and I was not always a servant. I am the daughter of Pope Urban X and the Princess of Palestrina. Until I was fourteen I was brought up in a palace to which all the castles of your German Barons would not have served as stables; and one of my dresses cost more than all the magnificence of Westphalia. I increased in beauty, in grace, in talents, among pleasures, respect and hopes; already I inspired love, my breasts were forming; and what breasts! White, firm, carved like those of the Venus de' Medici. And what eyes! What eyelids! What black eyebrows! What fire shone from my two eyeballs, and dimmed the glitter of the stars, as the local poets pointed out to me. The women who dressed and undressed me fell into ecstasy when they beheld me in front and behind; and all the men would have liked to be in their place. I was betrothed to a ruling prince of Massa-Carrara. What a prince! As beautiful as I was, formed of gentleness and charms, brilliantly witty and burning with love; I loved him with a first love, idolatrously and extravagantly. The marriage ceremonies were arranged with unheard-of pomp and magnificence; there were continual fêtes, revels and comic operas; all Italy wrote sonnets for me and not a good one among them. I reached the moment of my happiness when an old marchioness who had been my prince's mistress invited him to take chocolate with her; less than two hours afterwards he died in horrible convulsions; but that is only a trifle. My mother was in despair, though less distressed than I, and wished to absent herself for a time from a place so disastrous. She had a most beautiful estate near Gaeta; we embarked on a galley, gilded like the altar of St. Peter's at Rome. A Salle pirate swooped down and boarded us; our soldiers defended us like soldiers of the Pope; they threw down their arms, fell on their knees and asked the pirates for absolution *in articulo mortis*. They were immediately stripped as naked as monkeys and my mother, our ladies of honor and myself as well. The diligence with which these gentlemen strip people is truly admirable, but I was still more surprised by their inserting a finger in a place belonging to all of us where we women usually only allow the end of a syringe. This appeared to me a very strange ceremony; but that is how we judge everything when we leave our own country. I soon learned that it was to find out if we had hidden any diamonds there; 'tis a custom established from time immemorial among the civilized nations who roam the seas.

"I have learned that the religious Knights of Malta never fail in it when they capture Turks and Turkish women; this is an international law which has never been broken. I will not tell you how hard it is for a young princess to be taken with her mother as a slave to Morocco; you will also guess all we had to endure in the pirates' ship. My mother was still very beautiful; our ladies of honor, even our waiting-maids possessed more charms than could be found in all Africa; and I was ravishing, I was beauty, grace itself, and I was a virgin; I did not remain so long; the flower which had been reserved for the handsome prince of Massa-Carrara was ravished from me by a pirate captain; he was an abominable Negro who thought he was doing me a great honor. The Princess of Palestrina and I must indeed have been strong to bear up against all we endured before our arrival in Morocco! But let that pass; these things are so common that they are not worth mentioning. Morocco was swimming in blood when we arrived. The fifty sons of the Emperor Muley Ismael had each a faction; and this produced fifty civil wars, of blacks against blacks, browns against browns, mulattoes against mulattoes. There was continual carnage throughout the whole extent of the empire. Scarcely had we landed when the blacks of a party hostile to that of my pirate arrived with the purpose of depriving him of his booty. After the diamonds and the gold, we were the most valuable possessions. I witnessed a fight such as is never seen in your European climates. The blood of the northern peoples is not sufficiently ardent; their madness for women does not reach the point which is common in Africa. The Europeans seem to have milk in their veins; but vitriol and fire flow in the veins of the inhabitants of Mount Atlas and the neighboring countries. They fought with the fury of the lions, tigers and serpents of the country to determine who should have us. A Moor grasped my mother by the right arm, my captain's lieutenant held her by the left arm; a Moorish soldier held one leg and one of our pirates seized the other. In a moment nearly all our women were seized in the same way by four soldiers. My captain kept me hidden behind him; he had a scimitar in his hand and killed everybody who opposed his fury. I saw my mother and all our Italian women torn in pieces, gashed, massacred by the monsters who disputed them. The prisoners, my companions, those who had captured them, soldiers, sailors, blacks, browns, whites, mulattoes and finally my captain were all killed and I remained expiring on a heap of corpses. As every one knows, such scenes go on in an area of more than three hundred square leagues and yet no one ever fails to recite the five daily prayers ordered by Mahomet. With great difficulty I extricated myself from the bloody heaps of corpses and dragged myself to the foot of a large orange-tree on the bank of a stream; there I fell down with terror, weariness, horror, despair and hunger. Soon afterwards, my exhausted senses fell into a sleep which was more like a swoon than repose. I was in this state of weakness and insensibility between life and death when I felt myself oppressed by something which moved on my body. I opened my eyes and saw a white man of good appearance who was sighing and muttering between his teeth: *O che sciagura d'essere senza coglioni!*[1]

CHAPTER XII

Continuation of the old woman's misfortunes

"AMAZED and delighted to hear my native language, and not less surprised at the words spoken by this man, I replied that there were greater misfortunes than that of which he complained. In a few words I informed him of the horrors I had undergone and then swooned again. He carried me to a neighboring house, had me put to bed, gave me food, waited on me, consoled me, flattered me, told me he had never seen anyone so beautiful as I and that he had never so much regretted that which no one could give back to him. 'I was born at Naples,' he said, 'and every year they make two or three thousand children there into capons; some die of it, others acquire voices more beautiful than women's, and others become the governors of States. This operation was

---

[1]"What a pity to have no testicles!"

performed upon me with very great success and I was a
musician in the chapel of the Princess of Palestrina.' 'Of my
mother,' I exclaimed. 'Of your mother!' cried he, weeping.
'What! Are you that young princess I brought up to the age
of six and who even then gave promise of being as beautiful as you are?' 'I am! my mother is four hundred yards
from here, cut into quarters under a heap of corpses . . .' I
related all that had happened to me; he also told me his
adventures and informed me how he had been sent to the
King of Morocco by a Christian power to make a treaty
with that monarch whereby he was supplied with powder,
cannons and ships to help to exterminate the commerce of
other Christians. 'My mission is accomplished,' said this
honest eunuch, 'I am about to embark at Ceuta and I will
take you back to Italy. *Ma che sciagura d'essere senza coglioni!*' I thanked him with tears of gratitude; and instead of
taking me back to Italy he conducted me to Algiers and sold
me to the Dey. I had scarcely been sold when the plague
which had gone through Africa, Asia and Europe, broke out
furiously in Algiers. You have seen earthquakes; but have
you ever seen the plague?" "Never," replied the Baroness.
"If you had," replied the old woman, "you would admit
that it is much worse than an earthquake. It is very common in Africa; I caught it. Imagine the situation of a Pope's
daughter aged fifteen, who in three months had undergone
poverty and slavery, had been raped nearly every day, had
seen her mother cut into four pieces, had undergone hunger
and war, and was now dying of the plague in Algiers. However, I did not die; but my eunuch and the Dey and almost
all the seraglio of Algiers perished. When the first ravages
of this frightful plague were over, the Dey's slaves were
sold. A merchant bought me and carried me to Tunis; he
sold me to another merchant who re-sold me at Tripoli;
from Tripoli I was re-sold to Alexandria, from Alexandria

re-sold to Smyrna, from Smyrna to Constantinople. I was finally bought by an Aga of the Janizaries, who was soon ordered to defend Azov against the Russians who were besieging it. The Aga, who was a man of great gallantry, took his whole seraglio with him, and lodged us in a little fort on the Islands of Palus-Maeotis, guarded by two black eunuchs and twenty soldiers. He killed a prodigious number of Russians but they returned the compliment as well. Azov was given up to fire and blood, neither sex nor age was pardoned; only our little fort remained; and the enemy tried to reduce it by starving us. The twenty Janizaries had sworn never to surrender us. The extremities of hunger to which they were reduced forced them to eat our two eunuchs for fear of breaking their oath. Some days later they resolved to eat the women. We had with us a most pious and compassionate Imam who delivered a fine sermon to them by which he persuaded them not to kill us altogether. 'Cut,' said he, 'only one buttock from each of these ladies and you will have an excellent meal; if you have to return, there will still be as much left in a few days; Heaven will be pleased at so charitable an action and you will be saved.' He was very eloquent and persuaded them. This horrible operation was performed upon us; the Imam anointed us with the same balm that is used for children who have just been circumcised; we were all at the point of death. Scarcely had the Janizaries finished the meal we had supplied when the Russians arrived in flat-bottomed boats; not a Janizary escaped. The Russians paid no attention to the state we were in. There are French doctors everywhere; one of them who was very skillful, took care of us; he healed us and I shall remember all my life that, when my wounds were cured, he made propositions to me. For the rest, he told us all to cheer up; he told us that the same thing had happened in several sieges and that it was a law of war. As soon as my companions could walk they were sent to Moscow. I fell to the lot of a Boyar who made me his gardener and gave me twenty lashes a day. But at the end of two years this lord was broken on the wheel with thirty other Boyars owing to some court disturbance, and I profited by this adventure; I fled; I crossed all Russia; for a long time I was a servant in an inn at Riga, then at Rostock, at Wismar, at Leipzig, at Cassel, at Utrecht, at Leyden, at the Hague, at Rotterdam; I have grown old in misery and in shame, with only half a backside, always remembering that I was the daughter of a Pope; a hundred times I wanted to kill myself but I still loved life. This ridiculous weakness is perhaps the most disastrous of our inclinations; for is there anything sillier than to desire to bear continually a burden one always wishes to throw on the ground; to look upon oneself with horror and yet to cling to oneself; in short, to caress the serpent which devours us until he has eaten our heart? In the countries it has been my fate to traverse and in the inns where I have served I have seen a prodigious number of people who hated their lives; but I have only seen twelve who voluntarily put an end to their misery: three Negroes, four Englishmen, four Genevans and a German professor named Robeck. I ended up as servant to the Jew, Don Issachar; he placed me in your service, my fair young lady; I attached myself to your fate and have been more occupied with your adventures than with my own. I should never even have spoken of my misfortunes, if you had not piqued me a little and if it had not been the custom on board ship to tell stories to pass the time. In short, Mademoiselle, I have had experience, I know the world; provide yourself with an entertainment, make each passenger tell you his story; and if there is one who has not often cursed his life, who has not often said to himself that he was the most unfortunate of men, throw me head-first into the sea."

CHAPTER XIII

*How Candide was obliged to separate from
the fair Cunegonde and the old woman*

THE fair Cunegonde, having heard the old woman's story,
treated her with all the politeness due to a person of her
rank and merit. She accepted the proposition and persuaded
all the passengers one after the other to tell her their adventures. She and Candide admitted that the old woman was
right. "It was most unfortunate," said Candide, "that the
wise Pangloss was hanged contrary to custom at an *auto-da-
fé;* he would have said admirable things about the physical
and moral evils which cover the earth and the sea, and I
should feel myself strong enough to urge a few objections
with all due respect." While each of the passengers was
telling his story the ship proceeded on its way. They arrived
at Buenos Ayres. Cunegonde, Captain Candide and the
old woman went to call on the governor, Don Fernando
d'Ibaraa y Figueora y Mascarenes y Lampourdos y Souza.
This gentleman had the pride befitting a man who owned so
many names. He talked to men with a most noble disdain,
turning his nose up so far, raising his voice so pitilessly,
assuming so imposing a tone, affecting so lofty a carriage,
that all who addressed him were tempted to give him a
thrashing. He had a furious passion for women. Cunegonde
seemed to him the most beautiful woman he had ever seen.
The first thing he did was to ask if she were the Captain's
wife. The air with which he asked the question alarmed
Candide; he did not dare say that she was his wife, because
as a matter of fact she was not; he dared not say she was

his sister, because she was not that either; and though this
official lie was formerly extremely fashionable among the
ancients, and might be useful to the moderns, his soul was
too pure to depart from truth. "Mademoiselle Cunegonde,"
said he, "is about to do me the honor of marrying me, and
we beg your excellency to be present at the wedding." Don
Fernando d'Ibaraa y Figueora y Mascarenes y Lampourdos
y Souza twisted his moustache, smiled bitterly and ordered
Captain Candide to go and inspect his company. Candide
obeyed; the governor remained with Mademoiselle Cunegonde. He declared his passion, vowed that the next day he
would marry her publicly, or otherwise, as it might please
her charms. Cunegonde asked for a quarter of an hour to
collect herself, to consult the old woman and to make up
her mind. The old woman said to Cunegonde: "You have
seventy-two quarterings and you haven't a shilling; it is in
your power to be the wife of the greatest Lord in South
America, who has an exceedingly fine moustache; is it for
you to pride yourself on a rigid fidelity? You have been
raped by Bulgarians, a Jew and an Inquisitor have enjoyed
your good graces; misfortunes confer certain rights. If I
were in your place, I confess I should not have the least
scruple in marrying the governor and making Captain Candide's fortune." While the old woman was speaking with all
that prudence which comes from age and experience, they
saw a small ship come into the harbor; an Alcayde and
some Alguazils were on board, and this is what had happened. The old woman had guessed correctly that it was a
long-sleeved monk who stole Cunegonde's money and jewels
at Badajoz, when she was flying in all haste with Candide.
The monk tried to sell some of the gems to a jeweller. The
merchant recognized them as the property of the Grand
Inquisitor. Before the monk was hanged he confessed that
he had stolen them, he described the persons and the direc- .

tion they were taking. The flight of Cunegonde and Candide was already known. They were followed to Cadiz; without any waste of time a vessel was sent in pursuit of them. The vessel was already in the harbor at Buenos Ayres. The rumor spread that an Alcayde was about to land and that he was in pursuit of the murderers of His Lordship the Grand Inquisitor. The prudent old woman saw in a moment what was to be done. "You cannot escape," she said to Cunegonde, "and you have nothing to fear; you did not kill His Lordship; moreover, the governor is in love with you and will not allow you to be maltreated; stay here." She ran to Candide at once. "Fly," said she, "or in an hour's time you will be burned." There was not a moment to lose; but how could he leave Cunegonde and where could he take refuge?

CHAPTER XIV

How Candide and Cacambo were received by the Jesuits in Paraguay

CANDIDE had brought from Cadiz a valet of a sort which is very common on the coasts of Spain and in colonies. He was one-quarter Spanish, the child of a half-breed in Tucuman; he had been a choir-boy, a sacristan, a sailor, a monk, a postman, a soldier and a lackey. His name was Cacambo and he loved his master because his master was a very good man. He saddled the two Andalusian horses with all speed. "Come, master, we must follow the old woman's advice; let us be off and ride without looking behind us."

Candide shed tears. "O my dear Cunegonde! Must I abandon you just when the governor was about to marry us! Cunegonde, brought here from such a distant land, what will become of you?" "She will become what she can," said Cacambo. "Women never trouble about themselves; God will see to her; let us be off." "Where are you taking me? Where are we going? What shall we do without Cunegonde?" said Candide. "By St. James of Compostella," said Cacambo, "you were going to fight the Jesuits; let us go and fight for them; I know the roads, I will take you to their kingdom, they will be charmed to have a captain who can drill in the Bulgarian fashion, you will make a prodigious fortune; when a man fails in one world, he succeeds in another. 'Tis a very great pleasure to see and do new things." "Then you have been in Paraguay?" said Candide. "Yes, indeed," said Cacambo. "I was servitor in the College of the Assumption, and I know the government of *Los Padres* as well as I know the streets of Cadiz. Their government is a most admirable thing. The kingdom is already more than three hundred leagues in diameter and is divided into thirty provinces. *Los Padres* have everything and the people have nothing; 'tis the masterpiece of reason and justice. For my part, I know nothing so divine as *Los Padres* who here make war on the Kings of Spain and Portugal and in Europe act as their confessors; who here kill Spaniards and at Madrid send them to Heaven; all this delights me; come on; you will be the happiest of men. What a pleasure it will be to *Los Padres* when they know there is coming to them a captain who can drill in the Bulgarian manner!" As soon as they reached the first barrier, Cacambo told the sentry that a captain wished to speak to the Commandant. This information was carried to the main guard. A Paraguayan officer ran to the feet of the Commandant to tell him the news. Candide and Cacambo were disarmed and their two

Andalusian horses were taken from them. The two strangers
were brought in between two ranks of soldiers; the Commandant was at the end, with a three-cornered hat on his
head, his gown tucked up, a sword at his side and a spon-
toon in his hand. He made a sign and immediately the two
new-comers were surrounded by twenty-four soldiers. A
sergeant told them that they must wait, that the Commandant could not speak to them, that the reverend provincial
father did not allow any Spaniard to open his mouth in his
presence or to remain more than three hours in the country. "And where is the reverend provincial father?" said
Cacambo. "He is on parade after having said Mass, and you
will have to wait three hours before you will be allowed to
kiss his spurs." "But," said Cacambo, "the captain who is
dying of hunger just as I am, is not a Spaniard but a German; can we not break our fast while we are waiting for his
reverence?" The sergeant went at once to inform the Commandant of this. "Blessed be God!" said that lord. "Since he
is a German I can speak to him; bring him to my arbor."
Candide was immediately taken to a leafy summer-house
decorated with a very pretty colonnade of green marble and
gold, and lattices enclosing parrots, humming-birds, colibris, guinea-hens and many other rare birds. An excellent
breakfast stood ready in gold dishes; and while the Paraguayans were eating maize from wooden bowls, out of doors
and in the heat of the sun, the reverend father Commandant entered the arbor. He was a very handsome young
man, with a full face, a fairly white skin, red cheeks, arched
eyebrows, keen eyes, red ears, vermilion lips, a haughty air,
but a haughtiness which was neither that of a Spaniard nor
of a Jesuit. Candide and Cacambo were given back the arms
which had been taken from them and their two Andalusian
horses; Cacambo fed them with oats near the arbor, and
kept his eye on them for fear of a surprise. Candide first

kissed the hem of the Commandant's gown and then they sat down to table. "So you are a German?" said the Jesuit in that language. "Yes, reverend father," said Candide. As they spoke these words they gazed at each other with extreme surprise and an emotion they could not control. "And what part of Germany do you come from?" said the Jesuit. "From the filthy province of Westphalia," said Candide; "I was born in the castle of Thunder-ten-tronckh." "Heavens! Is it possible!" cried the Commandant. "What a miracle!" cried Candide. "Can it be you?" said the Commandant. "'Tis impossible!" said Candide. They both fell over backwards, embraced and shed rivers of tears. "What! Can it be you, reverend father? You, the fair Cunegonde's brother! You, who were killed by the Bulgarians! You, the son of My Lord the Baron! You, a Jesuit in Paraguay! The world is indeed a strange place! O Pangloss! Pangloss! How happy you would have been if you had not been hanged!" The Commandant sent away the Negro slaves and the Paraguayans who were serving wine in goblets of rock-crystal. A thousand times did he thank God and St. Ignatius; he clasped Candide in his arms; their faces were wet with tears. "You would be still more surprised, more touched, more beside yourself," said Candide, "if I were to tell you that Mademoiselle Cunegonde, your sister, whom you thought disembowelled, is in the best of health." "Where?" "In your neighborhood, with the governor of Buenos Ayres; and I came to make war on you." Every word they spoke in this long conversation piled marvel on marvel. Their whole souls flew from their tongues, listened in their ears and sparkled in their eyes. As they were Germans, they sat at table for a long time, waiting for the reverend provincial father; and the Commandant spoke as follows to his dear Candide.

CHAPTER XV

How Candide killed his dear Cunegonde's brother

"I shall remember all my life the horrible day when I saw my father and mother killed and my sister raped. When the Bulgarians had gone, my adorable sister could not be found, and my mother, my father and I, two maid-servants and three little murdered boys were placed in a cart to be buried in a Jesuit chapel two leagues from the castle of my fathers. A Jesuit sprinkled us with holy water; it was horribly salt; a few drops fell in my eyes; the father noticed that my eyelids trembled, he put his hand on my heart and felt that it was still beating; I was attended to and at the end of three weeks was as well as if nothing had happened. You know, my dear Candide, that I was a very pretty youth, and I became still prettier; and so the Reverend Father Croust, the Superior of the house, was inspired with a most tender friendship for me; he gave me the dress of a novice and some time afterwards I was sent to Rome. The Father General wished to recruit some young German Jesuits. The sovereigns of Paraguay take as few Spanish Jesuits as they can; they prefer foreigners, whom they think they can control better. The Reverend Father General thought me apt to labor in his vineyard. I set off with a Pole and a Tyrolese. When I arrived I was honored with a sub-deaconship and a lieutenancy; I am now colonel and priest. We shall give the King of Spain's troops a warm reception; I guarantee they will be excommunicated and beaten. Providence has sent you to help us. But is it really true that my dear sister Cunegonde is in the neighborhood with the governor of

Buenos Ayres?" Candide assured him on oath that nothing could be truer. Their tears began to flow once more. The Baron seemed never to grow tired of embracing Candide; he called him his brother, his saviour. "Ah! My dear Candide," said he, "perhaps we shall enter the town together as conquerors and regain my sister Cunegonde." "I desire it above all things," said Candide, "for I meant to marry her and I still hope to do so." "You, insolent wretch!" replied the Baron. "Would you have the impudence to marry my sister who has seventy-two quarterings! I consider you extremely impudent to dare to speak to me of such a foolhardy intention!" Candide, petrified at this speech, replied: "Reverend Father, all the quarterings in the world are of no importance; I rescued your sister from the arms of a Jew and an Inquisitor; she is under considerable obligation to me and wishes to marry me. Mr. Pangloss always said that men are equal and I shall certainly marry her." "We shall see about that, scoundrel!" said the Jesuit Baron of Thunder-ten-tronckh, at the same time hitting him violently in the face with the flat of his sword. Candide promptly drew his own and stuck it up to the hilt in the Jesuit Baron's belly; but, as he drew it forth smoking, he began to weep. "Alas! My God," said he, "I have killed my old master, my friend, my brother-in-law; I am the mildest man in the world and I have already killed three men, two of them priests." Cacambo, who was acting as sentry at the door of the arbor, ran in. "There is nothing left for us but to sell our lives dearly," said his master. "Somebody will certainly come into the arbor and we must die weapon in hand." Cacambo, who had seen this sort of thing before, did not lose his head; he took off the Baron's Jesuit gown, put it on Candide, gave him the dead man's square bonnet, and made him mount a horse. All this was done in the twinkling of an eye. "Let us gallop, master; every one will take you for a Jesuit carrying orders and we shall have passed the frontiers before they can pursue us." As he spoke these words he started off at full speed and shouted in Spanish: "Way, way for the Reverend Father Colonel . . ."

CHAPTER XVI

What happened to the two travelers with two girls, two monkeys, and the savages called Oreillons

CANDIDE and his valet were past the barriers before anybody in the camp knew of the death of the German Jesuit. The vigilant Cacambo had taken care to fill his saddle-bag with bread, chocolate, ham, fruit, and several bottles of wine. On their Andalusian horses they plunged into an unknown country where they found no road. At last a beautiful plain traversed by streams met their eyes. Our two travelers put their horses to grass. Cacambo suggested to his master that they should eat and set the example. How can you expect me to eat ham," said Candide, "when I have killed the son of My Lord the Baron and find myself condemned never to see the fair Cunegonde again in my life? What is the use of prolonging my miserable days since I must drag them out far from her in remorse and despair? And what will the Journal de Trévoux say?"[1] Speaking thus, he began to eat. The sun was setting. The two wanderers heard faint cries which seemed to be uttered by women. They could not tell whether these were cries of pain or of

[1]The Jesuit *Journal de Trévoux*, founded in 1701, frequently denounced Voltaire and his works.

joy; but they rose hastily with that alarm and uneasiness caused by everything in an unknown country. These cries came from two completely naked girls who were running gently along the edge of the plain, while two monkeys pursued them and bit their buttocks. Candide was moved to pity; he had learned to shoot among the Bulgarians and could have brought down a nut from a tree without touching the leaves. He raised his double-barrelled Spanish gun, fired, and killed the two monkeys. "God be praised, my dear Cacambo, I have delivered these two poor creatures from a great danger; if I committed a sin by killing an Inquisitor and a Jesuit, I have atoned for it by saving the lives of these two girls. Perhaps they are young ladies of quality and this adventure may be of great advantage to us in this country." He was going on, but his tongue clove to the roof of his mouth when he saw the two girls tenderly kissing the two monkeys, shedding tears on their bodies and filling the air with the most piteous cries. "I did not expect so much human kindliness," he said at last to Cacambo, who replied: "You have performed a wonderful masterpiece; you have killed the two lovers of these young ladies." "Their lovers! Can it be possible? You are jesting at me, Cacambo; how can I believe you?" "My dear master," replied Cacambo, "you are always surprised by everything; why should you think it so strange that in some countries there should be monkeys who obtain ladies' favors? They are quarter men, as I am a quarter Spaniard." "Alas!" replied Candide, "I remember to have heard Dr. Pangloss say that similar accidents occurred in the past and that these mixtures produce Aigypans, fauns and satyrs; that several eminent persons of antiquity have seen them; but I thought they were fables." "You ought now to be convinced that it is true," said Cacambo, "and you see how people behave when they have not received a proper education; the only thing I fear is that these ladies may get us into difficulty." These wise reflections persuaded Candide to leave the plain and to plunge into the woods. He ate supper there with Cacambo and, after having cursed the Inquisitor of Portugal, the governor of Buenos Ayres and the Baron, they went to sleep on the moss. When they woke up they found they could not move; the reason was that during the night the Oreillons, the inhabitants of the country, to whom they had been denounced by the two ladies, had bound them with ropes made of bark. They were surrounded by fifty naked Oreillons, armed with arrows, clubs and stone hatchets. Some were boiling a large cauldron, others were preparing spits and they were all shouting: "Here's a Jesuit, here's a Jesuit! We shall be revenged and have a good dinner; let us eat Jesuit, let us eat Jesuit!" "I told you so, my dear master," said Cacambo sadly. "I knew those two girls would play us a dirty trick." Candide perceived the cauldron and the spits and exclaimed: "We are certainly going to be roasted or boiled. Ah! What would Dr. Pangloss say if he saw what the pure state of nature is? All is well, granted; but I confess it is very cruel to have lost Mademoiselle Cunegonde and to be spitted by the Oreillons." Cacambo never lost his head. "Do not despair," he said to the wretched Candide. "I understand a little of their dialect and I will speak to them." "Do not fail," said Candide, "to point out to them the dreadful inhumanity of cooking men and how very unchristian it is." "Gentlemen," said Cacambo, "you mean to eat a Jesuit today? 'Tis a good deed; nothing could be more just than to treat one's enemies in this fashion. Indeed the law of nature teaches us to kill our neighbor and this is how people behave all over the world. If we do not exert the right of eating our neighbor, it is because we have other means of making good cheer; but you have not the same resources as we, and it is certainly better to eat our enemies than to abandon the fruits of victory to ravens and crows. But, gentlemen, you would not wish to eat your friends. You believe you are about to place a Jesuit on the spit, and 'tis your defender, the enemy of your enemies you are about to roast. I was born in your country; the gentleman you see here is my master and, far from being a Jesuit, he has just killed a Jesuit and is wearing his clothes; which is the cause of your mistake. To verify what I say, take his gown, carry it to the first barrier of the kingdom of *Los Padres* and inquire whether my master has not killed a Jesuit officer. It will not take you long and you will have plenty of time to eat us if you find I have lied. But if I have told the truth, you are too well acquainted with the principles of public law, good morals and discipline, not to pardon us." The Oreillons thought this a very reasonable speech; they deputed two of their notables to go with all diligence and find out the truth. The two deputies acquitted themselves of their task like intelligent men and soon returned with the good news. The Oreillons unbound their two prisoners, overwhelmed them with civilities, offered them girls, gave them refreshment, and accompanied them to the frontiers of their dominions, shouting joyfully: "He is not a Jesuit, he is not a Jesuit!" Candide could not cease from wondering at the cause of his deliverance. "What a nation," said he. "What men! What manners! If I had not been so lucky as to stick my sword through the body of Mademoiselle Cunegonde's brother I should infallibly have been eaten. But, after all, there is something good in the pure state of nature, since these people, instead of eating me, offered me a thousand civilities as soon as they knew I was not a Jesuit."

CHAPTER XVII

*Arrival of Candide and his valet in the country
of Eldorado and what they saw there*

WHEN they reached the frontiers of the Oreillons,
Cacambo said to Candide: "You see this hemisphere is no
better than the other; take my advice, let us go back to
Europe by the shortest road." "How can we go back," said
Candide, "and where can we go? If I go to my own country,
the Bulgarians and the Abares are murdering everybody; if
I return to Portugal I shall be burned; if we stay here,
we run the risk of being spitted at any moment. But how
can I make up my mind to leave that part of the world
where Mademoiselle Cunegonde is living?" "Let us go to
Cayenne," said Cacambo, "we shall find Frenchmen there,
for they go all over the world; they might help us. Perhaps
God will have pity on us." It was not easy to go to
Cayenne. They knew roughly the direction to take, but
mountains, rivers, precipices, brigands and savages were
everywhere terrible obstacles. Their horses died of fatigue;
their provisions were exhausted; for a whole month they
lived on wild fruits and at last found themselves near a little
river fringed with cocoanut-trees which supported their lives
and their hopes. Cacambo, who always gave advice as prudent as the old woman's, said to Candide: "We can go no
farther, we have walked far enough; I can see an empty
canoe in the bank, let us fill it with cocoanuts, get into the
little boat and drift with the current; a river always leads to
some inhabited place. If we do not find anything pleasant,
we shall at least find something new." "Come on then," said

Candide, "and let us trust to Providence." They drifted for some leagues between banks which were sometimes flowery, sometimes bare, sometimes flat, sometimes steep. The river continually became wider; finally it disappeared under an arch of frightful rocks which towered up to the very sky. The two travelers were bold enough to trust themselves to the current under this arch. The stream, narrowed between walls, carried them with horrible rapidity and noise. After twenty-four hours they saw daylight again; but their canoe was wrecked on reefs; they had to crawl from rock to rock for a whole league and at last they discovered an immense horizon, bordered by inaccessible mountains. The country was cultivated for pleasure as well as for necessity; everywhere the useful was agreeable. The roads were covered or rather ornamented with carriages of brilliant material and shape, carrying men and women of singular beauty, who were rapidly drawn along by large red sheep whose swiftness surpassed that of the finest horses of Andalusia, Tetuan, and Mequinez. "This country," said Candide, "is better than Westphalia." He landed with Cacambo near the first village he came to. Several children of the village, dressed in torn gold brocade, were playing horseshoes outside the village. Our two men from the other world amused themselves by looking on; their horseshoes were large round pieces, yellow, red and green which shone with peculiar lustre. The travelers were curious enough to pick up some of them; they were of gold, emeralds and rubies, the least of which would have been the greatest ornament in the Mogul's throne. "No doubt," said Cacambo, "these children are the sons of the King of this country playing horseshoes." At that moment the village schoolmaster appeared to call them into school. "This," said Candide, "is the tutor of the Royal Family." The little beggars immediately left their game, abandoning their horseshoes and everything with which they had been playing. Candide picked them up, ran to the tutor, and presented them to him humbly, giving him to understand by signs that their Royal Highnesses had forgotten their gold and their precious stones. The village schoolmaster smiled, threw them on the ground, gazed for a moment at Candide's face with much surprise and continued on his way. The travelers did not fail to pick up the gold, the rubies and the emeralds. "Where are we?" cried Candide. "The children of the King must be well brought up, since they are taught to despise gold and precious stones." Cacambo was as much surprised as Candide. At last they reached the first house in the village, which was built like a European palace. There were crowds of people round the door and still more inside; very pleasant music could be heard and there was a delicious smell of cooking. Cacambo went up to the door and heard them speaking Peruvian; it was his maternal tongue, for everyone knows that Cacambo was born in a village of Tucuman where nothing else is spoken. "I will act as your interpreter," he said to Candide, "this is an inn, let us enter." Immediately two boys and two girls of the inn, dressed in cloth of gold, whose hair was bound up with ribbons, invited them to sit down to the table d'hôte. They served four soups each garnished with two parrots, a boiled condor which weighed two hundred pounds, two roast monkeys of excellent flavor, three hundred colibris in one dish and six hundred humming-birds in another, exquisite ragouts and delicious pastries, all in dishes of a sort of rock-crystal. The boys and girls brought several sorts of drinks made of sugar-cane. Most of the guests were merchants and coachmen, all extremely polite, who asked Cacambo a few questions with the most delicate discretion and answered his in a satisfactory manner. When the meal was over, Cacambo, like Candide, thought he could pay the reckoning by throwing on the table two of the large pieces of gold he had picked up; the host and hostess laughed until they had to hold their sides. At last they recovered themselves. "Gentlemen," said the host, "we perceive you are strangers; we are not accustomed to seeing them. Forgive us if we began to laugh when you offered us in payment the stones from our highways. No doubt you have none of the money of this country, but you do not need any to dine here. All the hotels established for the utility of commerce are paid for by the government. You have been ill-entertained here because this is a poor village; but everywhere else you will be received as you deserve to be." Cacambo explained to Candide all that the host had said, and Candide listened in the same admiration and disorder with which his friend Cacambo interpreted. "What can this country be," they said to each other, "which is unknown to the rest of the world and where all nature is so different from ours? Probably it is the country where everything is for the best; for there must be one country of that sort. And, in spite of what Dr. Pangloss said, I often noticed that everything went very ill in Westphalia."

CHAPTER XVIII

What they saw in the land of Eldorado

CACAMBO informed the host of his curiosity, and the host said, "I am a very ignorant man and am all the better for it; but we have here an old man who has retired from the court and who is the most learned and most communicative man in the kingdom." And he at once took

Cacambo to the old man. Candide now played only the second part and accompanied his valet. They entered a very simple house, for the door was only of silver and the paneling of the apartments in gold, but so tastefully carved that the richest decorations did not surpass it. The antechamber indeed was only encrusted with rubies and emeralds; but the order with which everything was arranged atoned for this extreme simplicity. The old man received the two strangers on a sofa padded with colibri feathers, and presented them with drinks in diamond cups; after which he satisfied their curiosity in these words: "I am a hundred and seventy-two years old and I heard from my late father, the King's equerry, the astonishing revolutions of Peru of which he had been an eyewitness. The kingdom where we now are is the ancient country of the Incas, who most imprudently left it to conquer part of the world and were at last destroyed by the Spaniards. The princes of their family who remained in their native country had more wisdom; with the consent of the nation, they ordered that no inhabitants should ever leave our little kingdom, and this it is that has preserved our innocence and our felicity. The Spaniards had some vague knowledge of this country, which they called Eldorado, and about a hundred years ago an Englishman named Raleigh came very near to it; but, since we are surrounded by inaccessible rocks and precipices, we have hitherto been exempt from the rapacity of the nations of Europe who have an inconceivable lust for the pebbles and mud of our land and would kill us to the last man to get possession of them." The conversation was long; it touched upon the form of the government, manners, women, public spectacles and the arts. Finally Candide, who was always interested in metaphysics, asked through Cacambo whether the country had a religion. The old man blushed a little.

"How can you doubt it?" said he. "Do you think we are ingrates?" Cacambo humbly asked what was the religion of Eldorado. The old man blushed again. "Can there be two religions?" said he. "We have, I think, the religion of every one else; we adore God from evening until morning." "Do you adore only one God?" said Cacambo, who continued to act as the interpreter of Candide's doubts. "Manifestly," said the old man, "there are not two or three or four. I must confess that the people of your world ask very extraordinary questions." Candide continued to press the old man with questions; he wished to know how they prayed to God in Eldorado. "We do not pray," said the good and respectable sage, "we have nothing to ask from him; he has given us everything necessary and we continually give him thanks." Candide was curious to see the priests, and asked where they were. The good old man smiled. "My friends," said he, "we are all priests; the King and all the heads of families solemnly sing praises every morning, accompanied by five or six thousand musicians." "What! Have you no monks to teach, to dispute, to govern, to intrigue and to burn people who do not agree with them?" "For that, we should have to become fools," said the old man; "here we are all of the same opinion and do not understand what you mean with your monks." At all this Candide was in an ecstasy and said to himself: "This is very different from Westphalia and the castle of His Lordship the Baron; if our friend Pangloss had seen Eldorado, he would not have said that the castle of Thunder-ten-tronckh was the best of all that exists on the earth; certainly, a man should travel." After this long conversation the good old man ordered a carriage to be harnessed with six sheep and gave the two travelers twelve of his servants to take them to court. "You will excuse me," he said, "if my age deprives me of the honor of accompanying you. The King will receive you in a manner which will not displease you and doubtless you will pardon the customs of the country if any of them disconcert you." Candide and Cacambo entered the carriage; the six sheep galloped off and in less than four hours they reached the King's palace, which was situated at one end of the capital. The portal was two hundred and twenty feet high and a hundred feet wide; it is impossible to describe its material. Anyone can see the prodigious superiority it must have over the pebbles and sand we call *gold* and *gems*. Twenty beautiful maidens of the guard received Candide and Cacambo as they alighted from the carriage, conducted them to the baths and dressed them in robes woven from the down of colibris; after which the principal male and female officers of the Crown led them to his Majesty's apartment through two files of a thousand musicians each, according to the usual custom. As they approached the throne-room, Cacambo asked one of the chief officers how they should behave in his Majesty's presence; whether they should fall on their knees or flat on their faces, whether they should put their hands on their heads or on their backsides; whether they should lick the dust of the throne-room; in a word, what was the ceremony? "The custom," said the chief officer, "is to embrace the King and to kiss him on either cheek." Candide and Cacambo threw their arms round his Majesty's neck; he received them with all imaginable favor and politely asked them to supper. Meanwhile they were carried to see the town, the public buildings rising to the very skies, the market-places ornamented with thousands of columns, the fountains of rose-water and of liquors distilled from sugar-cane, which played continually in the public squares paved with precious stones which emitted a perfume like that of cloves and cinnamon. Candide asked to see the law courts; he was told there were none, and that nobody ever went to law. He asked if there were prisons and was told there were none. He was still more surprised and pleased by the palace of sciences, where he saw a gallery two thousand feet long, filled with instruments of mathematics and physics. After they had explored all the afternoon about a thousandth part of the town, they were taken back to the King. Candide sat down to table with his Majesty, his valet Cacambo and several ladies. Never was there a better supper, and never was anyone wittier at supper than his Majesty. Cacambo explained the King's witty remarks to Candide and even when translated they still appeared witty. Among all the things which amazed Candide, this did not amaze him the least. They enjoyed this hospitality for a month. Candide repeatedly said to Cacambo: "Once again, my friend, it is quite true that the castle where I was born cannot be compared with this country; but then Mademoiselle Cunegonde is not here and you probably have a mistress in Europe. If we remain here, we shall only be like everyone else; but if we return to our own world with only twelve sheep laden with Eldorado pebbles, we shall be richer than all the kings put together; we shall have no more Inquisitors to fear and we can easily regain Mademoiselle Cunegonde." Cacambo agreed with this; it is so pleasant to be on the move, to show off before friends, to make a parade of the things seen on one's travels, that these two happy men resolved to be so no longer and to ask his Majesty's permission to depart. "You are doing a very silly thing," said the King. "I know my country is small; but when we are comfortable anywhere we should stay there; I certainly have not the right to detain foreigners, that is a tyranny which does not exist either in our manners or our laws; all men are free, leave when you please, but the way

out is very difficult. It is impossible to ascend the rapid
river by which you miraculously came here and which flows
under arches of rock. The mountains which surround the
whole of my kingdom are ten thousand feet high and are
perpendicular like walls; they are more than ten leagues
broad, and you can only get down from them by way of
precipices. However, since you must go, I will give orders to
the directors of machinery to make a machine which will
carry you comfortably. When you have been taken to the
other side of the mountains, nobody can proceed any farther
with you; for my subjects have sworn never to pass this
boundary and they are too wise to break their oath. Ask
anything else of me you wish." "We ask nothing of your
Majesty," said Cacambo, "except a few sheep laden with
provisions, pebbles and the mud of this country." The King
laughed. "I cannot understand," said he, "the taste you people of Europe have for our yellow mud; but take as much as
you wish, and much good may it do you." He immediately
ordered his engineers to make a machine to hoist these two
extraordinary men out of his kingdom. Three thousand
learned scientists worked at it; it was ready in a fortnight
and only cost about twenty million pounds sterling in the
money of that country. Candide and Cacambo were placed
on the machine; there were two large red sheep saddled and
bridled for them to ride on when they had passed the
mountains, twenty pack sheep laden with provisions, thirty
carrying presents of the most curious productions of the
country and fifty laden with gold, precious stones and diamonds. The King embraced the two vagabonds tenderly.
Their departure was a splendid sight and so was the ingenious manner in which they and their sheep were hoisted
onto the top of the mountains. The scientists took leave of
them after having landed them safely, and Candide's only
desire and object was to go and present Mademoiselle

Cunegonde with his sheep. "We have sufficient to pay the governor of Buenos Ayres," said he, "if Mademoiselle Cunegonde can be bought. Let us go to Cayenne, and take ship, and then we will see what kingdom we will buy."

CHAPTER XIX

*What happened to them at Surinam and how
Candide made the acquaintance of Martin*

OUR two travelers' first day was quite pleasant. They were encouraged by the idea of possessing more treasures than all Asia, Europe and Africa could collect. Candide in rapture carved the name of Cunegonde on the trees. On the second day two of the sheep stuck in a marsh and were swallowed up with their loads; two other sheep died of fatigue a few days later; then seven or eight died of hunger in a desert; several days afterwards others fell off precipices. Finally, after they had traveled for a hundred days, they had only two sheep left. Candide said to Cacambo: "My friend, you see how perishable are the riches of this world; nothing is steadfast but virtue and the happiness of seeing Mademoiselle Cunegonde again." "I admit it," said Cacambo, "but we still have two sheep with more treasures than the King of Spain will ever have, and in the distance I see a town I suspect is Surinam, which belongs to the Dutch. We are at the end of our troubles and the beginning of our happiness." As they drew near the town they came upon a Negro lying on the ground wearing only half his clothes, that is to say, a pair of blue cotton drawers; this poor man had no left leg and no right hand. "Good heavens!" said Candide to him in Dutch, "what are you doing there, my friend, in that horrible state?" "I am waiting for my master, the famous merchant Monsieur Vanderdendur." "Was it Monsieur Vanderdendur," said Candide, "who treated you in that way?" "Yes, sir," said the Negro, "it is the custom. We are given a pair of cotton drawers twice a year as clothing. When we work in the sugar-mills and the grindstone catches our fingers, they cut off the hand; when we try to run away, they cut off a leg. Both these things happened to me. This is the price paid for the sugar you eat in Europe. But when my mother sold me for ten patagons on the coast of Guinea, she said to me: 'My dear child, give thanks to our fetishes, always worship them, and they will make you happy; you have the honor to be a slave of our lords the white men and thereby you have made the fortune of your father and mother.' Alas! I do not know whether I made their fortune, but they certainly did not make mine. Dogs, monkeys and parrots are a thousand times less miserable than we are; the Dutch fetishes who converted me tell me that we are all of us, whites and blacks, the children of Adam. I am not a genealogist, but if these preachers tell the truth, we are all second cousins. Now, you will admit that no one could treat his relatives in a more horrible way." "O Pangloss!" cried Candide. "This is an abomination you had not guessed; this is too much, in the end I shall have to renounce optimism." "What is optimism?" said Cacambo. "Alas!" said Candide, "it is the mania of maintaining that everything is well when we are wretched." And he shed tears as he looked at his Negro; and he entered Surinam weeping. The first thing they inquired was whether there was any ship in the port which could be sent to Buenos Ayres. The person they addressed happened to be a Spanish captain, who offered to strike an honest bargain with them.

He arranged to meet them at an inn. Candide and the faithful Cacambo went and waited for him with their two sheep. Candide, who blurted everything out, told the Spaniard all his adventures and confessed that he wanted to elope with Mademoiselle Cunegonde. "I shall certainly not take you to Buenos Ayres," said the captain. "I should be hanged and you would, too. The fair Cunegonde is his Lordship's favorite mistress." Candide was thunderstruck; he sobbed for a long time; then he took Cacambo aside. "My dear friend," said he, "this is what you must do. We have each of us in our pockets five or six millions' worth of diamonds; you are more skillful than I am; go to Buenos Ayres and get Mademoiselle Cunegonde. If the governor makes any difficulties give him a million; if he is still obstinate give him two; you have not killed an Inquisitor so they will not suspect you. I will fit out another ship, I will go and wait for you at Venice; it is a free country where there is nothing to fear from Bulgarians, Abares, Jews or Inquisitors." Cacambo applauded this wise resolution; he was in despair at leaving a good master who had become his intimate friend; but the pleasure of being useful to him overcame the grief of leaving him. They embraced with tears. Candide urged him not to forget the good old woman. Cacambo set off that very same day; he was a very good man, this Cacambo. Candide remained some time longer at Surinam waiting for another captain to take him to Italy with the two sheep he had left. He engaged servants and bought everything necessary for a long voyage. At last Monsieur Vanderdendur, the owner of a large ship, came to see him. "How much do you want," he asked this man, "to take me straight to Venice with my servants, my baggage and these two sheep?" The captain asked for ten thousand piastres. Candide did not hesitate. "Oh! Ho!" said the prudent Vanderdendur to himself, "this foreigner gives ten thousand piastres immediately! He must be very rich." He returned a moment afterwards and said he could not sail for less than twenty thousand. "Very well, you shall have them," said Candide. "Whew!" said the merchant to himself, "this man gives twenty thousand piastres as easily as ten thousand." He came back again, and said he could not take him to Venice for less than thirty thousand piastres. "Then you shall have thirty thousand," replied Candide. "Oho!" said the Dutch merchant to himself again, "thirty thousand piastres is nothing to this man, obviously the two sheep are laden with immense treasures; I will not insist any further; first let me make him pay the thirty thousand piastres, and then we will see." Candide sold two little diamonds, the smaller of which was worth more than all the money the captain asked. He paid him in advance. The two sheep were taken on board. Candide followed in a little boat to join the ship which rode at anchor; the captain watched his time, set his sails and weighed anchor; the wind was favorable. Candide, bewildered and stupefied, soon lost sight of him. "Alas!" he cried, "this is a trick worthy of the old world." He returned to shore, in grief; for he had lost enough to make the fortunes of twenty kings. He went to the Dutch judge; and, as he was rather disturbed, he knocked loudly at the door; he went in, related what had happened and talked a little louder than he ought to have done. The judge began by fining him ten thousand piastres for the noise he had made; he then listened patiently to him, promised to look into his affair as soon as the merchant returned, and charged him another ten thousand piastres for the expenses of the audience. This behavior reduced Candide to despair; he had indeed endured misfortunes a thousand times more painful; but the calmness of the judge and of the captain who had robbed him, stirred up his bile and plunged him into a black melancholy. The malevolence of men revealed itself to his

mind in all its ugliness; he entertained only gloomy ideas.
At last a French ship was about to leave for Bordeaux and,
since he no longer had any sheep laden with diamonds to
put on board, he hired a cabin at a reasonable price and
announced throughout the town that he would give the passage, food and two thousand piastres to an honest man who
would make the journey with him, on condition that this
man was the most unfortunate and the most disgusted with
his condition in the whole province. Such a crowd of appli-
cants arrived that a fleet would not have contained them.
Candide, wishing to choose among the most likely, picked
out twenty persons who seemed reasonably sociable and
who all claimed to deserve his preference. He collected them
in a tavern and gave them supper, on condition that each
took an oath to relate truthfully the story of his life, promis-
ing that he would choose the man who seemed to him the
most deserving of pity and to have the most cause for being
discontented with his condition, and that he would give the
others a little money. The sitting lasted until four o'clock
in the morning. As Candide listened to their adventures he
remembered what the old woman had said on the voyage to
Buenos Ayres and how she had wagered that there was
nobody on the boat who had not experienced very great
misfortunes. At each story which was told him, he thought
of Pangloss. "This Pangloss," said he, "would have some
difficulty in supporting his system. I wish he were here.
Certainly, if everything is well, it is only in Eldorado and
not in the rest of the world." He finally determined in favor
of a poor man of letters who had worked ten years for the
booksellers at Amsterdam. He judged that there was no
occupation in the world which could more disgust a man.
This man of letters, who was also a good man, had been
robbed by his wife, beaten by his son, and abandoned by
his daughter, who had eloped with a Portuguese. He had

just been deprived of a small post on which he depended
and the preachers of Surinam were persecuting him because
they thought he was a Socinian. It must be admitted that
the others were at least as unfortunate as he was; but Candide hoped that this learned man would help pass the time
during the voyage. All his other rivals considered that Candide was doing them a great injustice; but he appeased them
by giving each of them a hundred piastres.

CHAPTER XX

What happened to Candide and Martin at sea

SO the old man, who was called Martin, embarked with
Candide for Bordeaux. Both had seen and suffered much;
and if the ship had been sailing from Surinam to Japan by
way of the Cape of Good Hope they would have been able
to discuss moral and physical evil during the whole voyage.
However, Candide had one great advantage over Martin,
because he still hoped to see Mademoiselle Cunegonde
again, and Martin had nothing to hope for; moreover, he
possessed gold and diamonds; and, although he had lost a
hundred large red sheep laden with the greatest treasures on
earth, although he was still enraged at being robbed by the
Dutch captain, yet when he thought of what he still had left
in his pockets and when he talked of Cunegonde, especially
at the end of a meal, he still inclined towards the system of
Pangloss. "But what do you think of all this, Martin?" said
he to the man of letters. "What is your view of moral and
physical evil?" "Sir," replied Martin, "my priests accused

me of being a Socinian; but the truth is I am a Manichæan."
"You are poking fun at me," said Candide, "there are no
Manichæans left in the world." "I am one," said Martin. "I
don't know what to do about it, but I am unable to think
in any other fashion." "You must be possessed by the
devil," said Candide. "He takes so great a share in the
affairs of this world," said Martin, "that he might well be in
me, as he is everywhere else; but I confess that when I consider this globe, or rather this globule, I think that God has
abandoned it to some evil creature—always excepting Eldorado. I have never seen a town which did not desire the ruin
of the next town, never a family which did not wish to
exterminate some other family. Everywhere the weak loathe
the powerful before whom they cower and the powerful
treat them like flocks of sheep whose wool and flesh are to
be sold. A million drilled assassins go from one end of
Europe to the other murdering and robbing with discipline
in order to earn their bread, because there is no more honest occupation; and in the towns which seem to enjoy peace
and where the arts flourish, men are devoured by more
envy, troubles and worries than the afflictions of a besieged
town. Secret griefs are even more cruel than public miseries.
In a word, I have seen so much and endured so much that I
have become a Manichæan." "Yet there is some good,"
replied Candide. "There may be," said Martin, "but I do
not know it." In the midst of this dispute they heard the
sound of cannon. The noise increased every moment. Every
one took his telescope. About three miles away they saw
two ships engaged in battle; and the wind brought them so
near the French ship that they had the pleasure of seeing
the fight at their ease. At last one of the two ships fired a
broadside so accurately and so low down that the other ship
began to sink. Candide and Martin distinctly saw a hundred
men on the main deck of the sinking ship; they raised their

hands to Heaven and uttered frightful shrieks; in a moment all were engulfed. "Well!" said Martin, "that is how men treat each other." "It is certainly true," said Candide, "that there is something diabolical in this affair." As he was speaking, he saw something of a brilliant red swimming near the ship. They launched a boat to see what it could be; it was one of his sheep. Candide felt more joy at recovering this sheep than grief at losing a hundred all laden with large diamonds from Eldorado. The French captain soon perceived that the captain of the remaining ship was a Spaniard and that the sunken ship was a Dutch pirate; the captain was the very same who had robbed Candide. The immense wealth this scoundrel had stolen was swallowed up with him in the sea and only a sheep was saved. "You see," said Candide to Martin, "that crime is sometimes punished; this scoundrel of a Dutch captain has met the fate he deserved." "Yes," said Martin, "but was it necessary that the other passengers on his ship should perish too? God punished the thief, and the devil punished the others." Meanwhile the French and Spanish ships continued on their way and Candide continued his conversation with Martin. They argued for a fortnight and at the end of the fortnight they had got no further than at the beginning. But after all, they talked, they exchanged ideas, they consoled each other. Candide stroked his sheep. "Since I have found you again," said he, "I may very likely find Cunegonde."

CHAPTER XXI

AT last they sighted the coast of France. "Have you ever been to France, Monsieur Martin?" said Candide. "Yes," said Martin, "I have traversed several provinces. In some half the inhabitants are crazy, in others they are too artful, in some they are usually quite gentle and stupid, and in others they think they are clever; in all of them the chief occupation is making love, the second scandal-mongering and the third talking nonsense." "But, Monsieur Martin, have you seen Paris?" "Yes, I have seen Paris; it is a mixture of all the species; it is a chaos, a throng where everybody hunts for pleasure and hardly anybody finds it, at least so far as I could see. I did not stay there long; when I arrived there I was robbed of everything I had by pickpockets at Saint-Germain's fair; they thought I was a thief and I spent a week in prison; after which I became a printer's reader to earn enough to return to Holland on foot. I met the scribbling rabble, the intriguing rabble and the fanatical rabble. We hear that there are very polite people in the town; I am glad to think so." "For my part, I have not the least curiosity to see France," said Candide. "You can easily guess that when a man has spent a month in Eldorado he cares to see nothing else in the world but Mademoiselle Cunegonde. I shall go and wait for her at Venice; we will go to Italy by way of France; will you come with me?" "Willingly," said Martin. "They say that Venice is only for the Venetian nobles but that foreigners are nevertheless well received when they have plenty of money; I have none, you have plenty, I will follow you anywhere." "By the way," said Candide, "do you think the earth was originally a sea, as we are assured by that large book belonging to the captain?" "I don't believe it in the least," said Martin, "any more than all the other whimsies we have been pestered with recently!" "But to what end was this world formed?" said Candide. "To infuriate us," replied Martin. "Are you not very much surprised," continued Candide, "by the love those girls of the country of the Oreillons had for those two monkeys, whose adventure I told you?" "Not in the least," said Martin. "I see nothing strange in their passion; I have seen so many extraordinary things that nothing seems extraordinary to me." "Do you think," said Candide, "that men have always massacred each other, as they do today? Have they always been liars, cheats, traitors, brigands, weak, flighty, cowardly, envious, gluttonous, drunken, grasping, and vicious, bloody, back-biting, debauched, fanatical, hypocritical and stupid?" "Do you think," said Martin, "that sparrow-hawks have always eaten the pigeons they came across?" "Yes, of course," said Candide. "Well," said Martin, "if sparrow-hawks have always possessed the same nature, why should you expect men to change theirs?" "Oh!" said Candide, "there is a great difference; free-will . . ." Arguing thus, they arrived at Bordeaux.

CHAPTER XXII

What happened to Candide and Martin in France

CANDIDE remained in Bordeaux only long enough to sell a few Eldorado pebbles and to provide himself with a two-seated post-chaise, for he could no longer get on without his philosopher Martin; but he was very much grieved at having to part with his sheep, which he left with the Academy of Sciences at Bordeaux. The Academy offered as the subject for a prize that year the cause of the redness of the sheep's fleece; and the prize was awarded to a learned man in the North, who proved by A plus B minus C divided by Z that the sheep must be red and die of the sheep-pox. However all the travelers Candide met in taverns on the way said to him: "We are going to Paris." This general eagerness at length made him wish to see that capital; it was not far out of the road to Venice. He entered by the Faubourg Saint-Marceau and thought he was in the ugliest village of Westphalia. Candide had scarcely reached his inn when he was attacked by a slight illness caused by fatigue. As he wore an enormous diamond on his finger, and a prodigiously heavy strong-box had been observed in his baggage, he immediately had with him two doctors he had not asked for, several intimate friends who would not leave him and two devotees who kept making him broth. Said Martin: "I remember that I was ill too when I first came to Paris; I was very poor; so I had no friends, no devotees, no doctors, and I got well." However, with the aid of medicine and blood-letting, Candide's illness became serious. An inhabitant of the district came and gently asked him for a

note payable to bearer in the next world; Candide would
have nothing to do with it. The devotees assured him that it
was a new fashion; Candide replied that he was not a fashionable man. Martin wanted to throw the inhabitant out the
window; the clerk swore that Candide should not be buried;
Martin swore that he would bury the clerk if he continued
to annoy them. The quarrel became heated; Martin took
him by the shoulders and turned him out roughly; this
caused a great scandal, and they made an official report on
it. Candide got better; and during his convalescence he had
very good company to supper with him. They gambled for
high stakes. Candide was vastly surprised that he never
drew an ace; and Martin was not surprised at all. Among
those who did the honors of the town was a little abbé from
Périgord, one of those assiduous people who are always
alert, always obliging, impudent, fawning, accommodating,
always on the look-out for the arrival of foreigners, ready
to tell them all the scandals of the town and to procure
them pleasures at any price. This abbé took Candide and
Martin to the theatre. A new tragedy was being played.
Candide was seated near several wits. This did not prevent
his weeping at perfectly played scenes. One of the argumentative bores near him said during an interval: "You
have no business to weep, this is a very bad actress, the
actor playing with her is still worse, the play is still worse
than the actors; the author does not know a word of Arabic
and yet the scene is in Arabia; moreover, he is a man who
does not believe in innate ideas; tomorrow I will bring you
twenty articles written against him." "Sir," said Candide to
the abbé, "how many plays have you in France?" "Five or
six thousand," he replied. "That's a lot," said Candide,
"and how many good ones are there?" "Fifteen or sixteen,"
replied the other. "That's a lot," said Martin. Candide was
greatly pleased with an actress who took the part of Queen

Elizabeth in a rather dull tragedy which is sometimes played. "This actress," said he to Martin, "pleases me very much; she looks rather like Mademoiselle Cunegonde; I should be very glad to pay her my respects." The abbé offered to introduce her to him. Candide, brought up in Germany, asked what was the etiquette, and how queens of England were treated in France. "There is a distinction," said the abbé, "in the provinces we take them to a tavern; in Paris we respect them when they are beautiful and throw them in the public sewer when they are dead." "Queens in the public sewer!" said Candide. "Yes, indeed," said Martin, "the abbé is right; I was in Paris when Mademoiselle Monime departed, as they say, this life; she was refused what people here call the *honors of burial*—that is to say, the honor of rotting with all the beggars of the district in a horrible cemetery; she was buried by herself at the corner of the Rue de Burgoyne; which must have given her extreme pain, for her mind was very lofty."[1] "That was very impolite," said Candide. "What do you expect?" said Martin. "These people are like that. Imagine all possible contradictions and incompatibilities; you will see them in the government, in the law-courts, in the churches and the entertainments of this absurd nation." "Is it true that people are always laughing in Paris?" said Candide. "Yes," said the abbé, "but it is with rage in their hearts, for they complain of everything with roars of laughter and they even commit with laughter the most detestable actions." "Who is that fat pig," said Candide, "who said so much ill of the play I cried at so much and of the actors who gave me so much pleasure?" "He is a living evil," replied the abbé, "who earns his living by abusing all plays and all books; he hates any-

[1]Mademoiselle Monime is the actress Adrienne Lecouvreur. On her death in 1730 she was denied burial in consecrated ground. According to some reports, Voltaire helped to bury her secretly by night.

one who succeeds, as eunuchs hate those who enjoy; he is one of the serpents of literature who feed on filth and venom; he is a scribbler." "What do you mean by a scribbler?" said Candide. "A scribbler of periodical sheets," said the abbé. "A Fréron."[2] Candide, Martin and the abbé from Périgord talked in this manner on the stairway as they watched everybody going out after the play. "Although I am most anxious to see Mademoiselle Cunegonde again," said Candide, "I should like to sup with Mademoiselle Clairon, for I thought her admirable." The abbé was not the sort of man to know Mademoiselle Clairon, for she saw only good company. "She is engaged this evening," he said, "but I shall have the honor to take you to the house of a lady of quality, and there you will learn as much of Paris as if you had been here for four years." Candide, who was naturally curious, allowed himself to be taken to the lady's house at the far end of the Faubourg Saint-Honoré; they were playing faro; twelve gloomy punters each held a small hand of cards, the dog-eared register of their misfortunes. The silence was profound, the punters were pale, the banker was uneasy, and the lady of the house, seated beside this pitiless banker, watched with lynx's eyes every double stake, every seven-and-the-go, with which each player marked his cards; she had them un-marked with severe but polite attention, for fear of losing her customers; the lady called herself Marquise de Parolignac. Her fifteen-year-old daughter was among the punters and winked to her to let her know the tricks of the poor people who attempted to repair the cruelties of fate. The abbé from Périgord, Candide and Martin entered; nobody rose, nobody greeted them, nobody looked at them; everyone was profoundly occupied with the cards. "Her Ladyship, the Baroness of Thunder-ten-tronckh, was

---

[2]Fréron was a literary journalist of the day who ceaselessly scribbled attacks on Voltaire.

more civil," said Candide. However the abbé whispered in
the ear of the Marquise, who half rose, honored Candide
with a gracious smile and Martin with a most noble nod.
Candide was given a seat and a hand of cards, and lost fifty
thousand francs in two hands; after which they supped very
merrily and everyone was surprised that Candide was not
more disturbed by his loss. The lackeys said to each other,
in the language of lackeys: "He must be an English
Milord." The supper was like most suppers in Paris; first
there was a silence and then a noise of indistinguishable
words, then jokes, most of which were insipid, false news,
false arguments, some politics and a great deal of scandal;
there was even some talk of new books. "Have you seen,"
said the abbé from Périgord, "the novel by Gauchat, the
doctor of theology?" "Yes," replied one of the guests, "but I
could not finish it. We have a crowd of silly writings, but
all of them together do not approach the silliness of
Gauchat, doctor of theology. I am so weary of this immen-
sity of detestable books which inundates us that I have
taken to faro." "And what do you say about the *Mélanges*
by Archdeacon T.?"[3] said the abbé. "Ah!" said Madame de
Parolignac, "the tiresome creature! How carefully he tells
you what everybody knows! How heavily he discusses what
is not worth the trouble of being lightly mentioned! How
witlessly he appropriates other people's wit! How he spoils
what he steals! How he disgusts me! But he will not disgust
me any more; it is enough to have read a few pages by the
Archdeacon." There was a man of learning and taste at
table who confirmed what the marchioness had said. They
then talked of tragedies; the lady asked why there were
tragedies which were sometimes played and yet were
unreadable. The man of taste explained very clearly how a
play might have some interest and hardly any merit; in a

[3]The allusion is to another of Voltaire's enemies, the Abbé Trublet.

few words he proved that it was not sufficient to bring in
one or two of the situations which are found in all novels
and which always attract the spectators; but that a writer of
tragedies must be original without being bizarre, often sublime and always natural, must know the human heart and
be able to give it speech, must be a great poet but not let
any character in his play appear to be a poet, must know
his language perfectly, speak it with purity, with continual
harmony and never allow the sense to be spoilt for the sake
of the rhyme. "Anyone," he added, "who does not observe
all these rules may produce one or two tragedies applauded
in the theatre, but he will never be ranked among good
writers; there are a very few good tragedies; some are idylls
in well-written and well-rhymed dialogue; some are political
arguments which send one to sleep, or repulsive amplifica-
tions; others are the dreams of an enthusiast, in a barbarous
style, with broken dialogue, long apostrophes to the gods
(because he does not know how to speak to men), false
maxims and turgid commonplaces." Candide listened attentively to these remarks and thought highly of the speaker;
and, as the marchioness had been careful to place him
beside her, he leaned over to her ear and took the liberty of
asking her who was the man who talked so well. "He is a
man of letters," said the lady, "who does not play cards and
is sometimes brought here to supper by the abbé; he has a
perfect knowledge of tragedies and books and he has written
a tragedy which was hissed and a book of which only one
copy has ever been seen outside his bookseller's shop and
that was one he gave me." "The great man!" said Candide.
"He is another Pangloss." Then, turning to him, Candide
said: "Sir, no doubt you think that all is for the best in the
physical world and in the moral, and that nothing could be
otherwise than as it is?" "Sir," replied the man of letters, "I

do not think anything of the sort. I think everything goes awry with us, that nobody knows his rank or his office, nor what he is doing, nor what he ought to do, and that except at supper, which is quite gay and where there appears to be a certain amount of sociability, all the rest of their time is passed in senseless quarrels: Jansenists with Molinists, lawyers with churchmen, men of letters with men of letters, courtiers with courtiers, financiers with the people, wives with husbands, relatives with relatives—'tis an eternal war." Candide replied: "I have seen worse things; but a wise man, who has since had the misfortune to be hanged, taught me that it is all for the best; these are only the shadows in a fair picture." "Your wise man who was hanged was poking fun at the world," said Martin; "and your shadows are horrible stains." "The stains are made by men," said Candide, "and they cannot avoid them." "Then it is not their fault," said Martin. Most of the gamblers, who had not the slightest understanding of this kind of talk, were drinking; Martin argued with the man of letters and Candide told the hostess some of his adventures. After supper the marchioness took Candide into a side room and made him sit down on a sofa. "Well!" said she, "so you are still madly in love with Mademoiselle Cunegonde of Thunder-ten-tronckh?" "Yes, madame," replied Candide. The marchioness replied with a tender smile: "You answer like a young man from Westphalia. A Frenchman would have said: 'It is true that I was in love with Mademoiselle Cunegonde, but when I see you, madame, I fear that I should cease to love her.'" "Alas! madame," said Candide, "I will answer as you wish." "Your passion for her," said the marchioness, "began by picking up her handkerchief; I want you to pick up my garter." "With all my heart," said Candide; and he picked it up. "But I want you to put it on again," said the lady; and Candide put it on again. "You see," said the lady, "you are a foreigner; I sometimes make my lovers in Paris languish for a fortnight, but I give myself to you the very first night, because one must do the honors of one's country to a young man from Westphalia." The fair lady, having perceived two enormous diamonds on the young foreigner's hands, praised them so sincerely that they passed from Candide's fingers to the fingers of the marchioness. As Candide went home with his abbé from Périgord, he felt some remorse at having been unfaithful to Mademoiselle Cunegonde. The abbé sympathized with his distress; he had only had a small share in the fifty thousand francs Candide had lost at cards and in the value of the two half-given, half-extorted, diamonds. His plan was to profit as much as he could from the advantages which his acquaintance with Candide might procure for him. He talked a lot about Cunegonde and Candide told him that he should ask that fair one's forgiveness for his infidelity when he saw her at Venice. The abbé from Périgord redoubled his politeness and civilities and took a tender interest in all Candide said, in all he did, and in all he wished to do. "Then, sir," said he, "you are to meet her at Venice?" "Yes, sir," said Candide, "without fail I must go and meet Mademoiselle Cunegonde there." Then, carried away by the pleasure of talking about the person he loved, he related, as he was accustomed to do, some of his adventures with that illustrious Westphalian lady. "I suppose," said the abbé, "that Mademoiselle Cunegonde has a great deal of wit and that she writes charming letters." "I have never received any from her," said Candide, "for you must know that when I was expelled from the castle because of my love for her, I could not write to her; soon afterwards I heard she was dead, then I found her again and then I lost her, and now I have sent an express messenger to her two thousand five hundred leagues from here and am expecting her reply." The abbé listened attentively and seemed rather meditative. He soon took leave of the two foreigners, after having embraced them tenderly. The next morning when Candide woke up he received a letter composed as follows: "Sir, my dearest lover, I have been ill for a week in this town; I have just heard that you are here. I should fly to your arms if I could stir. I heard that you had passed through Bordeaux; I left the faithful Cacambo and the old woman there and they will soon follow me. The governor of Buenos Ayres took everything, but I still have your heart. Come, your presence will restore me to life or will make me die of pleasure." This charming, this unhoped-for letter, filled Candide with inexpressible joy; and the illness of his dear Cunegonde overwhelmed him with grief. Torn between these two sentiments, he took his gold and his diamonds and drove with Martin to the hotel where Mademoiselle Cunegonde was staying. He entered trembling with emotion, his heart beat, his voice was broken; he wanted to open the bed-curtains and to have a light brought. "Do nothing of the sort," said the waiting-maid. "Light would be the death of her." And she quickly drew the curtains. "My dear Cunegonde," said Candide, weeping, "how do you feel? If you cannot see me, at least speak to me." "She cannot speak," said the maid-servant. The lady then extended a plump hand, which Candide watered with his tears and then filled with diamonds, leaving a bag full of gold in the arm-chair. In the midst of these transports a police-officer arrived, followed by the abbé from Périgord and a squad of policemen. "So these are the two suspicious foreigners?" he said. He had them arrested immediately and ordered his bravoes to haul them off to prison. "This is not the way they treat travelers in Eldorado," said Candide. "I am more of a Manichæan than ever," said Martin. "But, sir, where are you taking us?" said Candide. "To the deepest dungeon," said the police-officer. Martin, having recovered his coolness, decided that the lady who pretended to be Cunegonde was a cheat, that the abbé from Périgord was a cheat who had abused Candide's innocence with all possible speed, and that the police-officer was another cheat of whom they could easily be rid. Rather than expose himself to judicial proceedings, Candide, enlightened by this advice and impatient to see the real Cunegonde again, offered the police-officer three little diamonds worth about three thousand pounds each. "Ah! sir," said the man with the ivory stick, "if you had committed all imaginable crimes you would be the most honest man in the world. Three diamonds! Each worth three thousand pounds each! Sir! I would be killed for your sake, instead of taking you to prison. All strangers are arrested here, but trust to me. I have a brother at Dieppe in Normandy, I will take you there; and if you have any diamonds to give him he will take as much care of you as myself." "And why are all strangers arrested?" said Candide. The abbé from Périgord then spoke and said: "It is because a scoundrel from Atrebatum listened to imbecilities;[4] this alone made him commit a parricide, not like that of May 1610, but like that of December 1594, and like several others committed in other years and in other months by other scoundrels who had listened to imbecilities." The police-officer then explained what it was all about. "Ah! the monsters!" cried Candide. "What! Can such horrors be in a nation which dances and sings! Can I not leave at once this country where monkeys

[4]A reference to Robert-François Damiens' attempted assassination of Louis XV in 1755. Atrebatum is the Latin name for the region of Arras where Damiens was born. In May 1610 François Ravaillac assassinated Henri IV; Jean Châtel's attempt of 1594 was unsuccessful.

torment tigers? I have seen bears in my own country; Eldorado is the only place where I have seen men. In God's
name, sir, take me to Venice, where I am to wait for Mademoiselle Cunegonde." "I can only take you to Lower
Normandy," said the officer. Immediately he took off their
irons, said there had been a mistake, sent his men away,
took Candide and Martin to Dieppe, and left them with his
brother. There was a small Dutch vessel in the port. With
the help of three other diamonds the Norman became the
most obliging of men and embarked Candide and his servants in the ship which was about to sail for Portsmouth in
England. It was not the road to Venice; but Candide felt as
if he had escaped from Hell, and he had every intention of
taking the road to Venice at the first opportunity.

CHAPTER XXIII

*Candide and Martin reach the coast of England;
and what they saw there*

"AH! Pangloss, Pangloss! Ah! Martin, Martin! Ah! my dear
Cunegonde! What sort of a world is this?" said Candide on
the Dutch ship. "Something very mad and very abominable," replied Martin. "You know England; are the people
there as mad as they are in France?" "'Tis another sort of
madness," said Martin. "You know these two nations are at
war for a few acres of snow in Canada, and that they are
spending more on this fine war than all Canada is worth, it
is beyond my poor capacity to tell you whether there are
more madmen in one country than in the other; all I know

is that in general the people we are going to visit are
extremely melancholic." Talking thus, they arrived at
Portsmouth. There were multitudes of people on the shore,
looking attentively at a rather fat man who was kneeling
down with his eyes bandaged on the deck of one of the
ships in the fleet; four soldiers placed opposite this man
each shot three bullets into his brain in the calmest manner
imaginable; and the whole assembly returned home with
great satisfaction. "What is all this?" said Candide. "And
what Demon exercises his power everywhere?" He asked
who was the fat man who had just been killed so ceremoni-
ously. "An admiral," was the reply. "And why kill the
admiral?" "Because," he was told, "he did not kill enough
people. He fought a battle with a French admiral and it was
held that the English admiral was not close enough to him."
"But," said Candide, "the French admiral was just as far
from the English admiral!" "That is indisputable," was the
answer, "but in this country it is a good thing to kill an
admiral from time to time to encourage the others."[1] Candide was so bewildered and so shocked by what he saw and
heard that he would not even set foot on shore, but bar-
gained with the Dutch captain (even if he had to pay him as
much as the Surinam robber) to take him at once to Venice.
The captain was ready in two days. They sailed down the
coast of France; and passed in sight of Lisbon, at which
Candide shuddered. They entered the Straits and the
Mediterranean and at last reached Venice. "Praised be
God!" said Candide, embracing Martin. "Here I shall see
the fair Cunegonde again. I trust Cacambo as I would
myself. All is well, all goes well, all goes as well as it possibly could."

[1]Voltaire here alludes to the execution of the English Admiral John Byng in
March 1757. He had interested himself in the case and made several appeals
on behalf of Byng to English authorities and friends.

CHAPTER XXIV

Paquette and Friar Giroflée

AS soon as he reached Venice, he inquired for Cacambo in all the taverns, in all the cafés, and of all the ladies of pleasure; and did not find him. Every day he sent out messengers to all ships and boats; but there was no news of Cacambo. "What!" said he to Martin, "I have had time to sail from Surinam to Bordeaux, to go from Bordeaux to Paris, from Paris to Dieppe, from Dieppe to Portsmouth, to sail along the coasts of Portugal and Spain, to cross the Mediterranean, to spend several months at Venice, and the fair Cunegonde has not yet arrived! Instead of her I have met only a jade and an abbé from Périgord! Cunegonde is certainly dead and the only thing left for me is to die too. Ah! It would have been better to stay in the Paradise of Eldorado instead of returning to this accursed Europe. How right you are, my dear Martin! Everything is illusion and calamity!" He fell into a black melancholy and took no part in the opera *à la mode* or in the other carnival amusements; not a lady caused him the least temptation. Martin said: "You are indeed simple-minded to suppose that a half-breed valet with five or six millions in his pocket will go and look for your mistress at the other end of the world and bring her to you at Venice. If he finds her, he will take her for himself; if he does not find her, he will take another. I advise you to forget your valet Cacambo and your mistress Cunegonde." Martin was not consoling. Candide's melancholy increased, and Martin persisted in proving to him that there was little virtue and small happiness in the world except perhaps in Eldorado where nobody could go. While arguing about this important subject and waiting for Cunegonde, Candide noticed a young Theatine monk in the Piazza San Marco, with a girl on his arm. The Theatine looked fresh, plump and vigorous; his eyes were bright, his air assured, his countenance firm, and his step lofty. The girl was very pretty and was singing; she gazed amorously at her Theatine and every now and then pinched his fat cheeks. "At least you will admit," said Candide to Martin, "that those people are happy. Hitherto I have only found unfortunates in the whole habitable earth, except in Eldorado; but I wager that this girl and the Theatine are very happy creatures." "I wager they are not," said Martin. "We have only to ask them to dinner," said Candide, "and you will see whether I am wrong." He immediately accosted them, paid his respects to them, and invited them to come to his hotel to eat macaroni, Lombardy partridges, and caviar, and to drink Montepulciano, Lacryma Christi, Cyprus and Samos wine. The young lady blushed, the Theatine accepted the invitation, and the girl followed, looking at Candide with surprise and confusion in her eyes which were filled with a few tears. Scarcely had they entered Candide's room when she said: "What! Monsieur Candide does not recognize Paquette!" At these words Candide, who had not looked at her very closely because he was occupied entirely by Cunegonde, said to her: "Alas! my poor child, so it was you who put Dr. Pangloss into the fine state I saw him in?" "Alas! sir, it was indeed," said Paquette. "I see you have heard all about it. I have heard of the terrible misfortunes which happened to Her Ladyship the Baroness's whole family and to the fair Cunegonde. I swear to you that my fate has been just as sad. I was very innocent when you knew me. A Franciscan friar who was my confessor easily seduced me. The results were dreadful; I was obliged to leave the castle shortly after His Lordship the Baron expelled you by kicking you hard and frequently in the backside. If a famous doctor had not taken pity on me I should have died. For some time I was the doctor's mistress from gratitude to him. His wife, who was madly jealous, beat me every day relentlessly; she was a fury. The doctor was the ugliest of men, and I was the most unhappy of all living creatures at being continually beaten on account of a man I did not love. You know, sir, how dangerous it is for a shrewish woman to be the wife of a doctor. One day, exasperated by his wife's behavior, he gave her some medicine for a little cold and it was so efficacious that she died two hours afterwards in horrible convulsions. The lady's relatives brought a criminal prosecution against the husband; he fled and I was put in prison. My innocence would not have saved me if I had not been rather pretty. The judge set me free on condition that he take the doctor's place. I was soon supplanted by a rival, expelled without a penny, and obliged to continue the abominable occupation which to you men seems so amusing and which to us is nothing but an abyss of misery. I came to Venice to practice this profession. Ah! sir, if you could imagine what it is to be forced to caress impartially an old tradesman, a lawyer, a monk, a gondolier, an abbé; to be exposed to every insult and outrage; to be reduced often to borrow a petticoat in order to go and find some disgusting man who will lift it; to be robbed by one of what one has earned with another, to be despoiled by the police, and contemplate for the future nothing but a dreadful old age, a hospital and a dunghill, you would conclude that I am one of the most unfortunate creatures in the world." Paquette opened her heart in this way to Candide in a side room, in the presence of Martin, who said to Candide: "You see, I have already won half my wager." Friar Giroflée had remained in the dining room, drinking a glass while he waited for dinner. "But," said Candide to Paquette, "when I met you, you looked so gay, so happy; you were singing, you were caressing the Theatine so naturally; you seemed to me to be as happy as you are unfortunate." "Ah! sir," replied Paquette, "that is one more misery of our profession. Yesterday I was robbed and beaten by an officer, and today I must seem to be in a good humor to please a monk." Candide wanted to hear no more; he admitted that Martin was right. They sat down to table with Paquette and the Theatine. The meal was quite amusing and towards the end they were talking with some confidence. "Father," said Candide to the monk, "you seem to me to enjoy a fate which everybody should envy; the flower of health shines on your cheek, your face is radiant with happiness; you have a very pretty girl for your recreation and you appear to be very well pleased with your state of life as a Theatine." "Faith, sir," said Friar Giroflée, "I wish all the Theatines were at the bottom of the sea. A hundred times I have been tempted to set fire to the monastery and to go and be a Turk. My parents forced me at the age of fifteen to put on this detestable robe, in order that more money might be left to my cursed elder brother, whom God confound! Jealousy, discord, fury, inhabit the monastery. It is true, I have preached a few bad sermons which bring me in a little money, half of which is stolen from me by the prior; the remainder I spend on girls; but when I go back to the monastery in the evening I feel ready to smash my head against the dormitory walls, and all my colleagues are in the same state." Martin turned to Candide and said with his usual calm: "Well, have I not won the whole wager?" Candide gave two thousand piastres to Paquette and a thousand to Friar Giroflée. "I warrant," said he, "that they will be happy with that." "I don't believe it in the very least," said Martin. "Perhaps you will make them still more unhappy with those piastres." "That may be," said Candide, "but I am consoled by one thing; I see that we often meet people we thought we should never meet again; it may very well be that as I met my red sheep and Paquette, I may also meet Cunegonde again." "I hope," said Martin, "that she will one day make you happy; but I doubt it very much." "You are very hard," said Candide. "That's because I have lived," said Martin. "But look at these gondoliers," said Candide, "they sing all day long." "You do not see them at home, with their wives and their brats of children," said Martin. "The Doge has his troubles, the gondoliers have theirs. True, looking at it all round, a gondolier's lot is preferable to a Doge's; but I think the difference so slight that it is not worth examining." "They talk," said Candide, "about Senator Pococurante who lives in that handsome palace on the Brenta and who is hospitable to foreigners. He is supposed to be a man who has never known a grief." "I should like to meet so rare a specimen," said Martin. Candide immediately sent a request to Lord Pococurante for permission to wait upon him the next day.

CHAPTER XXV

Visit to the noble Venetian, Lord Pococurante[1]

CANDIDE and Martin took a gondola and rowed to the noble Pococurante's palace. The gardens were extensive and ornamented with fine marble statues; the architecture of the

[1]The name Pococurante means "caring little."

palace was handsome. The master of this establishment, a
very wealthy man of about sixty, received the two visitors
very politely but with very little cordiality, which discon-
certed Candide but did not displease Martin. Two pretty
and neatly dressed girls served them with very frothy
chocolate. Candide could not refrain from praising their
beauty, their grace and their skill. "They are quite good
creatures," said Senator Pococurante, "and I sometimes
make them sleep in my bed, for I am very tired of the ladies
of the town, with their coquetries, their jealousies, their
quarrels, their humors, their meanness, their pride, their
folly, and the sonnets one must write or have written for
them; but, after all, I am getting very tired of these two
girls." After lunch, Candide was walking in a long gallery
and was surprised by the beauty of the pictures. He asked
what master had painted the two first. "They are by
Raphael," said the Senator. "Some years ago I bought them
at a very high price out of mere vanity; I am told they are
the finest in Italy, but they give me no pleasure; the color
has gone very dark, the faces are not sufficiently rounded
and do not stand out enough; the draperies have not the
least resemblance to material; in short, whatever they may
say, I do not consider them a true imitation of nature. I
shall only like a picture when it makes me think it is nature
itself; and there are none of that kind. I have a great many
pictures, but I never look at them now." While they waited
for dinner, Pococurante gave them a concert. Candide
thought the music delicious. "This noise," said Pococurante, "is amusing for half an hour; but if it lasts any
longer, it wearies everybody although nobody dares to say
so. Music nowadays is merely the art of executing difficulties and in the end that which is only difficult ceases to
please. Perhaps I should like the opera more, if they had not

made it a monster which revolts me. Those who please may go to see bad tragedies set to music, where the scenes are only composed to bring in clumsily two or three ridiculous songs which show off an actress's voice; those who will or can, may swoon with pleasure when they see a eunuch humming the part of Cæsar and Cato as he awkwardly treads the boards; for my part, I long ago abandoned such trivialities, which nowadays are the glory of Italy and for which monarchs pay so dearly." Candide demurred a little, but discreetly. Martin entirely agreed with the Senator. They sat down to table and after an excellent dinner went into the library. Candide saw a magnificently bound Homer and complimented the Illustrissimo on his good taste. "That is the book," said he, "which so much delighted the great Pangloss, the greatest philosopher of Germany." "It does not delight me," said Pococurante coldly; "formerly I was made to believe that I took pleasure in reading it; but this continual repetition of battles which are all alike, these gods who are perpetually active and achieve nothing decisive, this Helen who is the cause of the war and yet scarcely an actor in the piece, this Troy which is always besieged and never taken—all bore me extremely. I have sometimes asked learned men if they were as bored as I am by reading it; all who were sincere confessed that the book fell from their hands, but it must be in every library, as a monument of antiquity, and like those rusty coins which cannot be put into circulation." "Your Excellency has a different opinion of Virgil?" said Candide. "I admit," said Pococurante, "that the second, fourth and sixth books of his Æneid are excellent, but as for his pious Æneas and the strong Cloanthes and the faithful Achates and the little Ascanius and the imbecile king Latinus and the middle-class Amata and the insipid Lavinia, I think there could be nothing more frigid

and disagreeable. I prefer Tasso and the childish tales of
Ariosto." "May I venture to ask you, sir," said Candide, "if
you do not take great pleasure in reading Horace?" "He has
two maxims," said Pococurante, "which might be useful to
a man of the world, and which, being compressed in ener-
getic verses, are more easily impressed upon the memory;
but I care very little for his Journey to Brundisium, and his
description of a Bad Dinner, and the street brawlers' quarrel between—what is his name?—Rupilius, whose words, he
says, were full of pus, and another person whose words were
all vinegar. I was extremely disgusted with his gross verses
against old women and witches; and I cannot see there is
any merit in his telling his friend Mæcenas that, if he is
placed by him among the lyric poets, he will strike the stars
with his lofty brow. Fools admire everything in a celebrated
author. I only read to please myself, and I only like what
suits me." Candide, who had been taught never to judge
anything for himself, was greatly surprised by what he
heard; and Martin thought Pococurante's way of thinking
quite reasonable. "Oh! There is a Cicero," said Candide. "I
suppose you are never tired of reading that great man?" "I
never read him," replied the Venetian. "What do I care that
he pleaded for Rabirius or Cluentius. I have enough cases to
judge myself; I could better have endured his philosophical
works; but when I saw that he doubted everything, I concluded I knew as much as he and did not need anybody else
in order to be ignorant." "Ah! There are eighty volumes of
the Proceedings of an Academy of Sciences," exclaimed
Martin, "there might be something good in them." "There
would be," said Pococurante, "if a single one of the authors
of all that rubbish had invented even the art of making pins;
but in all those books there is nothing but vain systems and
not a single useful thing." "What a lot of plays I see there,"

said Candide. "Italian, Spanish, and French!" "Yes," said the Senator, "there are three thousand and not three dozen good ones. As for those collections of sermons, which all together are not worth a page of Seneca, and all those large volumes of theology, you may well suppose that they are never opened by me or anybody else." Martin noticed some shelves filled with English books. "I should think," he said, "that a republican would enjoy most of those works written with so much freedom." "Yes," replied Pococurante, "it is good to write as we think; it is the privilege of man. In all Italy, we write only what we do not think; those who inhabit the country of the Cæsars and the Antonines dare not have an idea without the permission of a Dominican monk. I should applaud the liberty which inspires Englishmen of genius if passion and party spirit did not corrupt everything estimable in that precious liberty." Candide, in noticing a Milton, asked him if he did not consider that author to be a very great man. "Who?" said Pococurante. "That barbarian who wrote a long commentary on the first chapter of Genesis in ten books of harsh verses? That gross imitator of the Greeks, who disfigures the Creation, and who, while Moses represents the Eternal Being as producing the world by speech, makes the Messiah take a large compass from the heavenly cupboard in order to trace out his work? Should I esteem the man who spoiled Tasso's hell and devil; who disguises Lucifer sometimes as a toad, sometimes as a pigmy; who makes him repeat the same things a hundred times; makes him argue about theology; and imitates seriously Ariosto's comical invention of firearms by making the devils fire a cannon in Heaven? Neither I nor anyone else in Italy could enjoy such wretched extravagances. The marriage of Sin and Death and the snakes which sin brings forth nauseate any man of delicate taste, and his long description of a hospital would only please a grave-digger. This obscure, bizarre and disgusting poem was despised at its birth; I treat it today as it was treated by its contemporaries in its own country. But then I say what I think, and care very little whether others think as I do." Candide was distressed by these remarks; he respected Homer and rather liked Milton. "Alas," he whispered to Martin, "I am afraid this man would have a sovereign contempt for our German poets." "There wouldn't be much harm in that," said Martin. "Oh! What a superior man!" said Candide under his breath. "What a great genius this Pococurante is! Nothing can please him." After they had thus reviewed all his books they went down into the garden. Candide praised all its beauties. "I have never met anything more tasteless," said the owner. "We have nothing but trifles; but tomorrow I shall begin to plant a garden on a more noble plan." When the two visitors had taken farewell of his Excellency, Candide said to Martin: "Now you will admit that he is the happiest of men, for he is superior to everything he possesses." "Do you not see," said Martin, "that he is disgusted with everything he possesses? Plato said long ago that the best stomachs are not those which refuse all food." "But," said Candide, "is there not pleasure in criticising, in finding faults where other men think they see beauty?" "That is to say," answered Martin "that there is pleasure in not being pleased." "Oh! Well," said Candide, "then there is no one happy except me— when I see Mademoiselle Cunegonde again." "It is always good to hope," said Martin. However, the days and weeks went by; Cacambo did not return and Candide was so much plunged in grief that he did not even notice that Paquette and Friar Giroflée had not once come to thank him.

CHAPTER XXVI

How Candide and Martin supped with six strangers
and who they were

ONE evening when Candide and Martin were going to sit down to table with the strangers who lodged in the same hotel, a man with a face the color of soot came up to him from behind and, taking him by the arm, said: "Get ready to come with us, and do not fail." He turned round and saw Cacambo. Only the sight of Cunegonde could have surprised and pleased him more. He was almost wild with joy. He embraced his dear friend. "Cunegonde is here, of course? Where is she? Take me to her, let me die of joy with her." "Cunegonde is not here," said Cacambo. "She is in Constantinople." "Heavens! In Constantinople! But were she in China, I would fly to her, let us start at once!" "We will start after supper," replied Cacambo. "I cannot tell you any more; I am a slave, and my master is waiting for me; I must go and serve him at table! Do not say anything; eat your supper, and be in readiness." Candide, torn between joy and grief, charmed to see his faithful agent again, amazed to see him a slave, filled with the idea of seeing his mistress again, with turmoil in his heart, agitation in his mind, sat down to table with Martin (who met every strange occurrence with the same calmness), and with six strangers, who had come to spend the Carnival at Venice. Cacambo, who acted as butler to one of the strangers, bent down to his master's head towards the end of the meal and said: "Sire, your Majesty can leave when you wish, the ship is ready." After saying this, Cacambo withdrew. The guests looked at each other with surprise without saying a word, when another servant came up to his master and said: "Sire, your Majesty's post-chaise is at Padua, and the boat is ready." The master made a sign and the servant departed. Once more all the guests looked at each other, and the general surprise doubled. A third servant went up to the third stranger and said: "Sire, believe me, your Majesty cannot remain here any longer; I will prepare everything." And he immediately disappeared. Candide and Martin had no doubt that this was a Carnival masquerade. A fourth servant said to the fourth master: "Your Majesty can leave when you wish." And he went out like the others. The fifth servant spoke similarly to the fifth master. But the sixth servant spoke differently to the sixth stranger who was next to Candide, and said: "Faith, sire, they will not give your Majesty any more credit nor me either, and we may very likely be jailed to-night, both of us; I am going to look to my own affairs, good-bye." When the servants had all gone, the six strangers, Candide and Martin remained in profound silence. At last it was broken by Candide. "Gentlemen," said he, "this is a curious jest. How is it you are all kings? I confess that neither Martin nor I are kings." Cacambo's master then gravely spoke and said in Italian: "I am not jesting, my name is Achmet III. For several years I was Sultan; I dethroned my brother; my nephew dethroned me; they cut off the heads of my viziers; I am ending my days in the old seraglio; my nephew, Sultan Mahmoud, sometimes allows me to travel for my health, and I have come to spend the Carnival at Venice." A young man who sat next to Achmet spoke after him and said: "My name is Ivan; I was Emperor of all the Russias; I was dethroned in my cradle; my father and mother were imprisoned and I was brought up in prison; I sometimes have permission to travel, accompanied by those who guard me, and I have come to spend the Carnival at Venice." The third said: "I am Charles Edward, King of England; my father gave up his rights to the throne to me and I fought a war to assert them; the hearts of eight hundred of my adherents were torn out and dashed in their faces. I have been in prison; I am going to Rome to visit the King, my father, who is dethroned like my grandfather and me; and I have come to spend the Carnival at Venice." The fourth then spoke and said: "I am the King of Poland; the chance of war deprived me of my hereditary states; my father endured the same reverse of fortune; I am resigned to Providence like the Sultan Achmet, the Emperor Ivan and King Charles Edward, to whom God grant long life; and I have come to spend the Carnival at Venice." The fifth said: "I also am the King of Poland; I have lost my kingdom twice; but Providence has given me another state in which I have been able to do more good than all the kings of the Sarmatians together have been ever able to do on the banks of the Vistula; I also am resigned to Providence and I have come to spend the Carnival at Venice." It was now for the sixth monarch to speak. "Gentlemen," said he, "I am not so eminent as you; but I have been a king like anyone else. I am Theodore; I was elected King of Corsica; I have been called Your Majesty and now I am barely called Sir. I have coined money and do not own a farthing; I have had two Secretaries of State and now have scarcely a valet; I have occupied a throne and for a long time lay on straw in a London prison. I am much afraid I shall be treated in the same way here, although I have come, like your Majesties, to spend the Carnival at Venice." The five other kings listened to this speech with a noble compassion. Each of them gave King Theodore twenty sequins to buy clothes and shirts; Candide presented him with a diamond worth two thousand sequins. "Who is this man," said the five kings, "who is able to give a hundred times as much as any of us, and who gives it?" As they were leaving the table, there came to the same hotel four serene highnesses who had also lost their states in the chance of war, and who had come to spend the rest of the Carnival at Venice; but Candide did not even notice these newcomers. He could think of nothing but of going to Constantinople to find his dear Cunegonde.

CHAPTER XXVII

Candide's voyage to Constantinople

THE faithful Cacambo had already spoken to the Turkish captain who was to take Sultan Achmet back to Constantinople and had obtained permission for Candide and Martin to come on board. They both entered this ship after having prostrated themselves before his miserable Highness. On the way, Candide said to Martin: "So we have just supped with six dethroned kings! And among those six kings there was one to whom I gave charity. Perhaps there are many other princes still more unfortunate. Now, I have only lost a hundred sheep and I am hastening to Cunegonde's arms. My dear Martin, once more, Pangloss was right, all is well." "I hope so," said Martin. "But," said Candide, "this is a very singular experience we have just had at Venice. Nobody has ever seen or heard of six dethroned kings supping together in a tavern." "'Tis no more extraordinary," said Martin, "than most of the things which have happened to us. It is very common for kings to be dethroned; and as to the honor we have had of supping

with them, 'tis a trifle not deserving our attention." Scarcely
had Candide entered the ship when he threw his arms
round the neck of his old valet, of his friend Cacambo.
"Well!" said he, "what is Cunegonde doing? Is she still a
marvel of beauty? Does she still love me? How is she? Of
course you have bought her a palace in Constantinople?"
"My dear master," replied Cacambo, "Cunegonde is washing dishes on the banks of Propontis for a prince who
possesses very few dishes; she is a slave in the house of a
former sovereign named Ragotsky, who receives in his
refuge three crowns a day from the Grand Turk; but what
is even sadder is that she has lost her beauty and has
become horribly ugly." "Ah! beautiful or ugly," said Candide, "I am a man of honor and my duty is to love her
always. But how can she be reduced to so abject a condition with the five or six millions you carried off?" "Ah!"
said Cacambo, "did I not have to give two millions to Señor
Don Fernando d'Ibaraa y Figueora y Mascarenes y Lampourdos y Souza, Governor of Buenos Ayres, for permission
to bring away Mademoiselle Cunegonde? And did not a
pirate bravely strip us of all the rest? And did not this pirate
take us to Cape Matapan, to Milo, to Nicaria, to Samos, to
Petra, to the Dardanelles, to Marmora, to Scutari? Cunegonde and the old woman are servants to the prince I
mentioned, and I am slave to the dethroned Sultan." "What
a chain of terrible calamities!" said Candide. "But after all,
I still have a few diamonds; I shall easily deliver Cunegonde. What a pity she has become so ugly." Then, turning
to Martin, he said: "Who do you think is the most to be
pitied, the Sultan Achmet, the Emperor Ivan, King Charles
Edward, or me?" "I do not know at all," said Martin. "I
should have to be in your hearts to know." "Ah!" said Candide, "if Pangloss were here he would know and would tell
us." "I do not know," said Martin, "what scales your Pan-

gloss would use to weigh the misfortunes of men and to estimate their sufferings. All I presume is that there are millions of men on the earth a hundred times more to be pitied than King Charles Edward, the Emperor Ivan and the Sultan Achmet." "That may very well be," said Candide. In a few days they reached the Black Sea channel. Candide began by paying a high ransom for Cacambo and, without wasting time, he went on board a galley with his companions bound for the shores of Propontis, in order to find Cunegonde however ugly she might be. Among the galley slaves were two convicts who rowed very badly and from time to time the Levantine captain applied several strokes of a bull's pizzle to their naked shoulders. From a natural feeling of pity Candide watched them more attentively than the other galley slaves and went up to them. Some features of their disfigured faces appeared to him to have some resemblance to Pangloss and the wretched Jesuit, the Baron, Mademoiselle Cunegonde's brother. This idea disturbed and saddened him. He looked at them still more carefully. "Truly," said he to Cacambo, "if I had not seen Dr. Pangloss hanged, and if I had not been so unfortunate as to kill the Baron, I should think they were rowing in this galley." At the words Baron and Pangloss, the two convicts gave a loud cry, stopped on their seats and dropped their oars. The Levantine captain ran up to them and the lashes with the bull's pizzle were redoubled. "Stop! Stop, sir!" cried Candide. "I will give you as much money as you want." "What! Is it Candide?" said one of the convicts. "What! Is it Candide?" said the other. "Is it a dream?" said Candide. "Am I awake? Am I in this galley? Is that my Lord the Baron whom I killed? Is that Dr. Pangloss whom I saw hanged?" "It is, it is," they replied. "What! Is that the great philosopher?" said Martin. "Ah! sir," said Candide to the Levantine captain, "how much money do you want for My Lord

Thunder-ten-tronckh, one of the first Barons of the empire, and for Dr. Pangloss, the most profound metaphysician of Germany?" "Dog of a Christian," replied the Levantine captain, "since these two dogs of Christian convicts are Barons and metaphysicians, which no doubt is a high rank in their country, you shall pay me fifty thousand sequins." "You shall have them, sir. Row back to Constantinople like lightning and you shall be paid at once. But, no, take me to Mademoiselle Cunegonde." The captain, at Candide's first offer, had already turned the bow towards the town, and rowed there more swiftly than a bird cleaves the air. Candide embraced the Baron and Pangloss a hundred times. "How was it I did not kill you, my dear Baron? And, my dear Pangloss, how do you happen to be alive after having been hanged? And why are you both in a Turkish galley?" "Is it really true that my dear sister is in this country?" said the Baron. "Yes," replied Cacambo. "So once more I see my dear Candide!" cried Pangloss. Candide introduced Martin and Cacambo. They all embraced and all talked at the same time. The galley flew; already they were in the harbor. They sent for a Jew, and Candide sold him for fifty thousand sequins a diamond worth a hundred thousand, for which he swore by Abraham he could not give any more. The ransom of the Baron and Pangloss was immediately paid. Pangloss threw himself at the feet of his liberator and bathed them with tears; the other thanked him with a nod and promised to repay the money at the first opportunity. "But is it possible that my sister is in Turkey?" said he. "Nothing is so possible," replied Cacambo, "since she washes the dishes of a prince of Transylvania." They immediately sent for two Jews; Candide sold some more diamonds; and they all set out in another galley to rescue Cunegonde.

CHAPTER XXVIII

*What happened to Candide, to Cunegonde, to Pangloss,
to Martin, etc.*

"PARDON once more," said Candide to the Baron, "pardon me, reverend father, for having thrust my sword through your body." "Let us say no more about it," said the Baron. "I admit I was a little too sharp; but since you wish to know how it was you saw me in a galley, I must tell you that after my wound was healed by the brother apothecary of the college, I was attacked and carried off by a Spanish raiding party; I was imprisoned in Buenos Ayres at the time when my sister had just left. I asked to return to the Vicar-General in Rome. I was ordered to Constantinople to act as almoner to the Ambassador of France. A week after I had taken up my office I met towards evening a very handsome young page of the Sultan. It was very hot; the young man wished to bathe; I took the opportunity to bathe also. I did not know that it was a most serious crime for a Christian to be found naked with a young Mahometan. A cadi sentenced me to a hundred strokes on the soles of my feet and condemned me to the galley. I do not think a more horrible injustice has ever been committed. But I should very much like to know why my sister is in the kitchen of a Transylvanian sovereign living in exile among the Turks." "But, my dear Pangloss," said Candide, "how does it happen that I see you once more?" "It is true," said Pangloss, "that you saw me hanged; and in the natural course of events I should have been burned. But you remember, it poured with rain when they were going to roast me; the

storm was so violent that they despaired of lighting the fire;
I was hanged because they could do nothing better; a surgeon bought my body, carried me home and dissected me.
He first made a crucial incision in me from the navel to the
collar-bone. Nobody could have been worse hanged than I
was. The executioner of the holy Inquisition, who was a
sub-deacon, was marvellously skillful in burning people, but
he was not used to hanging them; the rope was wet and did
not slide easily and it was knotted; in short, I still breathed.
The crucial incision caused me to utter so loud a scream
that the surgeon fell over backwards and, thinking he was
dissecting the devil, fled away in terror and fell down the
staircase in his flight. His wife ran in from another room at
the noise; she saw me stretched out on the table with my
crucial incision; she was still more frightened than her husband, fled, and fell on top of him. When they had recovered
a little, I heard the surgeon's wife say to the surgeon: 'My
dear, what were you thinking of, to dissect a heretic? Don't
you know the devil always possesses them? I will go and get
a priest at once to exorcise him.' At this I shuddered and
collected the little strength I had left to shout: 'Have pity on
me!' At last the Portuguese barber grew bolder; he sewed
up my skin; his wife even took care of me, and at the end of
a fortnight I was able to walk again. The barber found me
a situation and made me lackey to a Knight of Malta who
was going to Venice; but, as my master had no money to
pay me wages, I entered the service of a Venetian merchant
and followed him to Constantinople. One day I took it into
my head to enter a mosque; there was nobody there except
an old Imam and a very pretty young devotee who was
reciting her prayers; her breasts were entirely uncovered;
between them she wore a bunch of tulips, roses, anemones,
ranunculus, hyacinths and auriculas; she dropped her bunch
of flowers; I picked it up and returned it to her with a most

respectful alacrity. I was so long putting them back that the
Imam grew angry and, seeing I was a Christian, called for
help. I was taken to the cadi, who sentenced me to receive
a hundred strokes on the soles of my feet and sent me to
the galleys. I was chained on the same seat and in the same
galley as My Lord the Baron. In this galley there were four
young men from Marseilles, five Neapolitan priests and two
monks from Corfu, who assured us that similar accidents
occurred every day. His Lordship the Baron claimed that
he had suffered a greater injustice than I; and I claimed that
it was much more permissible to replace a bunch of flowers between a woman's breasts than to be naked with one
of the Sultan's pages. We argued continually, and every day
received twenty strokes of the bull's pizzle, when the chain
of events of this universe led you to our galley and you ran-
somed us." "Well! my dear Pangloss," said Candide, "when
you were hanged, dissected, stunned with blows and made
to row in the galleys, did you always think that everything
was for the best in this world?" "I am still of my first opinion," replied Pangloss, "for after all I am a philosopher; and
it would be unbecoming for me to recant, since Leibnitz
could not be in the wrong and pre-established harmony is
the finest thing imaginable like the plenum and subtle matter."

CHAPTER XXIX

How Candide found Cunegonde and the old woman again

WHILE Candide, the Baron, Pangloss, Martin and Cacambo were relating their adventures, reasoning upon contingent or noncontingent events of the universe, arguing about effects and causes, moral and physical evil, free-will and necessity, and the consolations to be found in the Turkish galleys, they came to the house of the Transylvanian prince on the shores of Propontis. The first objects which met their sight were Cunegonde and the old woman hanging out towels to dry on the line. At this sight the Baron grew pale. Candide, that tender lover, seeing his fair Cunegonde sunburned, blear-eyed, flat-breasted, with wrinkles round her eyes and red, chapped arms, recoiled three paces in horror, and then advanced from mere politeness. She embraced Candide and her brother. They embraced the old woman; Candide bought them both. In the neighborhood was a little farm; the old woman suggested that Candide should buy it, until some better fate befell the group. Cunegonde did not know that she had become ugly, for nobody had told her so; she reminded Candide of his promises in so peremptory a tone that the good Candide dared not refuse her. He therefore informed the Baron that he was about to marry his sister. "Never," said the Baron, "will I endure such baseness on her part and such insolence on yours; nobody shall ever reproach me with this infamy; my sister's children could never enter the noble assemblies of Germany. No, my sister shall never marry anyone but a Baron of the Empire." Cunegonde threw herself at his feet and bathed them in tears; but he was inflexible. "Madman," said Candide, "I rescued you from the galleys, I paid your ransom and your sister's; she was washing dishes here, she is ugly, I am so kind as to make her my wife, and you pretend to oppose me! I should kill you again if I listened to my anger." "You may kill me again," said the Baron, "but you shall never marry my sister while I am alive."

CHAPTER XXX

Conclusion

AT the bottom of his heart Candide had not the least wish to marry Cunegonde. But the Baron's extreme impertinence determined him to complete the marriage, and Cunegonde urged it so warmly that he could not retract. He consulted Pangloss, Martin and the faithful Cacambo. Pangloss wrote an excellent memorandum by which he proved that the Baron had no rights over his sister and that by all the laws of the empire she could make a left-handed marriage with Candide. Martin advised that the Baron should be thrown into the sea; Cacambo decided that he should be returned to the Levantine captain and sent back to the galleys, after which he would be returned by the first ship to the Vicar-General at Rome. This was thought to be very good advice; the old woman approved it; they said nothing to the sister; the plan was carried out with the aid of a little money and they had the pleasure of duping a Jesuit and punishing the pride of a German Baron.

It would be natural to suppose that when, after so

many disasters, Candide was married to his mistress, and living with the philosopher Pangloss, the philosopher Martin, the prudent Cacambo and the old woman, having brought back so many diamonds from the country of the ancient Incas, he would lead the most pleasant life imaginable. But he was so cheated by the Jews that he had nothing left but his little farm; his wife, growing uglier every day, became shrewish and unendurable; the old woman was ailing and even more bad-tempered than Cunegonde. Cacambo, who worked in the garden and then went to Constantinople to sell vegetables, was overworked and cursed his fate. Pangloss was in despair because he did not shine in some German university. As for Martin, he was firmly convinced that people are equally uncomfortable everywhere; he accepted things patiently. Candide, Martin and Pangloss sometimes argued about metaphysics and morals. From the windows of the farm they often watched the ships going by, filled with effendis, pashas, and cadis, who were being exiled to Lemnos, to Mitylene and Erzerum. They saw other cadis, other pashas and other effendis coming back to take the place of the exiles and to be exiled in their turn. They saw the neatly impaled heads which were taken to the Sublime Porte. These sights redoubled their discussions; and when they were not arguing, the boredom was so excessive that one day the old woman dared to say to them: "I should like to know which is worse, to be raped a hundred times by Negro pirates, to have a buttock cut off, to run the gauntlet among the Bulgarians, to be whipped and flogged in an *auto-da-fé*, to be dissected, to row in a galley, in short, to endure all the miseries through which we have passed, or to remain here doing nothing?" "'Tis a great question," said Candide.

These remarks led to new reflections, and Martin especially concluded that man was born to live in the convulsions of distress or in the lethargy of boredom. Candide did not agree, but he asserted nothing. Pangloss confessed that he had always suffered horribly; but, having once maintained that everything was for the best, he had continued to maintain it without believing it.

One thing confirmed Martin in his detestable principles, made Candide hesitate more than ever, and embarrassed Pangloss. And it was this. One day there came to their farm Paquette and Friar Giroflée, who were in the most extreme misery; they had soon wasted their three thousand piastres, had left each other, made up, quarrelled again, been put in prison, escaped, and finally Friar Giroflée had turned Turk. Paquette continued her occupation everywhere and now earned nothing by it. "I foresaw," said Martin to Candide, "that your gifts would soon be wasted and would only make them the more miserable. You and Cacambo were once bloated with millions of piastres and you are no happier than Friar Giroflée and Paquette." "Ah! Ha!" said Pangloss to Paquette, "so Heaven brings you back to us, my dear child? Do you know that you cost me the end of my nose, an eye and an ear! What a plight you are in! Ah! What a world this is!" This new occurrence caused them to philosophize more than ever.

In the neighborhood there lived a very famous Dervish, who was supposed to be the best philosopher in Turkey; they went to consult him; Pangloss was the spokesman and said: "Master, we have come to beg you to tell us why so strange an animal as man was ever created." "What has it to do with you?" said the Dervish. "Is it your business?" "But, reverend father," said Candide, "there is a horrible amount of evil in the world." "What does it matter," said the Dervish, "whether there is evil or good? When his highness sends a ship to Egypt, does he worry about the comfort or discomfort of the rats in the ship?" "Then what should we do?" said Pangloss. "Hold your tongue," said the Dervish. "I flattered myself," said Pangloss, "that I should discuss with you effects and causes, this best of all possible worlds, the origin of evil, the nature of the soul and pre-established harmony." At these words the Dervish slammed the door in their faces.

During this conversation the news went round that at Constantinople two viziers and the mufti had been strangled and several of their friends impaled. This catastrophe made a prodigious noise everywhere for several hours. As Pangloss, Candide and Martin were returning to their little farm, they came upon an old man who was taking the air under a bower of orange-trees at his door. Pangloss, who was as curious as he was argumentative, asked him what was the name of the mufti who had just been strangled. "I do not know," replied the old man. "I have never known the name of any mufti or of any vizier. I am entirely ignorant of the occurrence you mention; I presume that in general those who meddle with public affairs sometimes perish miserably and that they deserve it, but I never inquire what is going on in Constantinople; I content myself with sending there for sale the produce of the garden I cultivate." Having spoken thus, he took the strangers into his house. His two daughters and his two sons presented them with several kinds of sherbet which they made themselves, caymac flavored with candied citron peel, oranges, lemons, limes, pineapples, dates, pistachios and Mocha coffee which had not been mixed with the bad coffee of Batavia and the Isles. After which this good Mussulman's two daughters perfumed the beards of Candide, Pangloss and Martin. "You must have a vast and magnificent estate?" said Candide to the Turk. "I have only twenty acres," replied the Turk. "I cultivate them with my children; and work keeps at bay three great evils: boredom, vice and need."

As Candide returned to his farm he reflected deeply on the Turk's remarks. He said to Pangloss and Martin: "That good old man seems to me to have chosen an existence preferable by far to that of the six kings with whom we had the honor to sup." "Exalted rank," said Pangloss, "is very dangerous, according to the testimony of all philosophers; for Eglon, King of the Moabites, was murdered by Ehud; Absalom was hanged by the hair and pierced by three darts; King Nadab, son of Jeroboam, was killed by Baasha; King Elah by Zimri; Ahaziah by Jehu; Athaliah by Jehoiada; the Kings Jehoiakim, Jeconiah and Zedekiah were made slaves. You know in what manner died Crœsus, Astyages, Darius, Denys of Syracuse, Pyrrhus, Perseus, Hannibal, Jugurtha, Ariovistus, Cæsar, Pompey, Nero, Otho, Vitellius, Domitian, Richard II of England, Edward II, Henry VI, Richard III, Mary Stuart, Charles I, the three Henrys of France, the Emperor Henry IV. You know . . ." "I also know," said Candide, "that we should cultivate our garden." "You are right," said Pangloss, "for, when man was placed in the Garden of Eden, he was placed there *ut operaretur eum*, to dress it and to keep it; which proves that man was not born for idleness." "Let us work without theorizing," said Martin; "'tis the only way to make life endurable."

The whole small fraternity entered into this praiseworthy plan, and each started to make use of his talents. The little farm yielded well. Cunegonde was indeed very ugly, but she became an excellent pastry-cook; Paquette embroidered; the old woman took care of the linen. Even Friar Giroflée performed some service; he was a very good carpenter and even became a man of honor; and Pangloss sometimes said to Candide: "All events are linked up in this best of all possible worlds; for, if you had not been expelled from the noble castle, by hard kicks in your backside for love of Mademoiselle Cunegonde, if you had not been clapped into the Inquisition, if you had not wandered about America on foot, if you had not stuck your sword in the Baron, if you had not lost all your sheep from the land of Eldorado, you would not be eating candied citrons and pistachios here." "That's well said," replied Candide, "but we must cultivate our garden."

PHILOSOPHICAL LETTERS

CONTENTS

INTRODUCTION

There are two things the *Philosophical Letters* can do for twentieth-century people besides amuse them. One is to introduce them (and for this purpose it is as good as any book I know) to the eighteenth century and to those two complementary strains of what, in our deadly provincialism, we call the Western Mind: the French and the English genius. The other is to remind them that there is hope for men because they have it in their power to be reasonable.

Professional philosophy the book is not; it is, however, a collection of critical reports by a *philosophe* of the Age of Reason—that is, a rational observer and free-thinking moralist—interested in the human meaning of all thought and action. The separate letters or chapters are written more or less as if to a friend in France (Nicolas Claude Thieriot), and the book first appeared, in an English translation by John Lockman, as *Letters Concerning the English Nation* (London, 1733). Voltaire himself referred to it often enough as the "English Letters," but it was as *Lettres Philosophiques*, with an additional letter on Pascal, that the book, on June 10, 1734, was condemned by the Parlement of Paris to be lacerated and burnt by the hangman, as "likely to inspire a license of thought most dangerous to religion and civil order." The true work of Voltaire had begun, and our lives are different because of it.

We think of Voltaire as having been, even in his cradle, a wit, a poet, a freely discursive mind. In the story of Ninon de Lenclos' leaving him 2,000 *écus* to buy books with, nothing is more interesting than that when she died, in 1705, he was no more than eleven years old. He was young enough when introduced into the urbane and hedonistic society of the Temple; at twenty-five he was famous as a tragic poet, the author of another *Oedipus*. Ambitious, inquisitive, always busy, he was also a brilliant speculator, and at thirty he had an independent fortune. His genius and individuality were irrepressible, and he was already, as the author of *La Ligue*, known as an epic poet, as well as a critic of powerful institutions and men, when he was called away from dinner with the Duc de Sully and cudgeled in the street by hirelings of the Chevalier de Rohan. After a comfortable stay in the Bastille (it was his second), where he was sent so that he might be protected from his own desire for revenge, he was released on the provision that he keep fifty leagues away from Paris. He went to England.

We do not know the dates of arrival and departure, but we may suppose his visit to have lasted from about the end of May, 1726, to September or October, 1728—that is, roughly two and a half years. Nor do we know much about his life in England, though he seems to have mixed with a fair number of notabilities if only because of the recommendations of Englishmen whom he had known in France—among them Bolingbroke and Horatio Walpole, the British ambassador. We hear of his being with Bubb Dodington, with Lord and Lady Hervey, with Pope, with Gay, and with Mrs. Conduit, the niece of Newton. He met the dowager Duchess of Marlborough; he talked with Berkeley and with Edward Young. It seems that he was, with Swift, for three months the guest of Lord Peterborough. He thought highly enough of Swift to write letters of introduction for him, in June of 1727, to du Noquet, treasurer-general at Calais; to the Comte de Morville, Secretary of State; and to the Marquis de Maisons. The first six months he spent in learning English, partly by means of constant attendance at the theater; by December of 1727 he had written and published two essays in English—one on epic poetry from Homer to Milton, the other on the civil wars in France.

Other travelers had written on the English, particularly during the previous half-century. The book Voltaire finished in 1733 was not so much a description of England and the English as a series of notes on the good life of men and nations. If he had pleased to comment at any length on English eccentricity, for instance, it would have been in the vein of this passage from a letter to Rolland Des Alleurs:

> I assure you again that a man of yr temper would not dislike a country, where one obeys to the laws only and to one's whims. Reason is free here and walks her own way, hippocondriaks especially are well come. No manner of living appears strange; we have men who walk six miles a day for their health, feed upon roots, never taste flesh, wear a coat in winter thinner than yr ladies do in the hottest days.[1]

Reason is free here and walks her own way. . . .

In the *Philosophical Letters*, Voltaire is on the trail of principles, though no book could seem more casual or be more informally put together. That is one of the principles. These letters are not to sound like art. He is talking, without guile or labor it would seem (though the guile will often step forth and preen itself for the pleasure of author and reader); he is talking to everyone who can pause long enough to listen. To a translator, doubly concerned with language, the vocabulary seems limited, repetitious; in the *Philosophical Letters* there are no great adventures in style: the grace of precision, the delicacy of strength will shine in

---

[1] Letter No. 321 in *Voltaire's Correspondence*, ed. Theodore Besterman (Geneva, 1953—).

works to come. This is mere life. And so Voltaire jerks his thumb at the subject with *ce, ce, ce*—this man, this book of this Jones; and so, the translator may now and then feel, the sentences go on, to end in the last murmurs of a subordinate clause. The translator finds that sentences constructed with such unconcern come over into English sounding absurdly ragged; but his infrequent and reluctant shifting of a clause only proves to him the colloquial beauty of the original, the style in style-lessness, the grace of mind when the mind is by nature full of ideas. There is possible triumph in being caught without one's wig.

And the immediate subject matter of these notes? English books and writers Voltaire reports on briefly, for the most part; it is important for his countrymen to know that this home of science and of political and religious liberty has poems and plays worth reading. He glances at their faults as well. The faults of literary works are not so mysterious as the beauties. A Butler makes a great comic poem out of subject matter near to him in place and time; too much of it is meaningless to foreigners and to Englishmen of a later generation. A Shakespeare—and Voltaire was to feel, with some justice, that it was he who had introduced Shakespeare, Newton, and inoculation to the French—a Shakespeare has marvelous beauties in him, but barbarism as well. Barbarism is the toleration or enjoyment of disorder, deformity, horror, and the truly civilized will not admire it as colorful, or excuse it because of poetic beauties elsewhere. Barbarism is indefensible, and the best that poetry can do is remind us of the fact. This classical view of things, absorbed by Voltaire from the air of France, from Boileau, and from the Jesuits who schooled him, is more rational than some moderns appear to think. It assumes that literature is not cut off from life, that poetry is necessarily social, that all things are vitally related to one another, that thought and action have consequences, and that what we admire is much of what we shall come to be.

Voltaire's interest in literature, then, while not unaesthetic, is broadly humane. He must survey and report on Bacon and Locke, even Pascal, for the same reason as he must report on the Parliament. He sees man at the center; he catches at what may make us free and throw light on the world for man's sake. Though granting the genius of Pascal, he sees in him a bent for the antihuman; though he admires the candid manliness of the Quakers, he scorns their artifices of spirituality; though he understands that mathematics paces off the immeasurable, he stares metaphysics in the eye and firmly, on a giddy planet, stakes out our claim. There is work to do on earth; it can be done only if enough men are sufficiently aware of their earthly circumstances. Voltaire is not a democrat but a liberator. He sits down to the subject of scientific method as to the practical questions of government. He is one of the great eighteenth-century popularizers, men who upheld with such passion the value of humanity that they forced the specialists out of their towers, and shamed them into lucid conversation.

For the rest, whether the subject is Quakers or Presbyterians, smallpox or universal gravitation, and whether we are simply enjoying the detail of the moment, we are hearing good news about man: that in his simplicity he is admirable; that he need not be superstitious; that slavery is not inevitable; that science is part of common sense; that reason and instinct are equally gifts of God; that there is no law by which we must make a hell of our earth rather than a garden; above all that we are on our own, helped by no providential hand, and that to be intelligent and just is our responsibility and our finest achievement.

ERNEST DILWORTH

PHILOSOPHICAL
LETTERS

LETTER ONE

ON THE QUAKERS

SINCE it seemed to me that the doctrine and history of so extraordinary a group as the Quakers deserved the curiosity of a thinking man, I went, in order to instruct myself, to visit one of the most famous Quakers in England, a man who, after thirty years in trade, had been able to set a limit to his fortune and to his desires, and had retired into the country near London. I sought him out in his retreat; it was a house small but well built, unornamented and decent throughout. The Quaker himself[1] was a fresh-looking old man who had never had an illness because he had always been a stranger to the passions and to intemperance. I have never in my life seen anyone with more noble, or more engaging, an air.

He was dressed, like all those of his religion, in a coat without pleats in the side, and without buttons on either pockets or sleeves, and he wore a large hat with the brim turned down like those of our clergy. He received me with his hat on his head, and advanced toward me without the slightest hint of a bow; but there was more politeness in the openness and humanity of his expression than there is in the habit of drawing one leg behind the other, and of carrying in the hand what was made to cover the head.

---

[1]In a note added in 1739, Voltaire identifies the Quaker as Andrew Pitt (died at Hampstead, April 16, 1736). They were on good terms, though the Quaker complained that the account went beyond the truth, and assured Voltaire that God was offended at the fun made of the Quakers.

"Friend," said he, "I see that thou art a stranger here; if I can be of any usefulness to thee, thou hast only to speak."

"Sir," said I, bending my body and sliding one foot toward him, according to our custom, "I flatter myself that my honest curiosity will not displease you, and that you will be so kind as to do me the honor of instructing me in your religion."

"The people of thy country," he replied, "make too many bows and compliments, but I have never yet seen one with such curiosity as thine. Come in, and let us first dine together."

I uttered a few more poor compliments, for one does not unmake one's habits all at once; and after a healthful and frugal repast which began and ended with a prayer to God, I set out interrogating my man. I began with the question that good Catholics have more than once asked of Huguenots: "My dear sir, have you been baptized?"

"No," said he, "and neither have my fellow Quakers."

"Zounds!" cried I. "Then you are not Christians?"

"My son," he answered gently, "do not swear. We are Christians and try to be good ones; but we do not think that Christianity consists in throwing cold water on the head, with a little seasoning."

"Good God!" cried I, outraged by this impiousness. "Have you forgotten, then, that Jesus Christ was baptized by John?"

"Friend," said the benign Quaker, "once more no swearing. Christ received baptism from John, but he baptized no one; we are the disciples not of John but of Christ."

"Gracious!" said I. "In an Inquisition country what a fire they would make of you, poor man. Do, for God's sake, let me baptize you and make a Christian out of you."

"If indulging thy weakness called only for that, we would do it willingly," was his grave answer. "We condemn no one for taking part in the ceremony of baptism, but we believe that those who profess a religion altogether holy and altogether spiritual must abstain as much as they can from Jewish rituals."

"That's a strange one," I exclaimed. "Jewish rituals?"

"Yes, my son," he continued, "and so much so that many Jews even today practice the baptism of John. Consult the ancient authors; they will teach thee that John only renewed an old practice which had been followed, among the Hebrews, long before his time, as the pilgrimage to Mecca had been among the Ishmaelites. Jesus consented to be baptized by John just as he submitted to circumcision, but circumcision and ceremonial washing were later to be done away with by the baptism of Christ, that baptism of the spirit, that ablution of the soul that saves mankind. Thus the forerunner John said, 'I indeed baptize you with water unto repentance: but he that cometh after me is mightier than I, whose shoes I am not worthy to bear: he shall baptize you with the Holy Ghost, and with fire.'[2] Thus the great apostle of the Gentiles, Paul, wrote to the Corinthians, 'Christ sent me not to baptize, but to preach the gospel.'[3] And Paul never did baptize any with water except two persons,[4] and that in spite of himself. He circumcised his disciple Timothy, and likewise the other apostles circumcised all who desired it. Art thou circumcised?" he added.

I replied that I had not had that honor.

"Very well, friend," said he, "thou art a Christian without being circumcised, and I without being baptized."

There was my holy man taking specious advantage of

[2]Matthew 3:11.
[3]I Corinthians 1:17.
[4]Crispus and Gaius (I Cor. 1:14-15).

three or four passages of Holy Writ that seemed to favor his sect, and forgetting, in the best of faith, a hundred passages that crushed it. I took care not to dispute anything he said, for there's no arguing with an Enthusiast. Better not take it into one's head to tell a lover the faults of his mistress, or a litigant the weakness of his cause—or to talk sense to a fanatic. And so I went on to other questions.

"With regard to the communion," said I, "what are your customs?"

"We haven't any," said he.

"What, no communion?"

"No. None but the communion of hearts."

Once more he quoted Scripture. He made me a fine sermon against the communion, and took on a tone of inspiration in proving to me that all the sacraments were merely human inventions, and that the word *sacrament* itself is not once to be found in the Gospel.

"Pardon my ignorance," he said. "I have not presented thee with a hundredth part of the proofs of my religion, but thou mayst find them in the exposition of our faith written by Robert Barclay,[5] one of the best books that ever came from the hand of man. Our enemies agree that it is highly dangerous, and that testifies to the honesty of its thought."

I promised to read this book, and my Quaker believed me already converted.

Later he explained to me briefly some of the peculiarities that expose this sect to the scorn of others.

"Confess," said he, "that it was all thou couldst do to keep from laughing when I replied to all thy courtesy in the

[5]Robert Barclay (1648-90), the great expositor of Quaker principles. His best known work is his "Apology." *Apology for the True Christian Divinity, as the same is set forth and preached by the people called in scorn Quakers:* such is the title of the 1678 English version of the work first published at Amsterdam (1676) as *Theologiae verae Christianae Apologia.*

second person singular and with my hat on. Yet thou
seemst too well educated not to know that in the time of
Christ no nation fell into the absurdity of substituting the
plural for the singular. To Augustus Caesar one said, *I love
thee, I beg thee, I thank thee*; he did not even allow anyone
to call him Mister, *Dominus*. It was not till long after his
day that people thought of addressing one another as *you*
instead of *thou*, as if they came in pairs, and of usurping the
impertinent titles of Lordship, Eminence, Holiness, which
earthworms give to other earthworms in assuring them that
they are, with profound respect and infamous falsity, their
most humble and most obedient servants. It is in order to
be more on our guard against this vile commerce of lies and
flattery that we say *thou* to both kings and cobblers, and
that we bow to no one, having nothing but kindness for
men, and respect only for the laws.

"Our clothing too is a little different from that of other
men, as a continual reminder to ourselves not to resemble
them. Others wear the signs of their rank and dignity; we
wear those of Christian humility. We turn away from gay
parties, from shows, from gambling, for we should be much
to be pitied if we filled with such frivolity those hearts that
God should dwell in. We never swear, not even in court,
feeling as we do that the name of the Most High should not
be bandied about in the wretched contests of mankind.
When it is necessary for us to appear before a magistrate in
the affairs of others (for we ourselves do not carry on lawsuits) we affirm the truth with a *yes* or a *no*, and the judges
accept our word, though so many Christians forswear themselves on the very Gospel. If we never go to war, it is not
that we fear death—on the contrary, we bless the moment
that unites us with the Being of Beings—but it's that we are
not wolves or tigers or watchdogs, but men and Christians.
Our Lord, who has commanded us to love our enemies and

to endure without complaint, certainly does not wish us to cross the sea and cut the throats of our brothers because some murderers dressed in red, and wearing hats two feet high, are enlisting citizens by making a noise with two little sticks on the tightly stretched skin of an ass. And when, after battles won, all London glitters with lights, when the sky blazes with fireworks, and the air resounds with the noise of thanksgiving, of bells, of organs, and of cannon, we mourn in silence over these murders, the cause of public gaiety."

LETTER TWO

ON THE QUAKERS

SUCH, in substance, was the conversation I had with that extraordinary man; but I was even more surprised when on the following Sunday he took me to the church of the Quakers. They have several chapels in London; the one I visited is near the famous pillar called the Monument. When I went in with my guide, the congregation had already assembled. There were about four hundred men in the church, and three hundred women; the women hid their faces with their fans, and the men were wearing their broad hats. All were seated, all in profound silence; I passed through the midst of them without causing a single person to look up at me. This silence lasted a quarter of an hour. Finally one of them rose, took off his hat, and after making some faces and heaving some sighs, began to intone, half through his mouth and half through his nose, a rigmarole which was taken, he thought, from the Gospel, and which was utterly meaningless to him and to everybody else. When this contortionist had finished his fine monologue, and the meeting had broken up with everyone both edified and in a stupor, I asked my companion why the more intelligent among them put up with such nonsense.

"We are obliged to tolerate it," he replied, "for it is impossible for us to know whether a man who rises to speak will be moved by the Spirit or by madness. Not knowing, we patiently listen to everything. We even allow women to speak. Often two or three of our devout females find themselves inspired at the same time, and then what a splendid noise there is in the house of the Lord!"

"Haven't you any priests?" I asked.

"No, friend," said the Quaker, "and we do very well without them. God forbid that we should presume to ordain anyone to receive the Holy Ghost on Sunday to the exclusion of the rest of the faithful. By God's grace we are the only ones on earth to have no priests. Would you deprive us of so happy a distinction? Why should we abandon our child to hired nurses when we have milk of our own to give it? Those hirelings would soon dominate our household and tyrannize over mother and child. Our Lord said, 'Freely ye have received; freely give.'[1] Shall we, after this command, bargain for the Gospel, put up the Holy Ghost for sale, and turn a Christian meeting-place into a market? We do not give money to men dressed in black to take care of our poor, bury our dead, and preach to the faithful; these sacred duties are too dear to us to be passed to the shoulders of others."

"But how can you tell," said I insistently, "whether it is the Spirit of God that moves you in your speeches?"

[1]Matthew 10:8.

"Whosoever prays that God enlighten him," he replied, "and then declares the Gospel truths that move him, may be sure that he has been inspired by God."

Whereupon he overwhelmed me with quotations from Scripture proving, so he said, that there is no such thing as Christianity without an immediate revelation. And he added these remarkable words:

"When thou movest one of thy limbs, does thine own power move it? Certainly not, for the same member often acts involuntarily. It is He who created thy body, then, who gives motion to this clay. And what of the ideas thy soul receives? Is it thou who forms them? Even less so, for they come in spite of thee. So it is the Creator of thy soul who gives thee thine ideas. But as he has left thy heart free, he gives thy mind such ideas as thy heart deserves. Thou livest in God; thou actest, thou thinkest in God; and so thou hast only to open thine eyes to that light which enlightens all men, and thou shalt see the truth and make it to be seen."

"Ah, it's the purest Father Malebranche!" I exclaimed.

"I know thy Malebranche," said he. "He was a bit of a Quaker, but not enough of one."[2]

Those are the most important things I have learned about the doctrine of the Quakers. In the next letter you shall have their history, which you will find even more singular than their doctrine.

---

[2]Nicolas de Malebranche (1638-1715), member of the congregation of secular priests known as *l'Oratoire*. His philosophical system, which he condensed in his *Entretiens sur la métaphysique et la religion* (1687), was started on its way by his study of Descartes. To him, human reason and the Divine Word are one: we see all things in God, and are unable to move except through the action of the divine upon us.

LETTER THREE

ON THE QUAKERS

YOU have already seen that the Quakers date from Jesus Christ, who was, according to them, the first Quaker.[1] Religion, they say, was corrupted almost immediately after his death, and remained in corruption some sixteen hundred years; but there were always a few Quakers hidden away in the world, who carefully fostered the sacred flame that was extinct wherever they were not, until finally the light spread to England in the year 1642.[2]

It was in the days when three or four sects were tearing Great Britain apart with wars undertaken in the name of God, that one George Fox, of the county of Leicester, son of a silkweaver, took it into his head to preach like a true Apostle, according to him—that is, without knowing how to read or write.[3] He was a young man of twenty-five, of irreproachable habits, and mad in a saintly way. Clothed in leather from head to foot, he went from village to village, shouting against war and the clergy. If he had only preached against the military, he would have had nothing to fear; but he attacked churchmen: he was promptly sent to prison.

[1] Voltaire's main source of information for this chapter is William Sewel, *The History of the Rise, Increase, and Progress of the Christian People Called Quakers* (1722). He makes some borrowings from Gerard Croese, *Historia Quakeriana* (1695), and he may have seen William Penn's *A Brief Account of the Rise and Progress of the People Called Quakers* (1694).

[2] Fox was born in 1624. In order for him to be twenty-five (see above), 1642 would have to be changed to 1649.

[3] He appears to have known at least how to read at that age; he never wrote like one of the learned, though in all he said he drew heavily on Scripture.

When they led him before the justice of the peace at Derby, he presented himself with his leather cap on his head. An officer gave him a smart box on the ear, saying,

"You beggar, don't you know enough to be bareheaded in the presence of his honor?"

Fox turned the other cheek, and begged the officer to hit him again for the love of God. The Derby justice tried to get him to take oath before being questioned.

"Friend," said he to the justice, "thou must know that I never take the name of the Lord in vain."

Hearing himself *thee'd* and *thou'd* by this man, the justice sent him to the Bedlam of Derby to be whipped. Praising God along the way, George Fox went to his lunatic asylum, where the sentence of the magistrate was rigorously carried out.[4] Those who inflicted on him the penance of the whip were much surprised when he begged them to flog him some more with a birch for the good of his soul. These gentlemen needed no begging, and Fox had his double dose, for which he thanked them cordially. He began to preach to them; first they laughed, then they listened, and, since the disease of Enthusiasm is catching, several were converted, and those who had whipped him became his first disciples.

Released from prison, he wandered about the country with a dozen proselytes, still preaching against the clergy, and having himself whipped from time to time. One day, having been set in the pillory,[5] he harangued the crowd so forcefully that he converted some fifty of his audience, and

[4]Fox was sent to a house of correction for blasphemy, as if for a kind of disorderly conduct. In the same place might be found vagrants, idlers, rogues, the infirm, and the mad. Voltaire has no trouble in turning "house of correction" into "the *Petites-Maisons* of Derby," and then—because in the Hospice des Petites-Maisons in Paris lunatics as well as beggars were lodged—into *"l'Hôpital des Fous."*

[5]Voltaire probably invented the instance of Fox in the pillory, piecing it together from other stories.

roused so much sympathy in the others that they freed him uproariously, sought out the Anglican clergyman through whose influence Fox had been condemned to stand, and pilloried him in his place.

He had the cheek to convert some of Cromwell's soldiers, whereupon they quit the service and refused to take the oath.[6] Cromwell wanted nothing to do with a sect whose members would not fight, as Sixtus the Fifth augured ill of a sect *dove non si chiavava*.[7] He took advantage of his power to persecute these newcomers; the prisons were filled with them. But persecution seldom has any other effect than to make new proselytes; they emerged from prison confirmed in their belief and followed by their jailers, whom they had converted. But here is what contributed most to the increase of the sect: Fox believed himself inspired. The consequence was that he thought he should speak in a different way from other men; he began to tremble, to contort his body and make wry faces, to hold his breath, and then to expel it violently. The Priestess of Delphi wouldn't have made a better job of it. In a short time, inspiration had become remarkably habitual with him, and soon afterward it was almost impossible for him to hold forth in any other way. This was the first gift he bestowed upon his disciples. With perfect sincerity, they made all the grimaces their Master did; they trembled as hard as they could in the moment of inspiration. Hence the name of Quakers. The crowd amused themselves with mimicking them. People trembled, talked through their noses, had convulsions, and fancied that the Holy Ghost was in them.

A few miracles seemed called for; they performed them.

[6]At the beginning of 1654 Cromwell required of his soldiers an oath of fidelity. Refusing to take the oath, then, would seem to come first here.

[7]"where there was no sexual intercourse." One of the bulls of Pope Sixtus the Fifth (1521-90) forbade eunuchs to marry.

Said the Patriarch Fox to a justice of the peace, before a large audience, "Friend, take care: God will soon punish thee for persecuting the Saints." This justice was a drunkard who every day drank altogether too much bad beer and brandy; he died of apoplexy two days after the warning, at the precise moment that he finished signing an order committing some Quakers to prison.[8] The sudden death of the justice was in no way attributed to his intemperance; everyone regarded it as an effect of the holy man's predictions.

That death made more Quakers than a thousand sermons and as many convulsions could have done. Cromwell, seeing that their number increased every day, wished to entice them into his party. He had them offered money, but they were incorruptible, and he said one day that theirs was the sole religion against which guineas had not enabled him to prevail.

They were sometimes persecuted under Charles II, not for their religion, but for refusing to pay tithes, for *theeing* and *thouing* magistrates, and refusing to take oath as prescribed by law.

At last, Robert Barclay, a Scot, presented to the King, in 1675, his *Apology* for the Quakers, as good a work as it could be. The dedication to Charles II contains, not base flattery, but bold truths and good counsel.

"Thou hast tasted of prosperity and adversity," he says to Charles at the end of this epistle; "thou knowest what it is to be banished thy native country, to be overruled, as well as to rule, and sit upon the throne; and being *oppressed*, thou hast reason to know how *hateful* the *oppressor* is both to God and man: If after all these warnings and advertisements, thou dost not turn unto the Lord with all thy heart, but forget him, who remembered thee in thy distress, and

[8]Voltaire's art has improved upon nature.

give up thyself to follow lust and vanity; surely great will be thy condemnation.

"Against which snare as well as the temptation of those that may or do feed thee, and prompt thee to evil, the most excellent and prevalent remedy will be, to apply thyself to that *Light of Christ*, which *shineth in thy conscience*, which neither can nor will flatter thee, nor suffer thee to be at ease in thy sins; but doth and will deal plainly and faithfully with thee, as those that are followers thereof have also done.

. . . Thy faithful friend and subject,
Robert Barclay."[9]

Yet more astonishing: this letter written to a King by an obscure private citizen had its effect and the persecution ceased.

---

[9]Barclay's English version of the *Apology* (pp. viii-ix, second stereotype edition, from the eighth London edition: New York, 1827). Voltaire has sensibly condensed the last paragraph. Here is his French version:

Tu as goûté, dit-il à Charles à la fin de cette Épître, de la douceur et de l'amertume, de la prospérité et des plus grands malheurs; tu as été chassé des pays où tu règnes; tu as senti le poids de l'oppression, et tu dois savoir combien l'oppresseur est détestable devant Dieu et devant les hommes. Que si, après tant d'épreuves et de bénédictions, ton coeur s'endurcissait et oubliait le Dieu qui s'est souvenu de toi dans tes disgrâces, ton crime en serait plus grand et ta condamnation plus terrible. Au lieu donc d'écouter les flatteurs de ta Cour, écoute la voix de ta conscience, qui ne te flattera jamais. Je suis ton fidèle ami et sujet BARCLAY.

LETTER FOUR

ON THE QUAKERS

ABOUT this time there appeared on the scene the illustrious William Penn, who established the power of the Quakers in America, and who would have secured them respectability in Europe if men were able to respect virtue when it lies beneath a ridiculous exterior. He was the only son of Vice-Admiral Penn, a favorite of the Duke of York who was later James II.

At the age of fifteen, William Penn met a Quaker at Oxford, where he was studying at the time. This Quaker made a proselyte of him, and the young man, who was lively and naturally eloquent, and had a certain nobility of feature and of manners, soon won over certain of his fellow students. There quietly grew up a society of young Quakers who met together at his rooms; so that at the age of sixteen he found himself at the head of a sect.

On his return home after leaving college, instead of kneeling before the Vice-Admiral his father and asking his blessing according to English custom, he confronted him with his hat on, and said to him, "I am happy, friend, to see thee in good health." The Vice-Admiral thought his son had gone mad, and then realized that he had become a Quaker. He used every means available to human prudence in order to induce him to live like other people. The young man's only reply was to exhort his father to become a Quaker himself.

At last the father gave way so far as to ask no more

than that he wait upon the King and the Duke of York with his hat under his arm, and without *theeing* and *thouing* them. William replied that his conscience would not permit it, and his father, in indignation and despair, drove him from the house. Young Penn gave thanks to God that he was already suffering in His cause, went to preach in the City, and made a large number of converts.

The sermons of the ministers grew more enlightening every day, and as Penn was young, handsome, and well made, the women of both court and town devotedly flocked to hear him. The Patriarch, George Fox, came from the other end of England to London to see him, on the strength of his reputation, and the two resolved to do missionary work in foreign countries. They embarked for Holland, having left behind them workers in sufficient numbers to take care of the London vineyard. Their labors had happy results in Amsterdam, but what redounded most to their honor, and put their humility most in danger, was the reception given them by Elizabeth, Princess Palatine, aunt of King George I of England, a woman renowned for her intelligence and her knowledge, to whom Descartes had dedicated his novel about philosophy.[1]

She was then living a retired life at the Hague,[2] where she welcomed these *friends*—for so the Quakers were called

[1]Elizabeth of Bohemia, Princess Palatine (1618-80), eldest daughter of Elizabeth "Queen of Hearts" and Frederick V. In 1667 she acquired and became abbess of the Lutheran monastery at Herford in old Westphalia, and turned it into the first school of Cartesianism. Her interest in the mystical attracted the attention of Quaker missionaries, among them Barclay, Penn, and Fox (Fox did not go to Herford). The visit described by Voltaire was in 1677; in 1644 her friend and correspondent Descartes had dedicated to her his *Principia Philosophiae*. Soon afterward he wrote his treatise on the passions (*Les Passions de l'Ame*) to meet certain of her objections to his thought. (See also Letter XIV, note 2.)

[2]Herford, rather.

in Holland at that time.[3] She had several discussions with them, they often preached to her household, and if they did not make a perfect Quakeress of her, they allowed at least that she was not far from the Kingdom of Heaven.

The Friends sowed in Germany too, but they reaped little. There was no taste for the fashion of *theeing* and *thouing* in a country where one must always have on the tip of the tongue such words as *Highness* and *Excellency*. Penn soon returned to England, having heard that his father was ill, and wishing to be with him in his last moments. The Vice-Admiral was reconciled with him, and embraced him tenderly even though he was of a different religion. William vainly exhorted his father not to receive the sacrament and to die a Quaker, and the old fellow fruitlessly advised William to wear buttons on his sleeves and ribbons on his hat.

William inherited great possessions, among them debts of the Crown for sums the Vice-Admiral had advanced for naval expeditions. Nothing was less certain at the time than money owed by the King; Penn was obliged more than once to go and *thee* and *thou* Charles II and his ministers for what was owing him. In 1680 the government gave him, in place of money, the ownership and sovereignty of a province in America south of Maryland. So now a Quaker had become a sovereign. He left for his new estates followed by two vessels loaded with Quakers.

From that time on, those lands have been called Pennsylvania, after him. He founded there the city of Philadelphia, today a very flourishing one. He began by making an alliance with the Americans, his neighbors. This is the only treaty between these peoples and the Christians that was never sworn to and has never been broken. The new

---

[3]In England as well, of course.

sovereign was also the legislator of Pennsylvania; he enacted wise laws, none of which has since been altered. The first is to mistreat no one for his religion, and to regard all those who believe in a God as brothers.

Hardly had he established his government, when a number of American merchants arrived to people this colony. The natives of the country, instead of fleeing into the forests, gradually got used to the peaceable Quakers; to the degree that they hated the other Christians, conquerors and destroyers of America, they loved these newcomers. Before long, delighted with the gentleness of their neighbors, a great crowd of these supposed savages came to ask William Penn if he would receive them as his vassals. It was quite a new sort of spectacle: a sovereign whom everyone familiarly *thee'd* and *thou'd*, and spoke to with one's hat on; a government without priests, people without weapons, citizens all of them equals—magistrates excepted—and neighbors free from jealousy.[4]

William Penn could boast of having brought forth on this earth the Golden Age that everyone talks so much about, and that probably never was, except in Pennsylvania. After the death of Charles II, he returned to England on business for his new country. King James, who had

---

[4]The Constitution of Pennsylvania, drawn up by Penn, was the first to guarantee liberty of conscience, though within limits that were taken for granted.

"35th: That all persons living in this province, who confess and acknowledge the one almighty and eternal God, to be the creator, upholder, and ruler of the world, and that hold themselves obliged in conscience to live peaceably and justly in civil society, shall in no ways be molested or prejudiced for their religious persuasion or practice in matters of faith and worship, nor shall they be compelled at any time to frequent or maintain any religious worship place or ministry whatever."—Penn's *First Frame of Government*, 1682.

Officials of various sorts had to profess faith in Jesus Christ. The Lord's Day was to be kept. There was "discouragement" and severe punishment of drunkenness, uncleanness, duels, stage plays, cards, dice, May-games, masques, revels, cockfighting, etc.

loved the father, had the same affection for the son, and considered him no longer as an obscure sectary but as a very great man. The politics of the King agreed, in this respect, with his own inclinations. He had a mind to please the Quakers by abolishing the laws against nonconformists, so as quietly, under cover of liberty, to bring Roman Catholicism in. All the sects in England saw the trap and took care not to be caught in it. They are always united against Catholicism, their common enemy; but Penn did not believe himself obliged to renounce his principles and take the part of Protestants who hated him against a King who loved him. He had established liberty of conscience in America; he had no desire to look as if he were destroying it in Europe. He therefore remained faithful to James II, so much so that he was generally accused of being a Jesuit. This calumny wounded him deeply, and he felt it necessary to justify himself in print. However, the unfortunate James II, who like almost all the Stuarts was a mixture of greatness and weakness, and who like them did both too much and too little, lost his kingdom without one's being able to say quite how it happened.

All the English sects accepted from William III and his parliament the same liberty they had been unwilling to owe to James. It was then that the Quakers began, by force of law, to enjoy all the privileges they are in possession of today. Penn, after having seen his sect at last firmly established in the land of his birth, returned to Pennsylvania. His own people and the Americans welcomed him with tears of joy as a father who had come home to his children. All his laws had been religiously observed during his absence—something that never happened to any legislator before him. He remained in Philadelphia for a number of years and departed at last, reluctantly, to solicit in London some new commercial advantages for the Pennsylvanians. He lived in

London from that time on into extreme old age, looked upon as the head of a people and of a religion. He did not die till 1718.

The ownership and government were reserved to his descendants, who sold the latter to the Crown for £12,000. The circumstances of the King permitted him to pay no more than a thousand. A French reader will perhaps expect that the ministry paid the rest in promises, and meanwhile took over the government. Not at all: since the Crown had been unable to complete payment within the prescribed time, the contract was declared void, and the Penn family resumed its rights.

I cannot guess at the future of the Quaker religion in America, but I see it daily declining in London. In every country the dominant religion, if it does not actually persecute all the others, swallows them up in the end. Quakers cannot be members of Parliament, nor can they hold office, for in either case one must take oath,[5] and they refuse to swear. They are reduced to making money by means of commerce. The children, made rich by the industry of their fathers, want to enjoy themselves, to acquire honors, buttons, and cuffs. They are ashamed to be called Quakers, and are turning Anglican to be in style.

---

[5]In 1696 an act was passed to accept the Quakers' "solemn affirmation and declaration. . . instead of an oath in the usual form." These are the words they were to use: "I, A. B., do declare in the presence of Almighty God, the witness of the truth of what I say. . . " They remained unqualified to give evidence in criminal causes, or serve on juries, or "bear any office or place of profit in the government."

LETTER FIVE

ON THE CHURCH OF ENGLAND

THIS is the country of sects. An Englishman, as a free man, goes to Heaven by whatever road he pleases.

Yet, though everyone here may serve God in his own fashion, their genuine Religion, the one in which people make their fortune, is the sect of Episcopalians, called the Church of England, or pre-eminently The Church. No one can hold office in England or in Ireland unless he is a faithful Anglican.[1] This argument, in itself a convincing proof, has converted so many noncomformists that today not a twentieth of the population lives outside the lap of the established Church.

The Anglican clergy has retained many of the Catholic ceremonies, particularly that of gathering in tithes with the most scrupulous attention. They also have the pious ambition of being the Masters.

Moreover, they work up in their flocks as much holy zeal against nonconformists as possible. This zeal was lively enough under the government of the Tories in the last years of Queen Anne, but it went no further than sometimes breaking the windows of heretical chapels; for the fury of the

---

[1]The Test Act of 1673 supported the Corporation Act (1661; obligation of magistrates to receive the sacrament in the Church of England), and the Act of Uniformity (1662; complete acceptance of the Book of Common Prayer by clergymen and teachers), by forbidding the holding of public office to those who refused to receive the sacrament in the Church of England and to deny transubstantiation. James II defied the Test Act by appointing Roman Catholics to office. This was political and religious subversion that aroused most Englishmen and gratified Louis XIV.

sects was over, in England, with the civil wars, and under Queen Anne nothing was left but the restless noises of a sea still heaving a long time after the storm. When Whigs and Tories were rending their native land as Guelphs and Ghibellines once had done, it was of course necessary that religion should become a party issue. The Tories were for episcopacy, the Whigs wanted to abolish it—but when they were on top they were content to humble it.

In the days when Harley, Earl of Oxford, and Lord Bolingbroke were having people drink the health of the Tories, the Church of England looked upon them as the defenders of its holy privileges. The lower house of convocation, which is a sort of house of commons made up of clergymen, had then some importance; at least they enjoyed the liberty of meeting, of arguing controversial points, and of now and then burning a few impious books—that is, books written against them. The ministry, which is a Whig one nowadays, does not even allow these gentlemen to hold their convocation; they are reduced, in the obscurity of their parishes, to the sad occupation of praying for a government they would not be sorry to distress. As for the bishops, who are twenty-six in all, they sit in the House of Lords in spite of the Whigs, for the old abuse of considering them the equivalent of barons still subsists; but they have no more power in the House than the ducal peers in the Parliament of Paris.

There is a clause in the oath that one must take to the state that sorely tries the Christian patience of these gentlemen: this is one's promise to be of the Church as it was established by law. There is hardly a bishop, a dean, an archdeacon, who does not think he holds his position by divine right; it is therefore highly mortifying to them to have to acknowledge that they owe everything to a miserable law made by profane laymen. A monk (Father

Courayer) recently wrote a book to confirm the validity and
the succession of ordinations in the Church of England.[2]
This work was condemned in France, but do you think it
pleased the English ministry? Not in the least. It's of very
little concern to these cursed Whigs whether the succession
of bishops has been interrupted in their country or not, and
whether Bishop Parker was consecrated in a tavern (as it is
rumored) or in a church. They prefer that bishops derive
their authority from parliament rather than from the Apostles. Lord B.[3] says that this concept of divine right can only
make tyrants in miters,[4] but that citizens are made by the
law.

With regard to morals, the Anglican clergy are better
ordered than those of France, and this is the reason: all clergymen are brought up in Oxford University, or in Cambridge,
far from the corruption of the capital. They are not called to
high station in the Church until very late, and at an age
when men have no other passion but avarice, if their ambition goes unfed. Positions of rank are here the reward of
long service in the Church just as in the army; one does not
see young fellows made bishops or colonels on leaving
school. Besides, the priests are almost all married; the awk-
wardness they pick up in the university, and the fact that,
socially, Englishmen have little to do with women, result in
a bishop's ordinarily being forced to content himself with
his own wife. Clergymen go to the tavern sometimes, for
custom allows it; if they get drunk they do so in a serious-
minded way and with perfect propriety.

[2]*Dissertation sur la validité des ordinations Anglicanes et sur la succession des
Evesques de l'Eglise Anglicane*, (Brussels, 1723).

[3]Sufficiently characteristic of Bolingbroke.

[4]Or camails and rochets, if the reader pleases.

That indefinable being which is neither ecclesiastical nor secular—in a word, that which is called an *Abbé*—is a species unknown in England. Clergymen here are all reserved, by temperament, and almost all pedantic. When they learn that in France young men, who are known for their debauchery and who have been raised to the prelacy by the plots of women, make love in public, divert themselves with the composing of sentimental songs, entertain daily with long and exquisite supper parties, and go from there to beseech the light of the Holy Spirit, and boldly to call themselves the successors of the Apostles—then the English thank God they are Protestants. But they are nasty heretics, fit to be burned to Hell and back, as Master François Rabelais says. That's why I keep out of it.

LETTER SIX

ON THE PRESBYTERIANS

THE Church of England is confined to England and Ireland. Presbyterianism is the predominant religion in Scotland. This Presbyterianism is nothing other than the purest Calvinism, as Calvinism was when it was established in France, and as it still is in Geneva. As the priests of this sect receive from their churches none but the meanest wages, and as consequently they are unable to live in the same luxury as bishops, they have taken the natural course of inveighing against a dignity they cannot attain to. Imagine the proud Diogenes treading under his feet the pride of

Plato: the Presbyterians of Scotland are not unlike that arrogant and beggarly dialectician. They treated King Charles II with a good deal less respect than Diogenes treated Alexander. For when they took up arms for him against Cromwell, who had deceived them, they made this poor king undergo four sermons a day, they forbade him to gamble, they made him stand in the corner—so that Charles was soon weary of being king of such pedants, and escaped as a boy slips away from school.

Compared with a young and lively French theological student, squalling at the university in the morning and singing with the ladies at night, an Anglican theologue is a Cato; but this Cato looks like a regular man-about-town if you set him beside a Scotch Presbyterian. The latter affects a solemn bearing, an air of displeasure; he wears a huge hat and a long cloak over a short coat, preaches through his nose, and gives the title of Whore of Babylon to all churches in which some of the clergy are fortunate enough to have an income of fifty thousand pounds, and where the people are so kind as to suffer it and call them My Lord, Your Grace, or Your Eminence.

These gentlemen, who also have some churches in England, have made grave airs and severe expressions all the fashion in this country. To them is owing the sanctification of Sunday in the three kingdoms. On that day it is forbidden to work and play, which is double the severity of the Catholic churches. No opera, no plays, no concerts in London on Sunday; even cards are so expressly forbidden that only the aristocracy, and those we call well-bred people, play on that day. The rest of the nation go to church, to the tavern, and to the brothel.

Although the Episcopalian and the Presbyterian are the two main sects in Great Britain, all others are welcome there and live pretty comfortably together, though most of their preachers detest one another almost as cordially as a Jansenist damns a Jesuit.

Go into the Exchange in London, that place more venerable than many a court, and you will see representatives of all the nations assembled there for the profit of mankind. There the Jew, the Mahometan, and the Christian deal with one another as if they were of the same religion, and reserve the name of infidel for those who go bankrupt. There the Presbyterian trusts the Anabaptist, and the Church of England man accepts the promise of the Quaker. On leaving these peaceable and free assemblies, some go to the synagogue, others in search of a drink; this man is on the way to be baptized in a great tub in the name of the Father, by the Son, to the Holy Ghost; that man is having the foreskin of his son cut off, and a Hebraic formula mumbled over the child that he himself can make nothing of; these others are going to their church to await the inspiration of God with their hats on; and all are satisfied.

If there were only one religion in England, there would be danger of tyranny; if there were two, they would cut each other's throats; but there are thirty, and they live happily together in peace.

ON THE SOCINIANS, OR ARIANS,
OR ANTI-TRINITARIANS

THERE is a little sect here composed of clergymen and of a few very learned laymen, who do not call themselves Arians, or Socinians either, but who are by no means of the opinion of St. Athanasius on the matter of the Trinity, and will tell you plainly that the Father is greater than the Son.

You remember hearing about a certain Orthodox bishop who, in order to convince an emperor of the truth of consubstantiation, ventured to take the emperor's son by the chin and pull his nose in the presence of His Sacred Majesty. The emperor was about to get angry with the bishop, when the good man delivered to him these fine and persuasive words: "My lord emperor, if your majesty is angry that a lack of respect has been shown your son, how do you suppose God the Father will behave toward those who refuse to Jesus Christ the titles that are his due?" The people I am discussing say that the holy bishop was most ill advised, that his argument was far from conclusive, and that the emperor ought to have replied to him, "Learn that there are two ways to be lacking in respect for me: first, in failing to pay sufficient honor to my son; second, in paying him as much as you do to me."

However that may be, the party of Arius is beginning to revive in England as well as in Holland and Poland. The great Mr. Newton did its doctrine the honor of favoring it; that philosopher thought the Unitarians reasoned more geometrically than we. But the strongest patron of the Arian doctrine is the famous Doctor Clarke. This is a man of rigid virtue and gentle disposition, more fond of his ideas than desirous of propagating them, wholly taken up with calculations and demonstrations: a veritable reasoning-machine.

It is he who is the author of a book, rather little understood but highly esteemed, on the existence of God, and of another, more intelligible but looked upon with some contempt, on the truth of the Christian religion.

He has not engaged in any splendid scholastic disputes, such as our friend . . .[1] calls *venerable humbug;* he has been content to publish a book containing all the testimony of the first centuries for and against the Unitarians, and left it to the reader to count the votes and pass sentence. This book of the Doctor's has won him many adherents but has prevented him from being Archbishop of Canterbury. I believe the Doctor made a mistake in his calculations, and that it is better to be an English Primate than an Arian curate.

See what revolutions occur in realms of opinion as well as in empires. The party of Arius, after three hundred years of triumph and twelve centuries of oblivion, is reborn at last from its ashes. But it has chosen its time very badly, to reappear in an age when the world is satiated with controversies and with sects. This one is still too small to obtain the liberty of holding public assemblies; it will obtain it, no doubt, if its numbers increase; but people are so lukewarm about all such matters nowadays that there is hardly a chance any more for a new or renovated religion to make its fortune. Isn't it amusing that Luther, Calvin, Zwingli, all of them unreadable writers, should have founded sects that portion out Europe among themselves; that the ignorant Mahomet should have given a religion to

[1]Rabelais? Bolingbroke? Voltaire himself?

Asia and Africa; and that Messrs. Newton, Clarke, Locke, Leclerc, *et al.*, the greatest philosophers and the best writers of their time, should just barely have managed to acquire a little flock of followers that, small as it is, dwindles every day?

That is what it means to come into the world at the right time. If Cardinal de Retz reappeared today, he would not be able to rouse up ten women in all Paris.

If Cromwell were born again, he who once had the head of his king cut off, and who made himself a sovereign, would be a plain London tradesman.

LETTER EIGHT

ON THE PARLIAMENT

THE members of the Parliament of England are fond of comparing themselves to the ancient Romans whenever the occasion arises.

Not long ago Mr. Shippen[1] began a speech in the House of Commons with these words: "The majesty of the English people would be wounded. . . ." The oddness of this expression raised a great shout of laughter; but without embarrassment Mr. Shippen repeated his words firmly, and the House was quiet. I confess that I see no resemblance between the majesty of the English people and that of the Roman, and even less between their governments. There is a senate in London, some of whose members are under sus-

[1]A Tory and Jacobite, adversary of Walpole.

picion, doubtless unjustly, of selling their votes on occasion, as was done in Rome: this is the only similarity. Otherwise, the two nations seem to me quite different as to both good and evil. Among the Romans the horrible madness of religious wars was unknown; that abomination was reserved for pious preachers of humility and patience. Marius and Sulla, Pompey and Caesar, Antony and Augustus did not fight over the question whether the Flamen should wear his shirt over his robe or his robe over his shirt; or whether, for auspices to be taken, the sacred chickens must both eat and drink or simply eat.[2] The English have in the past reciprocally hanged one another at their Assizes and destroyed one another in pitched battle over matters of this kind. Episcopalianism and Presbyterianism have turned these grave heads for a time. I suppose that no such foolishness will get control of them again, however, for they appear to me to have grown wiser at their own expense, and I see in them no longer any inclination to cut one another's throats over syllogisms.

There is a more essential difference between Rome and England which gives all the advantage to the latter, and that is that in Rome the fruit of civil wars was slavery, whereas in England it was freedom. The English are the only people on earth who have managed to prescribe limits to the power of kings by resisting them, and who by long endeavor have at last established that wise form of government in which the prince, all-powerful to do good, is restrained from doing evil;[3] in which the nobles are great without insolence or feudal power, and the people take part in the government without disorder.

[2]It was by the appetite of these birds that the augurs interpreted the divine will.

[3]See Fénelon's *Télémaque* (Book V), where the old Cretan is defining the royal authority. Voltaire has borrowed this particular antithesis almost word for word.

The House of Lords and that of the Commons are the arbiters of the nation, and the king is umpire. This balance the Romans lacked; there was always discord in Rome between the nobles and the common people, and no intermediary with power to reconcile them. The Senate of Rome, which had the unjust, the criminal arrogance to refuse to share anything with the plebeians, knew no other trick for keeping government out of their reach than to busy them continually with foreign wars. They regarded the People as a ferocious animal that had better be let loose upon the neighbors than kept at home to devour its master. Thus the greatest weakness in the government of the Romans made conquerors of them; it is because they were unhappy at home that they became the masters of the world—until domestic discord turned them into slaves.

The government of England was not made for such a burst of grandeur, nor for so disastrous an end. Its purpose is not the splendid folly of making conquests but to prevent its neighbors from making them. This people is not only jealous of its liberty, it is at the same time concerned about the liberty of others. The English were implacably opposed to Louis XIV for the sole reason that they thought him ambitious. They waged war against him with a light heart and surely without self-interest.

It has doubtless cost a good deal to establish liberty in England; the idol of arbitrary power was drowned in seas of blood. But the English do not believe that for good laws too high a price has been paid. Other nations have not had fewer troubles nor poured out less blood, but the blood they shed for liberty has only hardened their bondage.

What becomes a revolution in England is only a mutiny in other countries. In Spain, in Barbary, or in Turkey a city will take to arms to defend its privileges, and immediately it is subjugated by mercenary soldiers, and punished by executioners, and the rest of the nation kisses its chains. The French think that the government of this island is stormier than the sea that surrounds it, and so it is; but that is when the king provokes the tempest, when he wants to make himself master of the ship of which he is only the pilot. The civil wars of France have been longer, more ruthless, more productive of crimes than those of England, but not one of all these civil wars had a wise liberty for its object.

In the detestable days of Charles IX and Henri III the only question was whether one was going to be the slave of the Guise family. As for the last war of Paris, it deserves only catcalls. I seem to see a crowd of schoolboys rioting against their headmaster, and being whipped for it. Cardinal de Retz, a man who had much wit and courage and used them badly, a rebel without a cause, a dissident without a plan, head of a faction without an army, intrigued for the sake of intrigue, and seemed to foment civil war for his own pleasure. The Parlement knew neither what it had in mind nor what it didn't have in mind. It raised troops by decree and discharged them; it threatened, it apologized; it put a price on the head of Cardinal Mazarin and then came to compliment him in state. Our civil wars under Charles VI had been savage; those of the Ligue were abominable; that of the Fronde was ridiculous.

What the French chiefly reproach the English for is the execution of Charles I, who was treated by his vanquishers as he would have treated them if he had been lucky.

After all, consider on the one hand Charles I defeated in pitched battle, made prisoner, tried, sentenced at Westminster; and on the other hand the emperor Henry VII[4]

---

[4]Thirty-first Holy Roman Emperor; of the house of Luxembourg, he died near Siena in 1313. The crime, as Voltaire says in *Annals of the Empire,* is difficult to prove. But that does little harm to the argument.

poisoned by his chaplain while receiving the sacrament; Henri III killed by a monk, minister to the fury of a whole faction; thirty plots to assassinate Henri IV, several set going, and the last one depriving France of that great king forever. Weigh these outrages, and then judge.

LETTER NINE

ON THE GOVERNMENT

THIS happy mixture in the government of England, this union of commons, lords, and king, has not always been in effect. England was long a slave; it was enslaved to the Romans, the Saxons, the Danes, the French. William the Conqueror, more than others, governed with an iron scepter; he disposed of the property and the life of his new subjects like some Oriental monarch. He forbade, on pain of death, any Englishman to be so presumptuous as to have any fire or light in his house after eight in the evening—either expecting by such measures to prevent their assembling at night, or else wishing to discover, by so bizarre a prohibition, just how far the power of one man over other men could go.

It is true that before and after William the Conqueror the English had parliaments; they boast about it, as if the assemblies then called parliaments, composed as they were of ecclesiastical tyrants and of plunderers known as barons—as if those assemblies were the guardians of liberty and public bliss.

The barbarians, who from the shores of the Baltic Sea

poured into the rest of Europe, brought with them the custom of these legislative bodies or parliaments that so much fuss is made about and are so little known. The kings at the time were not despotic, it is true, but the people only groaned the more for it in a wretched state of bondage. The chiefs of these savages who had devastated France, Italy, Spain, and England made themselves kings; their captains shared among themselves the lands of the conquered: hence these margraves, these lairds, these barons, these under-tyrants who often squabbled with their king over what they had plundered from the peoples. They were birds of prey battling an eagle to suck the blood of doves. Each people had a hundred tyrants instead of one master. The priests soon joined the party. It had always been the fate of the Gauls, the Germans, and the islanders of England to be ruled by their druids and by the chiefs of their villages, an ancient species of baron, less tyrannical than what came after. These druids professed to be mediators between the deity and mankind; they made laws, they excommunicated people, they condemned people to death. The bishops gradually succeeded to their temporal authority in the Goth and Vandal governments. The popes put themselves at the head of them, and with breves, bulls, and monks, made kings tremble, deposed them, had them assassinated, and drew to themselves as much of the money of Europe as they could. The imbecile Ina, one of the tyrants of the English Heptarchy, was the first who on a pilgrimage to Rome consented to pay Peter pence (which would amount to about an *écu* in our money) for every house in his lands. The whole island promptly followed his example, England little by little became a province of the pope, and the Holy Father sent his legates there from time to time to levy exorbitant taxes. At last, John Lackland, following regulations, ceded his realm to His Holiness, who had excommunicated him; and the barons, who found that not exactly to their interest, drove out their miserable king. They put in his place Louis VIII, the father of St. Louis of France, but they soon sickened of this newcomer and sent him back across the water.

While barons, bishops, and popes were in this way pulling apart an England of which they all wanted control, the people, the most numerous, the most virtuous even, and consequently the most respectable class of men, composed of those who devote themselves to the laws and the sciences, of merchants, of craftsmen—in a word, of all that was not tyrannical—the people, I say, were regarded by them as animals on a plane below the human. The commons were then far from having any part in the government; they were villeins: their labor, their blood belonged to their masters, who were called nobles. Most men were, throughout Europe then, what they still are in several parts of the North, serfs of a lord, a species of cattle bought and sold with the land. It has taken centuries to do justice to humanity, to feel it was horrible that the many should sow and the few should reap. And isn't it a good thing for the human race that the authority of those little brigands was stamped out in France by the legitimate power of our kings, and in England by the legitimate power of the kings and the people?

Fortunately, in the shaking that the strife between kings and nobles gave to empires, the chains of the nations have been more or less loosened. Liberty was born in England of the quarrels between tyrants. The barons forced John Lackland and Henry III to grant that famous Charter whose main purpose was really to make the kings subordinate to the lords but in which the rest of the nation was favored a little, so that when the occasion arose they would range themselves on the side of their pretended protectors. That Great Charter, which is regarded as the consecrated source of English liberty, shows very clearly in itself how little liberty was known. The title alone proves that the King thought himself absolute by right, and that the barons and even the clergy were able to force him to relax his hold on this pretended right only by being stronger than he.

This is how the Great Charter begins: "We grant of our own free will the following rights to archbishops, bishops, abbots, priors, and barons of our realm," etc.[1]

In the articles of that Charter not a word is said about the House of Commons, which is proof that it did not yet exist, or that it existed in impotence. The "freemen" of England are specified there, sad evidence that there were some who were not that. It is clear by Article 32 that these supposedly free men owed services to their lord. Such liberty had a remarkable resemblance to slavery.

In Article 21 the king orders that his officers no longer be permitted to seize by force the horses and carts of free men unless payment is made, and this regulation struck the people as true liberty, because it removed a greater kind of tyranny.

Henry VII, a successful usurper and great politician, who pretended to love the barons but who hated and feared them, had the idea of securing the alienation of their lands. As a result, as time went on, the villeins who by means of hard work had acquired some capital, bought the castles of the noble peers, who had ruined themselves through their own folly. Little by little all the lands changed masters.

The House of Commons became daily more powerful; the older noble families in time died out; and since in En-

[1]Voltaire's information about the charter comes from the condensation of Rapin de Thoyras.

gland according to the rigor of the law only peers are noble, there would be no more nobility in that country at all if the kings had not created new lords from time to time, and preserved the order of peers, which they once had been so much afraid of, so as to oppose it to that of the commons, now grown too formidable.

All these new peers who compose the upper house receive from the king their title and nothing more; hardly any of them owns the land whose name he bears. One is Duke of Dorset and hasn't an inch of ground in Dorsetshire. Another is Earl of a village and scarcely knows where the village is situated. They have power in parliament but nowhere else.

You hear no talk in this country of high, middle, and low justice, nor of the right of hunting over the property of a citizen who himself has not the liberty of firing a shot in his own field.

A man is not exempt here from paying certain taxes because he is a nobleman or a priest. All taxes are levied by the House of Commons, which, though second in rank, is first in importance.

It is quite within the power of the lords and bishops to reject a tax bill presented by the Commons, but they are not permitted to alter it in any way; they must either pass it or throw it out altogether and without reserve. When a bill is confirmed by the Lords and approved by the king, then everyone pays, each giving not according to his rank (which is absurd) but according to his income: there is no *taille* or arbitrary poll tax, but a real tax on lands, all of which were evaluated under the famous King William III and classified accordingly.

The tax rate remains the same as it was, though the revenues from land have gone up, and so nobody is downtrodden and nobody complains. The feet of the peasant are not tortured by wooden shoes, he eats white bread, he is well clothed, and he is not afraid to increase the number of his cattle or to cover his roof with tile, lest his taxes be raised next year. There are many peasants here who own property amounting to some 200,000 francs, and who do not disdain to keep on cultivating the soil that enriched them and on which they live free.

LETTER TEN

ON COMMERCE

COMMERCE, which has brought wealth to the citizenry of England, has helped to make them free, and freedom has developed commerce in its turn. By means of it the nation has grown great; it is commerce that little by little has strengthened the naval forces that make the English the masters of the seas. At present they have nearly two hundred warships. Posterity may learn with some surprise that a little island with nothing of its own but a bit of lead, tin, fuller's earth, and coarse wool, became, by means of its commerce, powerful enough by 1723 to send three fleets at one time to three different ends of the earth—one to guard Gibraltar, conquered and kept by its arms; another to Portobello to dispossess the King of Spain of the treasures of the Indies; and the third to the Baltic Sea to prevent the Northern Powers from fighting.[1]

[1]The three fleets go back to the days of Queen Anne; the specific event took place in June of 1726. (Lanson.)

When Louis XIV was shaking Italy, and his armies, already in possession of Savoy and Piedmont, were ready to capture Turin, it was up to Prince Eugene to march from the depths of Germany to the aid of the Duke of Savoy. He had no money at all, a thing without which towns are neither taken nor defended. He appealed to some English merchants. In half an hour he had a loan of fifty millions; whereupon he delivered Turin, beat the French, and wrote this little note to those who had loaned him that sum: "Gentlemen, I have received your money, and I flatter myself that I have employed it to your satisfaction."

All this makes an English merchant justly proud, and allows him boldly to compare himself, not without some reason, to a Roman citizen; moreover, the younger brother of a peer of the realm does not scorn to enter into trade. Lord Townshend, Minister of State, has a brother who is content to be a merchant in the City. When Lord Oxford was governing England, his younger brother was a factor at Aleppo; he did not want to return home, and died there.

This custom, which unfortunately is beginning to go out of fashion, appears monstrous to Germans infatuated with their quarterings. They are unable to imagine how the son of a peer of England could be only a rich and powerful bourgeois, whereas Germany is all Prince: there have been at one time as many as thirty Highnesses of the same name, with nothing to show for it but pride and a coat of arms.

In France anybody who wants to can be a marquis; and whoever arrives in Paris from the remotest part of some province with money to spend and an *ac* or an *ille* at the end of his name, may indulge in such phrases as "a man of my sort," "a man of my rank and quality," and with sovereign eye look down upon a wholesaler. The merchant himself so often hears his profession spoken of disdainfully that he is fool enough to blush. Yet I don't know which is the more useful to a state, a well-powdered lord who knows precisely what time the king gets up in the morning and what time he goes to bed, and who gives himself airs of grandeur while playing the role of slave in a minister's antechamber, or a great merchant who enriches his country, sends orders from his office to Surat and to Cairo, and contributes to the well-being of the world.

LETTER ELEVEN

ON INOCULATION WITH SMALLPOX

IN Christian Europe people gently aver that the English are fools and madmen: fools because they give their children smallpox to keep them from having it; madmen because they lightheartedly communicate to these children a disease that is certain and frightful, with a view to preventing an evil that may never befall them. The English, on their side, say, "The other Europeans are cowardly and unnatural: they are cowardly in fearing to hurt their children a little; unnatural in exposing them to the danger of dying some day of smallpox." To help decide who is right on this question, here is the story of that famous practice of inoculation, which outside England people speak of with such horror.

The women of Circassia have from time immemorial had the custom of giving smallpox to their children, when as little as six months old, by making an incision on the arm and inserting in that incision a pustule that they have carefully removed from the body of another child. That pustule has, in the arm into which it has been slipped, the effect of yeast in dough; it ferments there and spreads through the mass of the blood the characteristics with which it is marked. The pustules of the child who has been given this artificial smallpox are used to carry the same disease to others. The circulation of the disease goes on in Circassia almost without pause; and when unfortunately there is no smallpox at all in the country, people are as much troubled as they are in a bad year elsewhere.

What caused the rise in Circassia of a custom that appears so strange to other peoples was nevertheless something that the whole earth shares with them, and that is mother-love and self-interest.

The Circassians are poor and their daughters are beautiful, so most of their trade is in them; they furnish with beauties the harems of the Sultan, the Sophy of Persia, and such others as are rich enough to buy and maintain this precious merchandise. With the most honest and virtuous intentions, they bring up these girls to take the initiative with the male sex by caressing them, to improvise dances fraught with lust and voluptuousness, and, by all the most sensual artifices, to revive the appetite of the disdainful masters whom they are destined to serve. Every day these poor creatures rehearse their lessons with their mother, as our little girls recite their catechism, without understanding any of it.

Now it often happened that a father and a mother, after having taken great pains to give their children a good education, suddenly found themselves frustrated in their hopes. Smallpox broke out in the family; one daughter died of it, another lost an eye, a third recovered with a big nose; and the poor parents were ruined, all their resources gone. Often, what is more, when there was an actual epidemic of

smallpox, commerce was interrupted for several years, causing a notable diminution in the seraglios of Persia and of
Turkey.

A commercial nation is always quick to see its interest,
and neglects no branch of learning that may prove useful to
its trade. The Circassians observed that, out of a thousand
persons, hardly one could be found who had had a complete
case of smallpox twice; that in fact some people have undergone three or four light attacks, but never two unequivocal
and dangerous ones; that, in a word, no one really gets this
disease twice in a lifetime. They noticed also that when
smallpox is very benign, and when the eruptions have only
a fine and delicate skin to break through, no mark is left on
the face. From these natural observations they concluded
that if an infant of six months or a year old had a mild case
of smallpox, it would not die of it, would not be marked,
and would be done with that disease for the rest of its life.

And so, to preserve the life and the beauty of their children, what they had to do was give them smallpox early.
That is what they did, inserting in the body of a child a
pustule from as completely developed and yet mild a case of
smallpox as could be found. The experiment could not fail.
The Turks, who are sensible people, immediately adopted
the custom, and today there is not a Pasha in Constantinople who doesn't give smallpox to his son and his daughter
when they are being weaned.

There are some people who maintain that in ancient
times the Circassians learned this custom from the Arabs;
but we will leave this historical point to be cleared up by
some learned Benedictine, who will not fail to compose on
the subject several folio volumes along with the documents.
All I have to say on the matter is that at the beginning of
the reign of George I, Lady Mary Wortley Montagu, one of
the wittiest and most strong-minded women in England,

being with her husband on his embassy to Constantinople, took the step without hesitation, of giving smallpox to a child she had borne in that country. It was no use her chaplain telling her that the experiment was not Christian and could only succeed among infidels: Lady Mary's son recovered splendidly. The lady herself, on her return to London, told her story to the Princess of Wales, who is now queen. It must be acknowledged that, apart from titles and crowns, this princess was born to encourage all the arts and to do good to mankind; she is a gracious philosopher on a throne. She has never lost either a chance to learn or a chance to put her generosity to work. It is she who, having learned that a daughter of Milton was still living, and living in poverty, sent her at once the present of a considerable sum; it is she who is the protector of that poor Father Courayer; it is she who condescended to mediate between Dr. Clarke and Mr. Leibniz. As soon as she had heard of the inoculation or insertion of smallpox, she had it tested on dour criminals who had been condemned to death. Their lives she doubly saved, for not only did she deliver them from the gallows, but, by means of this artificial smallpox she prevented the natural kind, which they would probably otherwise have caught, and perhaps died of, at a more advanced age.

The princess, assured of the usefulness of her test, had her own children inoculated. England followed her example, and since that time at least ten thousand children of good family owe their lives, in the same way, to the Queen and to Lady Mary Wortley Montagu, and as many girls are indebted to them for their beauty.

Out of every hundred persons in the world, at least sixty get smallpox; of these sixty, twenty die of it in the most favorable years, and twenty keep unhappy traces of it with them for ever. That makes a fifth of mankind for certain, killed or disfigured by this disease. Of all those who are inoculated in Turkey or in England, not a one dies, unless he is infirm and condemned to death in other respects; no one is marked with it; no one gets smallpox a second time, so long as the inoculation was perfect.

Thus it is certain that if some French ambassadress had brought this secret from Constantinople to Paris, she would have rendered a service of everlasting benefit to the nation. The Duc de Villequier, father of the present Duc d'Aumont, the best set up and healthiest man in France, would not have died in the flower of his age; the Prince de Soubise, who enjoyed the most radiant health, would not have been carried off at the age of twenty-five; Monseigneur, the grandfather of Louis XV, would not have been buried in his fiftieth year; twenty thousand persons who died in Paris of smallpox in 1723 would still be alive. Well, then, have the French no liking for life? Don't their women care about their beauty? Really, we are odd people! Perhaps ten years from now we may adopt this English custom, if the curates and the doctors allow us; or who knows but that within three months the French will take up inoculation for a whim, if the English lose their taste for it through fickleness.

I find that the Chinese have practiced this custom for a hundred years; that is a great recommendation, the example of a country that passes for being the wisest and most civilized in the universe. It is true that the Chinese go about it in a different fashion; they make no incision but give smallpox through the nose, like snuff. This way is pleasanter, but it comes to the same thing, and serves equally to confirm the fact that if inoculation had been practiced in France, the lives of thousands would have been saved.

ON CHANCELLOR BACON

NOT long ago, in a company of well-known persons, the worn-out and frivolous old question was discussed as to who was the greatest man: Caesar, Alexander, Tamerlane, Cromwell, etc.

Someone replied that unquestionably it was Isaac Newton. The man was right; for if true greatness consists in having received a powerful genius from Heaven and in having used it to enlighten oneself and others, such a man as Mr. Newton, the like of whom is not seen in ten centuries, is truly the great man; and these politicians and conquerors, in whom no century has been wanting, are as a rule no more than eminent bad men. It is to him who holds sway over men's minds by force of truth, not to those who make slaves by violent means: it is to him who knows the universe, not to those who disfigure it, that we owe our esteem.

Since you have demanded that I speak about the famous men that England has produced, I must begin with the Bacons, Lockes, Newtons, etc. The generals and ministers will come along in their turn.

I should begin with the famous Lord Verulam, known in Europe under the name of Bacon, which was his family name. He was son of a Keeper of the Seals, and was for a long time Chancellor under King James I. Yet in the midst of court intrigues and the business of his high office, which themselves required a whole man, he found time to be a great philosopher, a good historian, and an elegant writer; and what is even more astonishing, he lived in a century in which the art of writing well was hardly known, and sound philosophy even less so. As is the way of the world, he was more highly valued after his death than during his lifetime: his enemies were courtiers in London; his admirers were found throughout Europe.

When Marquis d'Effiat accompanied to England Princess Marie, the daughter of Henry the Great who was to marry the Prince of Wales, that minister went to visit Bacon, who, being then ill in bed, received him with the curtains closed. "You are like the angels," said d'Effiat to him; "we are always hearing about them, we believe them quite superior to men, and we never have the consolation of seeing them."

You know, sir, how Bacon was accused of a crime which is hardly that of a philosopher—of having allowed himself to be corrupted by money. You know how he was sentenced by the House of Lords to pay a fine of about 400,000 livres in our money,[1] and to lose his station as Chancellor and as peer.

Today the English revere his memory to the point that they do not like to admit that he was guilty. If you ask me what I think, in order to answer you I will help myself to a fine thing I heard Lord Bolingbroke say. They were speaking in his presence of the avarice of which the Duke of Marlborough had been accused, and were citing instances for which they appealed to the testimony of Lord Bolingbroke, who, having been his declared enemy, might perhaps with propriety reveal the facts. "He was so great a man," replied Bolingbroke, "that I have forgotten his vices."

I shall confine myself, then, to speaking to you about what has earned Chancellor Bacon the esteem of Europe.

The most unusual and the best of his works is that

[1]The fine was 40,000 pounds sterling, equivalent to 1,000,000 French livres.

which is today the least read and the most useless; I have in mind his *Novum scientiarum organum*. This is the scaffolding by which the new philosophy[2] has been built; and when that edifice had been erected at least in part, the scaffolding was no longer of any use.

Chancellor Bacon was not yet familiar with nature, but he knew and pointed out all the paths that lead to her. He had early despised what the universities called Philosophy, and he did all that was in his power to prevent these corporations founded for the perfecting of human reason, from continuing to ruin it with their *quiddities,* their *abhorrence of a vacuum,* their *substantial forms,* and all the impertinent words that ignorance first made respectable, and that a ridiculous mixture with religion had rendered almost sacred.

He is the father of experimental philosophy. It is quite true that some wonderful discoveries had been made before his day. The mariner's compass had been invented; so had printing, engraving, oil painting, looking glasses; the art of restoring, to some extent, the sight of old people by glasses called spectacles; gunpowder, etc. A new world had been sought, found, and conquered. Who would not suppose that these sublime discoveries had been made by the greatest of philosophers, and in ages much more enlightened than our own? Not at all: it was in an age of the most stupid barbarism that these great changes were made on the earth. Chance alone produced almost all these inventions, and it is even very probable that what we call chance played a large part in the discovery of America. At least we have always believed that Christopher Columbus undertook his voyage solely on the faith of a naval captain whom a storm had driven into the latitude of the Caribbean islands.

[2]"Modern science."

At any rate, men knew how to go to the ends of the earth, they knew how to destroy towns with an artificial thunderbolt more terrible than the natural one; but they were not acquainted with the circulation of the blood, the weight of air, the laws of motion, the nature of light, the number of our planets, and so on; and a man who upheld a thesis on the categories of Aristotle, on the universal *à parte rei,* or some other such piece of nonsense, was regarded as a prodigy.

The most astonishing and most useful inventions are not those that do the most honor to the human mind.

It is to a mechanical bent, natural to most men, that we owe all the arts; we do not owe them to sound philosophy. The discovery of fire, the art of making bread, of smelting and working metals, of building houses, the invention of the weaver's shuttle, are of an entirely different order of necessity from printing and the mariner's compass; nevertheless, these arts were devised by men who were still savages.

Later on, what prodigious use the Greeks and the Romans made of mechanics! And yet in their day it was believed that the skies were of crystal, and that the stars were little lamps that sometimes fell into the sea; and one of their great philosophers, after much study, found that the heavenly bodies were pebbles that had broken away from the earth.[3]

In a word, nobody before Chancellor Bacon had understood experimental philosophy; and of all the physical experiments that have been made since his time, hardly one was not suggested in his book. Several of them he had made himself. He constructed pneumatic machines of some sort, by means of which he discovered the elasticity of the air; he went all around the discovery of its weight, he even grazed it,

[3]Voltaire, like a good modern, does less than justice to ancient science.

but Torricelli it was who seized upon that truth. Shortly afterward, experimental physics suddenly began to be cultivated in almost all parts of Europe at once. It was a hidden treasure of which Bacon had some expectations, and which all the philosophers, encouraged by his promise, labored to unearth.

But what has surprised me most has been to find in explicit terms in his book that novel theory of attraction which Mr. Newton is credited with inventing.

"We must try to discover," says Bacon, "whether there is not some kind of magnetic power which operates between the earth and heavy bodies, between the moon and the ocean, between the planets," etc.

In another place he says:

> It must be either that heavy bodies tend by their nature toward the center of the earth or else that they are mutually attracted by it; and, in this latter case, it is evident that the closer falling bodies approach to the earth, the more forcibly they are drawn to it.

He continues:

> We ought to find by experiment whether the same clock moved by weights will go faster on the top of a mountain or at the bottom of a mine. If the force of the weights diminishes on the mountain and increases in the mine, then it is likely that the earth has a real power of attraction.[4]

This precursor in philosophy was also an elegant writer, a historian, a wit.

His moral essays are highly regarded, but they were

[4]Voltaire has freely pieced together the original. For the first passage, see *Novum Organum*, II, xlv; for the second, II, xxxvi.

written to instruct rather than to please; and being neither a satire on human nature like the maxims of M. de La Rochefoucauld, nor a school for skepticism like Montaigne, they are less read than these two ingenious books.

His *History of Henry VII* has been considered a masterpiece; but I should be much mistaken if it deserved to be compared with the work of our excellent de Thou.

Discussing that famous impostor Perkin, a Jew by birth, who, encouraged by the Duchess of Burgundy, so boldly took the name of Richard IV, King of England, and disputed the crown with Henry VII, here is how Chancellor Bacon expresses himself:

> At this time the King began again to be haunted with sprites; by the magic and curious arts of the Lady Margaret; who raised up the ghost of Richard Duke of York . . . to walk and vex the King. . . .
>
> After such time as she thought he [Perkin] was perfect in his lesson, she began to cast with herself from what coast this blazing star should first appear, and at what time. It must be upon the horizon of Ireland; for there had the like meteor strong influence before."[5]

It seems to me that our sensible de Thou does not indulge in this fustian, which in the old days was taken for the sublime, but which we now rightly call galimatias.

[5]*The Works of Francis Bacon*, ed. Spedding, Ellis, and Heath (London, 1878), Vol. VI, pp. 132, 135. In his translation Voltaire found himself able to omit the last clause. (Also his eye picked up Edward IV in mistake for the son Richard.)

Environ ce temps, le roi Henri fut obsédé d'esprits malins par la magie de la duchesse de Bourgogne, qui évoqua des enfers l'ombre d'Édouard IV pour venir tourmenter le roi Henri. Quand la duchesse de Bourgogne eut instruit Parkins [sic], elle commença à délibérer par quelle région du Ciel elle ferait paraître cette comète, et elle résolut qu'elle éclaterait d'abord sur l'horizon de l'Irlande.

ON MR. LOCKE

PERHAPS there has never been a wiser, more orderly mind, or a logician more exact, than Mr. Locke; and yet he was no great mathematician. He never could submit to the drudgery of calculations, nor to the dryness of mathematical truths, which in themselves offer nothing concrete to the understanding; at the same time no one has better demonstrated than he that one may have a geometrical intellect without the help of geometry. Great philosophers before his time had positively determined what the soul of man is; but since they knew absolutely nothing about the matter, it is quite proper that they should all have been of different opinions.

In Greece, the cradle of arts and errors, where the grandeur and foolishness of the human mind were carried so far, people reasoned about the soul as we do.

The Divine Anaxagoras, to whom an altar was raised for teaching mankind that the sun is larger than the Peloponnesus, that snow is black, and that the heavens are made of stone, declared that the soul is an airy spirit but nevertheless immortal.

Diogenes—another than the one who became a cynic after having been a counterfeiter—asserted that the soul is a portion of the very substance of God, and that idea at least was a brilliant one.

Epicurus saw it as composed of parts, like the body; Aristotle, who has been explicated in a thousand ways because he was unintelligible, believed—if we can trust some of his disciples—that the human understanding is a single universal substance.

The divine Plato, master of the divine Aristotle; and the divine Socrates, master of the divine Plato, called the soul corporeal and eternal. No doubt the *daimon* of Socrates had told him all about it. It is true there are people who maintain that a man who bragged of having a familiar spirit was without question either a madman or a knave, but such people are too hard to please.

As for our Fathers of the Church, several of them in the earlier centuries believed the human soul, the angels, and God himself to be corporeal.

The world is getting subtler every day. St. Bernard, as Father Mabillon admits, taught that after death the soul did not see God in heaven but conversed only with the humanity of Jesus Christ. This time they did not take his word for it; the adventure of the Crusade had somewhat discredited his oracles. A thousand scholastic philosophers came after him, such as the Irrefragable Doctor, the Subtle Doctor, the Angelic Doctor, the Seraphic Doctor, the Cherubic Doctor,[1] all of whom have been quite sure they knew the soul through and through, but have never failed to discuss the subject as if they wanted nobody to understand a word of it.

Our Descartes, born to bring to light the errors of antiquity and to put his own in their place, being led astray by that spirit of system which blinds the greatest of men, imagined he had demonstrated that soul is the same thing as thought, just as matter, according to him, is the same as

[1]Alexander Hales, John Duns Scotus, St. Thomas Aquinas, St. Bonaventura, and, fifth, a joke borrowed from Rabelais.

extension. He maintained that we are perpetually thinking, and that the soul makes its arrival in the body already provided with every possible metaphysical notion, knowing God, space, and infinity, as well as the whole range of abstract ideas, and filled, in other words, with splendid knowledge all of which it unfortunately forgets as it leaves its mother's womb.

M. Malebranche, of the Oratory, in his sublime hallucinations, not only allowed the existence of innate ideas but was certain that all we perceive is in God and that God, so to speak, is our soul.

After so many deep thinkers had fashioned the romance of the soul, there came a wise man who modestly recounted its true history: Locke has unfolded to man the nature of human reason as a fine anatomist explains the powers of the body. Throughout his work he makes use of the torch of science. He dares sometimes to affirm, but he also dares to doubt. Instead of defining at once what we know nothing about, he examines, bit by bit, that which we want to understand. He takes a child at the moment of birth, he follows step by step the growth of its understanding, he marks what it has in common with animals, and in what ways it is superior to them. Above all, he consults his own experience, the consciousness of his own thought.

> But whether (he says) the soul be supposed to exist antecedent to, or coeval with, or some time after the first rudiments of organization, or the beginnings of life in the body, I leave to be disputed by those who have better thought of that matter. I confess myself to have one of those dull souls, that doth not perceive itself always to contemplate ideas; nor can conceive it any more necessary for the soul

always to think, than for the body always to move
. . . .[2]

As for me, I am proud of the honor of being in this respect as stupid as Locke, for no one will ever convince me that I am always thinking. And I am no more disposed than he is to imagine that a few weeks after my conception I was an exceedingly learned soul, knowing a thousand things that I later forgot in being born, having quite fruitlessly arrived *in utero* at mental attainments that were swept away as soon as I could have any use for them, and that I have never since been able to recover.

Having done away with innate ideas, having altogether renounced the vanity of believing that we are always thinking, Locke proves that all our ideas come to us through the senses, examines our ideas both simple and complex, follows the human mind in all its operations, and shows the imperfections of all the languages spoken by man, and our constant abuse of terms. He comes at last to consider the extent, or rather the nothingness, of human knowledge. It is in this chapter that he humbly ventures to suggest that "possibly we shall never be able to know whether any mere material being thinks or no."[3] These sage words struck more than one theologian as a scandalous declaration that the soul is material and mortal.

---

[2]*Essay Concerning Human Understanding.* Book II, Chapter 1, Section 10. Voltaire's version of this passage, drawn from the translation of Coste, is free yet not misleading.

"Je laisse, dit-il, à discuter à ceux qui en savent plus que moi, si notre âme existe avant ou après l'organisation de notre corps; mais j'avoue qu'il m'est tombé en partage une de ces âmes grossières qui ne pensent pas toujours, et j'ai même le malheur de ne pas concevoir qu'il soit plus nécessaire à l'âme de penser toujours qu'au corps d'etre toujours en mouvement."

[3]Book IV, Chapter III, Section 6. For "any mere material being" Locke had first written "matter."

Certain Englishmen, pious in their way, gave the alarm. The superstitious are in society what cowards are in an army: they are seized by, and they spread, panic terror. The cry went up that Locke was trying to overturn religion.[4] This was not a religious matter, though; it was a purely philosophic one, quite independent of faith and of revelation. All people had to do was to consider without bitterness whether there is any contradiction in saying, "Matter can think," and whether or not God is able to infuse thought into matter. But theologians have a bad habit of complaining that God is outraged when someone has simply failed to be of their opinion. They are too much like the bad poets who, because Boileau was making fun of them, accused him of speaking offensively of the King.

Doctor Stillingfleet[5] acquired the reputation of a moderate theologian by not saying anything positively abusive to Locke. He entered the lists against him but was beaten; for he argued as a man of learning, and Locke as a philosopher who was acquainted with the strength and weakness of the human mind and fought with weapons whose temper he knew.

If I were so bold as to speak after Mr. Locke on so ticklish a subject, I should say: Men have been wrangling for a long time over the nature and immortality of the soul. As for its immortality, that is impossible to prove since we are still arguing over its nature, and since, in order to determine whether something that exists is immortal or not, we surely must first be thoroughly familiar with it. The human reason

[4]See, for instance, Thomas Burnet, *Remarks upon an Essay Concerning Humane Understanding* (London, 1697-99); Henry Lee, *Antiscepticism, or Notes upon Each Chapter of Locke's Essay* (London, 1702).

[5]Edward Stillingfleet (1635-99), Bishop of Worcester, published three pamphlets (1696-97) in a controversy with Locke on the doctrine of the Trinity.

is so little capable of proving by its own means the immortality of the soul that religion has been obliged to reveal it to us. The common good of mankind requires that we believe the soul immortal; faith commands it; nothing more is necessary, and the question is settled. The nature of the soul is a different matter; religion cares little what the soul is made of so long as it is virtuous. It is a clock we have been given to regulate; but the craftsman who made it has not told us the composition of the spring.

I am a body, and I think; that is all I know. Shall I go and attribute to an unknown cause what I can so easily attribute to the only secondary cause I know? Here all the philosophers of the School[6] interrupt and say, "The body has only extension and solidity, and it is capable only of movement and of figure.[7] Now movement, figure, extension, and solidity cannot produce an idea, and thus the soul cannot be material." This great piece of reasoning, which has been so often repeated, may be reduced to these words:

> I am totally ignorant of the nature of matter; I make imperfect conjectures as to some of its properties. Now I am totally ignorant as to whether there is any possible connection between these properties and idea or thought. Thus, because I know nothing whatsoever, I positively affirm that matter is incapable of thought.

There, plainly, is the School's way of reasoning. Locke

---

[6]Cartesian. Voltaire, the reader may have guessed, admired "Our Descartes who was the greatest philosopher in Europe, before Sir Isaac Newton appeared. . ." (Dedication of *La Henriade* to the Queen of England, 1728), and wished that Descartes had more often followed his own Method, as laid down, for instance, in the first precept, "never to accept anything as true unless I know it certainly to be so."

[7]Shape, form, objectively describable bounds.

would say to these gentlemen with perfect simplicity, "Confess at least that you know as little as I. Your imagination no more than mine can conceive how it is that a body should have ideas; do you understand any better how any substance whatever should have them? You comprehend neither matter nor spirit; how then do you dare affirm anything?"

Then, in his turn, comes the superstitious man, and he says that those who suspect that thought is possible with the sole aid of the body ought to be burnt for the good of their souls. But what would such people say if it were they themselves that were guilty of irreligion? In fact, what man could venture to assert, without an absurd impiety, that it is impossible for the Creator to give thought and feeling to matter! See now, if you please, to what straits you are reduced, you who thus limit the power of the Creator! The animals have the same organs as we, the same feelings, the same perceptions; they have a memory, they combine certain ideas. If God has been unable to animate matter and to give it feeling, then one of two things is true: either animals are mere machines, or else they have a soul.

It appears to me almost certain that animals cannot be mere machines. Here is my proof: God made for them precisely the same sense organs as our own, and so if they do not feel, God has made a useless work. Now even you acknowledge that God does nothing in vain, and so He has not manufactured all those organs of feeling in order that no feeling should be done with them, and therefore animals are not mere machines.

Since according to you the animals cannot have a soul, there is, like it or not, nothing for you to say but that God gave to the organs of animals, which are matter, the faculty of feeling and perceiving, which in them you call instinct.

Well now, who can prevent God from imparting to our

more subtle organs that faculty of feeling, perceiving, and thinking which we call human reason? Wherever you turn you are obliged to confess your ignorance and the boundless power of the Creator; cease then to struggle against the wise and unassuming philosophy of Locke. Far from being opposed to religion, it would serve as proof if religion had need of it. For what philosophy is more religious than that which, affirming only what it clearly understands, and able to own to its weakness, tells us that no sooner do we examine first principles than we must have recourse to God.

Besides, we should never fear that any philosophical opinion could harm the religion of a country. Let our Mysteries be contrary to our demonstrations, they are no less revered for it by Christian philosophers, who know that matters of reason and matters of faith are different in nature. Never will philosophers set up a religious sect. Why? Because they do not write for the people, and because they are without enthusiasm.[8]

Divide the human race into twenty parts. Nineteen of them are composed of those who work with their hands, and will never know if there is a Locke in the world or not. In the remaining twentieth part how few men do we find who read! And among those who do read there are twenty who read novels for every one who studies philosophy. The number of those who think is exceedingly small, and they are not aiming to disturb the world.

It is not Montaigne, nor Locke, nor Bayle, nor Spinoza, nor Hobbes, nor Lord Shaftesbury, nor Mr. Collins, nor Mr. Toland, and so on, who have carried the torch of dis-

[8]Voltaire, in following Locke, is using the word "enthusiasm" in the then popular sense of "Fancied inspiration; 'a vain confidence of divine favour or communication,' " if not of "ill-regulated or misdirected religious emotion, extravagance of religious speculation." (O.E.D.)

cord in their native country; it is theologians, for the most part, who having first had the ambition of being leaders of their sect, have soon afterward desired to be heads of parties. Why, all the books of the modern philosophers put together will never make as much noise in the world as once was made just by the dispute of the Cordeliers[9] over the shape of their sleeve and their hood.

LETTER FOURTEEN

ON DESCARTES AND NEWTON

A Frenchman arriving in London finds quite a change, in philosophy as in all else. Behind him he left the world full; here he finds it empty. In Paris one sees the universe composed of vortices of subtle matter; in London one sees nothing of the sort. With us, it's the pressure of the moon that causes the rising of the tide; with the English, it's the sea gravitating toward the moon; so that when you think the moon ought to give us high tide, these gentlemen think it ought to be low; none of which unfortunately can be verified, for in order to know the truth of it we should have had to examine the moon and the tides at the first moment of creation.

You will also notice that the sun, which in France has nothing to do with the business, over here contributes his

[9]Greyfriars, Franciscans.

twenty-five per cent or so. According to your Cartesians, everything is done by means of an impulse that is practically incomprehensible; according to Mr. Newton it is by a kind of attraction, the reason for which is no better known. In Paris you picture the earth as shaped like a melon; in London it is flattened on both sides. Light, for a Cartesian, exists in the air; for a Newtonian it comes here from the sun in six and a half minutes. All the operations of your chemistry are owing to acids, alkalis, and subtile matter; in England, the concept of attraction dominates even in this.

The very essence of things is totally different. You agree neither on the definition of soul nor on that of matter. Descartes assures us that soul is the same thing as thought, and Locke pretty well demonstrates the contrary.

Descartes declares, again, that matter is nothing but extension; to that, Newton adds solidity. Here are some tremendous contrarieties.

Non nostrum inter vos tantas componere lites.[1]

This famous Newton, this destroyer of the Cartesian system, died in March of last year, 1727. In life he was honored by his countrymen, and he was buried like a king who had benefited his subjects.

The eulogy on Mr. Newton that was delivered by M. de Fontenelle before the Académie des Sciences has been read with eagerness, and has been translated into English. In England people looked forward to the opinion of M. de Fontenelle, expecting a solemn declaration of the superiority of English philosophy, but when they found him comparing Descartes to Newton, the whole Royal Society of London

---

[1] "It is not for me to settle such high debate as that between you."— Virgil, *Eclogues*, III, 108.

was aroused. Far from acquiescing in such a judgment, they found a good deal of fault with the discourse. Several even (and those by no means the most philosophical) were shocked at the comparison for the sole reason that Descartes was a Frenchman.

It must be confessed that these two great men were remarkably unlike in their way of life, in their fortune, and in their philosophy.

Descartes was born with a lively and strong imagination which made of him a man as extraordinary in his private life as in his thinking. That imagination could not be concealed even in his philosophical works, where at every moment one is struck by ingenious and sparkling comparisons. Nature had almost made him a poet, and as a matter of fact he did compose for the Queen of Sweden an entertainment in verse which, for the honor of his memory, has not been printed.

He tried the profession of arms for a while, and afterward, having become a philosopher altogether, thought it not unworthy of himself to have a love affair. He had by his mistress a daughter named Francine, who died young, and whose loss he deeply mourned. And so he experienced all that belongs to the human lot.

For a long time he believed that in order to philosophize freely he would have to escape from society, and especially from his native country. He was right; the men of his time knew too little to help him clarify his ideas, and were in fact capable of little more than doing him harm.

He left France because he followed after truth, which was persecuted there in those days by the miserable philosophy of scholasticism; but he found no more rationality in the universities of Holland, to which he retired. For while the sole propositions of his philosophy that were true were condemned in France, he was also persecuted by the pretended philosophers of Holland, who understood him no better, and who, having a nearer view of his glory, hated him personally even more. He was obliged to leave Utrecht. He had to undergo the accusation of atheism, the last resource of calumniators; he who had employed all his intellectual sagacity in a search for new proofs of the existence of a God was suspected of believing in none.

Such a deal of persecution presumes very great merit and a brilliant reputation; both were his. Reason even began to gleam a little in the world, piercing through the darkness of scholasticism and the prejudices of popular superstition. At last his name became so famous that there was some effort to attract him to France with the promise of rewards. A pension of a thousand *écus* was offered him. He came back with that expectation, paid the expenses of the patent (which was sold in those days), failed to receive the pension, and returned to philosophize in his North Holland solitude at the same time as the great Galileo, at the age of eighty, groaned in the prisons of the Inquisition for having proved the motion of the earth. In the end he died in Stockholm, prematurely, of a bad regimen, in the presence of a number of learned men, his enemies, and in the hands of a physician who loathed him.

The career of Sir Isaac Newton was altogether different. He lived for eighty-five years, always tranquil and happy, and held in honor in his own country. It was his great good fortune to have been born not only in a free country but in a time when, the irrelevancies of scholasticism being banished, reason alone was cultivated; and the world must needs be his pupil, not his enemy.

One curious difference between him and Descartes is, that in the course of so long a life he was free from both

passion and weakness. He never had intimacies with a
woman; this was confirmed to me by the doctor and the
surgeon in whose arms he died. One may admire Newton
for it, but one should not blame Descartes.

According to public opinion in England, of these two
philosophers the first was a dreamer and the other a sage.

Few people in London read Descartes, whose works, in
effect, have lost their utility; hardly any read Newton either,
for it takes considerable knowledge to understand him.
Nevertheless, everybody talks about them, granting nothing to the Frenchman and everything to the Englishman.
Some folk believe that if we are no longer satisfied with the
abhorrence of vacuums, if we know that air has weight, if
we use telescopes, we owe it all to Newton. Over here he is
the Hercules of fable, to whom the ignorant attributed all
the deeds of the other heroes.

In a criticism made in London of M. Fontenelle's discourse, somebody went so far as to say that Descartes was
not a great geometrician. Those who talk in this way may
reproach themselves for beating their nurse. Descartes made
as great progress, from the point at which he found geometry to the point to which he carried it, as Newton did after
him. He was the first who found the way to give the algebraic equations of curves. His geometry, which thanks to
him has by now become a commonplace, was in his time so
profound that no professor dared undertake to explain it,
and no one in Holland understood it but Schooten, and no
one in France but Fermat.

He carried the same spirit of geometry and inventive-
ness over into dioptrics, which in his hands became a new
art entirely; and if here or there he made a mistake, it is
clear that a man who discovers new lands cannot suddenly
know all there is to know about them. Those who come
after him and make those lands bear fruit at least owe their

discovery to him. I will not deny that all the other works of M. Descartes swarm with errors.

Geometry was a guide that, in a way, he himself had created and that would have conducted him safely through physics; he abandoned that guide in the end, however, and gave himself up to the systematizing spirit. From then on, his philosophy was no more than an ingenious romance,[2] at best seeming probable to the ignorant. He erred on the nature of the soul, on the proofs of the existence of God, on the subject of matter, on the laws of motion, on the nature of light. He admitted innate ideas, he invented new elements, he created a world, he made man according to his own fashion—in fact, it is rightly said that man according to Descartes is Descartes' man, far removed from man as he actually is.

He carried his errors in metaphysics so far as to assert that two and two make four only because God has willed it so. But it is not too much to say that he was admirable even in his aberrations. When he was wrong, at least he was systematically wrong, and with logical coherence. He got rid of the absurd chimeras with which we had infatuated our youth for two thousand years. He taught the men of his time how to reason, and how to fight him with his own weapons. If he has not paid in sterling, it is certainly something to have decried the counterfeit.

I do not think one can truly compare his philosophy in any way with that of Newton: the first is an experimental sketch, the second a finished masterpiece. But he who has set us on the road to truth is perhaps as worthy as he who since then has gone on to the end of it.

---

[2](See Letter IV, note 1.) Roger Cotes, in his preface (1713) to the second edition of Newton's *Principia*, uses this phrase to describe the work of philosophers who build accurately on hypotheses. James Thomson, in the unrevised "To the Memory of Sir Isaac Newton," as first published in folio, June, 1727, had referred to Descartes as "the French dreamer."

Descartes gave sight to the blind; they saw the faults of antiquity and their own as well. The course he opened to us has since become boundless. The little book of Rohaut[3] offered us for a while a complete system of physics; today, the collected works of all the academies of Europe do not amount even to the beginnings of a system. On going deep down into that abyss, we found it infinite.

Now we shall see what Mr. Newton dug out of it.

LETTER FIFTEEN

ON THE SYSTEM OF ATTRACTION

THE discoveries of Sir Isaac Newton,[1] which have brought him such universal fame, have to do with the system of the world, with light, with infinity in geometry, and last with chronology, which he played with for relaxation.

I will tell you (without verbiage, if I can) the little that I have been able to get hold of among all these sublime ideas.

As for the system of our world: there had long been dispute over what it is that causes all the planets to revolve, and what keeps them in their orbits, and also over what causes all bodies here below to come down to the surface of the earth.

---

[3]*Traite de physique* (1671), republished as late as 1730.

[1]In writing on Newton, Voltaire leaned heavily on Henry Pemberton's *A View of Sir Isaac Newton's Philosophy* (1728), on Fontenelle's *Éloge de Newton*, on the *Discours sur les différentes figures des astres* (1732) by Maupertuis, and on his correspondence with the latter.

The system of Descartes, expounded and much altered since his time, gave a plausible reason for these phenomena, and that reason appeared all the more true for being simple and intelligible to everybody. But in philosophy we must beware of what we think we understand too easily, as well as of what we do not understand at all.

Gravity, the increase of speed in bodies falling to earth, the revolution of the planets in their orbits, their rotation around their axes—all that is nothing but motion. Now motion cannot be conceived except by impulsion; hence all bodies are impelled. But by what? All space is full; then it is filled with a very subtile matter, for we do not perceive it; then this matter goes from west to east, since it is from west to east that all the planets are impelled. So, from conjecture to conjecture, and from probability to probability, there grew in the mind a vast vortex of subtile matter in which the planets are whirled around the sun. In addition an individual vortex is created, floating in the great one and turning daily around the planet. When all that is done, we assert that gravity is the result of this daily movement; for, we say, the subtile matter which turns about our little vortex must go seventeen times as fast as the earth; now if it goes seventeen times as fast as the earth, it must exert immensely more centrifugal force and, consequently, thrust all bodies toward the earth. And that is the cause of gravity according to the Cartesian system.

But before calculating the centrifugal force and speed of this subtile matter, they ought to have made sure that it exists at all; and supposing that it does, still the possibility of its being the cause of gravity has been shown to be false.

Mr. Newton seems utterly to annihilate all these vortices, great and small, the one that carries the planets about the sun as well as that which makes each planet turn on its own axis.

First, with regard to the supposed small vortex of the earth, it is established that little by little it must lose its motion; it is established that if the earth floats in a fluid, that fluid must be of the same density as the earth, and if that fluid is of the same density, all bodies that we move must encounter tremendous resistance—that is to say that to raise a pound's weight you would need a lever as long as the earth.

Secondly, as for great vortices, they are even more fantastic. It is impossible to reconcile them with the laws of Kepler, the truth of which has been proved. Mr. Newton shows that the revolution of the fluid in which Jupiter is supposedly rolled along is not to the revolution of the fluid of the earth as the revolution of Jupiter is to that of the earth.

He proves that, since all the planets revolve in ellipses, and consequently are much farther from one another at their aphelions and much nearer at their perihelions, the earth, for example, ought to go faster when it is nearer Venus and Mars, since the fluid that carries it along, being then under more pressure, must move faster; and yet it is just then that the motion of the earth is slower.

He proves that there is no such thing as a celestial matter that travels from west to east, since comets traverse these spaces sometimes from east to west, sometimes from north to south.

Finally, to settle the question more thoroughly if possible, he proves or at least shows it to be most likely (by means of experiments even) that the Plenum is impossible, and so he restores to us the Void, which Aristotle and Descartes had banished from the world.

Since, with these arguments and many others as well, he had upset the vortices of Cartesianism, he despaired of ever being in a position to know whether there is a secret principle in nature that is the cause of the movements of all the heavenly bodies and that also makes for gravity on the earth. Having withdrawn in 1666 into the country near Cambridge, one day as he walked in his garden and noticed fruit falling from a tree he drifted off into deep meditation on that problem of gravity, of which all the philosophers have so long vainly sought the cause, and in which the vulgar find nothing the slightest bit mysterious. He said to himself, "From whatever height in our hemisphere these bodies should fall, their descent would certainly be in the progression discovered by Galileo, and the distances covered by them would be as the squares of the times. This power that causes heavy bodies to go downward is the same, without any noticeable diminution, at whatever depth one may be within the earth and on the highest mountain. Why should this power not extend so far as the moon? And if it is true that it carries so far, is there not a great likelihood that this power holds it in its orbit and determines its movement? But if the moon does obey this power, whatever it may be, isn't it again very reasonable to suppose that the other planets are equally subject to it?

"If this power exists, it ought to increase (which has moreover been proved) inversely as the squares of the distances. All that remains is to compare the distance covered by a heavy body in falling to earth from a moderate height, with the distance covered in the same length of time by a body falling from the orbit of the moon. To learn what we wish to know we only need the measurements of the earth and the distance to it from the moon."

That is how Mr. Newton reasoned it out. But in England at the time the only measurements of the globe were very faulty ones; it was all left to the uncertain estimates of

pilots, who reckoned sixty English miles to a degree of latitude, whereas they should have reckoned nearly seventy.
Since this inaccurate calculation did not agree with the conclusions that Mr. Newton wished to draw, he abandoned
them. A mediocre philosopher, one filled only with vanity,
would have squared the measure of the earth with his own
system as well as he could. Mr. Newton preferred at the
time to abandon his project. But after M. Picart had mea-
sured the earth exactly, in tracing that Meridian which does
so much honor to France, Mr. Newton resumed his first
ideas and found what he wanted with the calculations of M.
Picart. It has always seemed extraordinary to me that such
sublime verities should have been discovered with the aid of
a quadrant and a little arithmetic.

The circumference of the earth is one hundred twenty-
three million two hundred forty-nine thousand six hundred
Paris feet.[2] From that alone may be derived the whole system of *attraction.*

We know the circumference of the earth, we know that
of the moon's orbit, and the diameter of that orbit. The
revolution of the moon in that orbit is completed in twenty-
seven days, seven hours, forty-three minutes. Thus it is
clear that the moon averages one hundred eighty-seven
thousand nine hundred and sixty Paris feet a minute; and,
by a familiar theorem, it is demonstrated that the central
force which would make a body fall from the height of the
moon would bring it down only fifteen Paris feet in the first
minute.

Now, if the law by which bodies bear down, gravitate,
are attracted in an inverse ratio to the squares of the distances is true; if it is the same power that acts according to

[2]Newton: *"pedum Parisiensium."* The French foot was .078 inches longer than
the English one.

this law throughout nature; it is evident that, the earth being sixty radii distant from the moon, a heavy body must fall to earth fifteen feet in the first second, and fifty-four thousand feet in the first minute.

It is a fact that a heavy body falls fifteen feet in the first second, and during the first minute covers fifty-four thousand feet, which figure is the square of sixty multiplied by fifteen; therefore, heavy bodies gravitate in an inverse ratio to the squares of the distances; therefore, the same power makes for gravity on the earth and holds the moon in its orbit.

Once it is demonstrated that the moon gravitates to the earth, which is the center of its particular motion, it is demonstrated that the earth and the moon gravitate to the sun, which is the center of their annual motion.

The other planets must equally be subject to this general law, and, if this law obtains, these planets must follow the laws discovered by Kepler. All these laws, all these relationships are in fact observed by the planets with the greatest exactitude; hence the power of gravitation pulls all the planets, like our own globe, toward the sun. Finally, since the reaction of every body is proportional to the action exerted upon it, we may be certain that the earth in its turn gravitates to the moon, and that the sun gravitates to both one and the other; that each of the satellites of Saturn gravitates to the other four and the other four to it, all five to Saturn, and Saturn to all five; that it is the same with Jupiter, and that all these globes are attracted by the sun, and the sun in turn by them.

This force of gravitation is exerted in proportion to the quantity of matter a body contains—a truth that Mr. Newton proved by experiment. This new discovery has served to show that the sun, the center of all the planets, attracts them all in direct proportion to their mass, combined with their distance. From there, rising by degrees to a kind of knowledge that seemed not to have been made for the human mind, he boldly calculates how much matter the sun contains, and how much is to be found in each planet; and thus he shows that, according to the simple laws of mechanics, every celestial globe must necessarily be just where it is. His principle of the laws of gravitation alone explains all the apparent irregularities in the motion of the heavenly bodies. The inequalities of the moon's motion follow necessarily from these laws. In addition, it becomes perfectly clear why the nodes of the moon's orbit complete their revolution in nineteen years, and those of the earth in about twenty-six thousand. The flux and reflux of the sea is another very simple result of attraction. The nearness of the moon when full and when new, and its remoteness at the quarters, combined with the influence of the sun, obviously explain the rise and fall of the ocean.

Once he had by means of his sublime theory accounted for the motion and inequalities of the planets, he bridled the comets with the same law. These beacons, so long a mystery which have terrified the world and shipwrecked philosophy, which were by Aristotle situated below the moon, and by Descartes ordered to stand above Saturn, have at last been put in their right place by Newton.

He proves that they are solid bodies, which move within the sphere of action of the sun, and describe an ellipse so eccentric and so nearly a parabola that certain comets take more than five hundred years to complete their course.

Mr. Halley believes that the comet of 1680 is the same as appeared in the time of Julius Caesar. That one is more useful than others in showing that comets are hard and opaque bodies. For it came so close to the sun as to be only a sixth of its diameter away from it; consequently, it had to rise to a degree of heat two thousand times greater than that of the fieriest iron. It would have been dissolved and consumed very shortly if it had not been an opaque body.

The fashion of foretelling the courses of comets was then beginning. The celebrated mathematician, Jacques Bernoulli, following his own system, concluded that the famous comet of 1680 would reappear on the 17th of May, 1719. Not an astronomer in Europe went to bed on that night of the 17th of May, but the famous comet failed to appear. There is at least more adroitness, if not more certainty, in giving it five hundred and seventy-five years to turn up again. An English geometrician named Wilston, no less fanciful than mathematical, seriously asserted that at the time of the Deluge there had been a comet, which he held responsible for the inundation of our globe; and he was so unjust as to be astonished when people laughed at him. The ancient world thought in much the same way as Wilston; it believed that comets were always the harbingers of some great earthly disaster. Newton, on the contrary, suspects that they all are most beneficent, and that their exhalations only serve to relieve and quicken the planets, which, in their courses, drink up all the particles that have been detached from comets by the sun. This sentiment is at least more probable than the other.

That is not all. If this force of gravitation, of attraction, is at work in all the celestial globes, it doubtless acts on all parts of those globes; for if bodies attract one another in proportion to their masses, it can only be in proportion to the quantity of their parts; and if this force resides in the whole, it certainly resides in the half, in the quarter, in the eighth part, and so on to infinity. In addition, if this power were not distributed equally in every part, there would always be some parts of the globe that would gravitate more than the others—which does not happen. Therefore this force really exists in all matter, and in the smallest particles of it.

So there is *attraction,* the great means by which all nature is moved.

Newton had rightly foreseen, after having demonstrated the reality of this principle, that there would be resistance to the mere name of it. In more than one place in his book he cautions his reader about attraction itself, warning him not to confuse it with the occult qualities of the ancients, and to content themselves with the knowledge that in all bodies there is a central force which, from one end of the universe to the other, acts on the nearest bodies and on the most remote, according to the immutable laws of mechanics.

It is surprising that after the solemn protestations of this great philosopher, M. Saurin and M. de Fontenelle, who themselves deserve the name, should have reproached him explicitly for holding to the absurdities of Peripateticism: M Saurin in the Memoirs of the Academy of 1709, and M. de Fontenelle in his very eulogy of Mr. Newton.

Almost all the French, whether learned or not, have repeated this reproach. Everywhere one hears them say: "Why didn't Newton use the word *impulsion,* which people understand so well, rather than *attraction,* which they don't understand at all?"

Newton could have replied to his critics: "In the first place, you don't understand the word *impulsion* any better than you do the word *attraction,* and if you cannot conceive how it is that one body is drawn toward the center of another, neither can you imagine by what means a body can push at that of another.

"Secondly, I have been unable to admit *impulsion;* for in order to do so I should have had to know that the planets are actually pushed by some sort of celestial matter;

whereas, not only am I not acquainted with any such matter, I have proved that it does not exist.

"Thirdly, I use the word *attraction* only to express an effect that I have discovered in nature: the certain and indisputable effect of an unknown principle, a quality inherent in matter, of which cleverer men than I will find the cause, if they can."

"What have you taught us, then," they go on doggedly, "and why all that figuring in order at last to inform us about something you yourself do not understand?"

"I have taught you," Newton might reply, "that the mechanics of central forces makes all bodies gravitate in proportion to the matter they contain, and that these central forces alone cause the planets and comets to move in marked proportion. I have demonstrated that it is impossible there should be another cause of gravity and of the movement of all the heavenly bodies; for with heavy bodies falling to earth according to the proved proportion of central forces, and the planets completing their courses following these same proportions, if there were yet another power acting on all these bodies it would increase their speeds or alter their directions. Now not one of these bodies ever shows a single degree of motion, of speed, of determination, which has not been demonstrated to be the effect of central forces. Thus it is impossible that there should be another power."

Permit me to give you another moment of Newton talking. Will he not be welcome when he says: "My position is very different from that of the ancients. They saw, for example, water rise in pumps, and they said, 'The water rises because it abhors a vacuum.' But I am in the position of the first person who ever noticed that water rises in pumps, and who left it to others to explain the cause of that effect. The first anatomist to say that the arm moves because the muscles contract, taught mankind an incon-

testable truth; do we owe him any the less for his not having known why the muscles contract? The cause of the
elasticity of air is unknown, but the man who discovered
this elasticity did a great service to the study of physics.
Since the force that I have discovered was both more hidden
and more universal, I ought to get all the more thanks. I
have discovered a new property of matter, one of the Creator's secrets; I have calculated, I have demonstrated its
effects; can they now cavil with me over the name I give it?

"It is vortices that can be called an occult quality, since
their existence has never been proved. Attraction, on the
contrary, is a reality, since its effects are demonstrated, and
proportions calculated. The cause of that cause is in the
bosom of God."

Procedes huc, et non ibis amplius.[3]

LETTER SIXTEEN

ON NEWTON'S OPTICS

A new universe was discovered by the philosophers of the
last century, one that was all the more difficult to understand as people did not even suspect that it existed. The
wisest felt that there was some temerity in so much as
dreaming that one could divine the laws by which the heavenly bodies move and by which light manifests itself.

---

[3]Should be *"Usque huc venies, et non procedes amplius"*: "Hitherto shalt thou
come, but no further."—Job 38:11.

Galileo, through his astronomical discoveries; Kepler, by means of his calculations; Descartes, at least in his dioptrics; and Newton in all his works, saw into the mechanics of the forces at work in the world. In geometry the infinite was subjected to calculation. The circulation of the blood in animals and of sap in plants changed our view of nature. In the air pump[1] a new mode of being was given to substances. With the aid of telescopes, distant objects were brought close to our eyes. Finally, what Newton discovered about light is equal to all that the curiosity of men could hope for in the way of something more exciting, after so many innovations.

Until Antonio de Dominis, the rainbow had seemed an inexplicable miracle; that philosopher discovered that it was a necessary effect of rain and sun. Descartes immortalized his name with the mathematical explanation of this most natural phenomenon; he tabulated the reflections of light in drops of water. There was something divine, then, in that sagacity of his.

But what would he have said if someone had informed him he was mistaken about the nature of light: that he had no reason at all to declare that it was a globulous matter; that it is false that this matter, spread throughout the universe, waits for the pressure of the sun in order to become manifest, as a blind man's stick does its work at one end when pressed at the other; that it is most certainly shot out by the sun and, in the end, transmitted from the sun to the earth in about seven minutes, whereas a cannon ball, maintaining the same speed all the way, could not make the trip in less than twenty-five years?

[1]Invented by Otto von Guericke by the middle of the 17th century. "In a tall glass well emptied of air," says Newton, "[small feathers] fall as fast as Lead or Gold."–*Opticks*, Book III, Part I, Query 28

What would have been his astonishment if he had been told: "It is false that light is reflected directly in rebounding from the solid parts of a body; it is false that bodies are transparent when they have large pores; and a man is coming who will prove these paradoxes and who will anatomize a single ray of light more dexterously than the most skillful artist dissects the human body!"

That man came. Newton, with the help of nothing more than a prism, opened our eyes to the fact that light is an agglomeration of colored rays which, all together, produce the color white. A single ray he divides into seven, which, on a piece of linen or white paper, range themselves in order, one above the other and at unequal distances. The first is the color of fire; the second, lemon;[2] the third, yellow; the fourth, green; the fifth, blue; the sixth, indigo; the seventh, violet. Each of these rays, though sifted afterward through a hundred other prisms, will keep its color unchanged, just as gold, once refined, changes no more in crucibles. And, for more than sufficient proof that each of these elementary rays bears within itself that which makes what we call its color, take a small piece of yellow wood, for example, and expose it to the fire-colored ray: the wood is instantly tinted fire-color; expose it to the green ray: it becomes green; and so with the others.

What then is the cause of the colors we find in the world? Nothing other than the disposition of bodies to reflect rays of a certain sort and to absorb all the others. What is this hidden disposition? He shows that it is only the thickness of the little parts of which a body is composed. And how is this reflection done? It used to be thought that the rays rebounded, like a ball, from the surface of a solid

[2] It is not known how red and orange become *couleur de feu* and *citron* in Voltaire.

body. Not at all. Newton taught the astonished philosophers that bodies are opaque only because their pores are large, that light is reflected to our eyes from the heart of those very pores; and that the smaller the pores of a body are, the more transparent is that body. Thus paper, which reflects light when it is dry, suffers it to pass through when it is oiled, because the oil, filling the pores, makes them much smaller.

It is there, in considering the extreme porosity of bodies, each part having its pores, and each part of its parts having its own, that he shows that we are not at all assured of there being a cubic inch of solid matter in the universe: so far is our intellect from conceiving what matter is.

Having thus decomposed light, and in the brilliance of his discoveries having gone so far as to demonstrate the means of knowing a compound color by its primary colors, he shows that these primary rays, separated by the agency of the prism, are in their particular order because they are refracted in that order; and it is this property, unknown before him, of breaking in proportion, it is this unequal refraction of rays, this property of refracting red less than orange, and so on, that he names refrangibility.

The most reflexible rays are the most refrangible; from that he shows that the causes of the reflection and refraction of light are one and the same.

Wondrous as these discoveries are, they are only the beginning. He discovered how to observe the vibrations and agitations of light, which come and go endlessly, and which transmit light or reflect it according to the thickness of the parts they encounter. He ventured to calculate the thickness of the particles of air necessary between two object-glasses set one upon the other—one of them flat, and the other convex on one side—to produce such and such a transmission or reflection, and to make such and such a color.

From all these contrivances he found the proportion

according to which light acts upon bodies and bodies act upon it.

He understood light so well that he determined the limits of the art of augmenting it and aiding our eyes with telescopes.

Descartes, with a noble confidence quite excusable in the heat of working on the early stages of an art practically discovered by him—Descartes hoped to see, with a spyglass, objects in the heavens as small as those we can discern on earth.

Newton showed, however, that we cannot go on improving dioptric telescopes, because of that very refraction and refrangibility, which, in bringing objects closer to us, causes too much dispersion of the primary rays. He figured out, in working with those object-glasses, the proportion of dispersion of red rays and blue rays; and carrying the demonstration over into matters whose existence even was not suspected, he examined the inequalities produced by the figure of the glass, and by refrangibility. He found that if the plane side of the object-glass of a telescope, convex on one side and plane on the other, is turned toward the object, the imperfection owing to the construction and the position of the glass is five thousand times less than that caused by refrangibility; and that thus, it is not the figure of the glasses that makes it impossible to perfect the telescope, but the nature of light itself.

That is why he invented a telescope that works by reflection rather than by refraction. This new kind of telescope is very difficult to make, and not exactly easy to operate, but they say in England that a five-foot reflecting telescope magnifies as much as a refracting telescope a hundred feet long.

ON INFINITY AND ON CHRONOLOGY

The labyrinth and the abyss of the infinite were another new territory surveyed by Newton, and it was he who gave us the thread by which we may find our way.

In this stunning innovation, Descartes again is found to be his precursor; in geometry he had been taking long strides in the direction of the infinite, but he stopped on the brink of it. Mr. Wallis, about the middle of the last century, was the first to reduce a fraction, by a perpetual division, to an infinite series.

Lord Brouncker made use of the series to square the hyperbola.

Mercator[1] published a demonstration of that quadrature. It was about this time that Newton, at the age of twenty-three, invented a general method of doing with all curves what had just been essayed with the hyperbola.

It is this method of submitting infinity everywhere to algebraic reckoning that is called differential calculus or fluxions and integral calculus. It is the art of exactly numbering and measuring that of which we cannot even conceive the existence.

In fact, wouldn't you think a man was making fun of you if he told you that there are lines infinite in extent that form an angle infinitely small? That a straight line,

---

[1]Not the geographer, but Nicholas Kauffmann (c. 1620-87).

which is straight so long as it is finite, in changing direction infinitely little, turns into an infinite curve; that a curve may become infinitely less a curve? That there are squares of infinity, cubes of infinity, and infinites of infinity, of which the next-to-last is nothing compared with the last?

All that, which strikes us at first as excess of unreason, is really the working of the human mind at its most delicately fine and most broadly encompassing, and the method of finding out truths till then unperceived.

Imposing as it is, this edifice is based on simple ideas. It is just a matter of measuring the diagonal of a square, of finding the area of a curve, of figuring out the square root of a number that in ordinary arithmetic hasn't any.

And, after all, so many orders of infinites ought not to shock the imagination more than that familiar proposition that one can always introduce more curves between a circle and its tangent; or that other to the effect that matter is endlessly divisible. These two facts were proved long ago, and are no more comprehensible than the rest.

Newton's claim to the invention of this famous calculus was for some time disputed. In Germany M. Leibniz was known as the discoverer of the differentials that Newton calls fluxions, and the integral calculus has been claimed by Bernoulli, but the honor of first discovery has remained Newton's, and to the others falls the glory of having made anyone doubt it.

It is thus that Harvey's right to the discovery of the circulation of the blood was contested, and M. Perrault's of the circulation of sap. Hartsoeker and Leeuwenhoek disputed the honor of having first seen the little grubs from which we come. Hartsoeker, again, disputed with M. Huyghens the invention of a new means of calculating the

distance of a fixed star. We still don't know which philosopher[2] first solved the problem of the cycloid.

At any rate, it is through that geometry of the infinite
that Newton arrived at the sublimest of discoveries.

I have still to speak to you about another work, one
more within the grasp of the human race, and that yet
shows the marks of that creative spirit which Newton carried into all his studies. This is a brand new chronology, for
in all his undertakings he had to alter the accepted ideas of
mankind.

Accustomed to bringing order out of chaos, he desired to shine at least a little light on the place where
ancient fables are confounded with history, and to fix an
unsettled chronology. The fact is that there is no family,
town, or nation that does not do what it can to push back
its date of origin; in addition, the first historians were the
most negligent of dates; books were then a thousand times
less common than they are today; consequently, being less
exposed to criticism the earlier historians found it less
inconvenient to deceive the world; and since it is clear
that they fabricated events, it is quite probable that they
fabricated dates as well.

Briefly, it seemed to Newton that the world was
younger than the chronologists said it was by five hundred
years. His idea was founded on the ordinary course of
nature and on astronomical observations.

By the course of nature, here, is meant the length of
each generation of men. The Egyptians were the first to
make use of this uncertain mode of counting. When they
wanted to write about the beginnings of their history, they
counted three hundred and forty-one generations from

[2]Torricelli, Father Mersenne, or G. P. de Roberval.

Menes[3] to Sethon;[4] and, having no fixed dates, they estimated three generations at a hundred years. Thus from the reign of Menes to that of Sethon they reckoned eleven thousand three hundred and forty years.

The Greeks, before counting by Olympiads, followed the Egyptian method and even slightly extended the length of a generation, stretching it to forty years.

Now the Egyptians and the Greeks were out in their reckoning here. It is true enough that in the ordinary course of nature three generations cover some hundred to a hundred and twenty years, but three reigns are not likely to come to that number. It is most evident that in general men live longer than kings reign. So anyone who desires to write history without being provided with exact dates, and who knows that a nation has had nine kings, will be much mistaken if he estimates for these nine kings three hundred years. Each generation is about thirty-six years; each reign is about twenty, on the average. Take the thirty kings of England from William the Conqueror to George I. They reigned six hundred and forty-eight years, which, divided among the thirty, gives each king a reign of twenty-one and a half years. Sixty-three kings of France have reigned, each, on the average, about twenty years. So much for the ordinary course of nature. The ancients, then, were wrong when they made the duration of reigns generally equivalent to that of generations; because of it they got too high a total; because of that it is appropriate to cut their figures down a bit.

Astronomical observations seem to lend even greater

[3]Founder of the first dynasty of Egypt (c. 3315 B.C.).

[4]Or Sethos: King of Egypt about 700 B.C. (?). According to Herodotus he was the priest of Hephaestus and a scorner of the warrior class. As a result, when the country was invaded by the armies of Sennacherib he found himself reduced to rallying an army of artisans and small tradesmen.

aid to our philosopher; he makes a better figure fighting on his own ground.

You know, Sir, that the earth, besides its annual course that takes it round the sun from west to east in the space of a year, has another remarkable kind of motion, one entirely unknown until recently. Its poles show a very slow movement of retrogradation from east to west, which causes their position not to match with the same points in the heavens every day. That discrepancy, imperceptible in one year, becomes quite large in time, and at the end of seventy-two years is found to amount to a degree—that is, a three hundred and sixtieth part of the heavens. Thus, after seventy-two years the colure of the spring equinox, which passed through one fixed star, will be in the same relationship to another. As a result the sun, instead of being in that part of the heavens where Aries[5] was in the days of Hipparchus, is found in that part where Taurus was, and where Taurus used to be, the Gemini are now. All the signs of the zodiac have shifted; yet we still hold on to the ancient manner of speaking: we say that in springtime the sun is in the Ram, with that amiable condescension with which we say that the sun rises and sets.

Hipparchus was the first among the Greeks to notice certain changes in the constellations in accordance with the equinoxes—or rather, he was the first to learn about it from the Egyptians. Philosophers attributed this movement to the stars, for at the time they were far from imagining the earth to be involved in such revolutions: they believed it to be in all senses immobile. And so they created a heaven to which they attached all the stars, and gave it a motion of its own that made it go toward the east, while all the stars seemed to make their daily journey from east to west. To this error

[5]Or the Ram.

they added a second that was much more important: they believed that the imaginary heaven of the fixed stars moved eastward by one degree in a hundred years. Thus they were mistaken in their astronomical calculations as well as in their physical system. For example, an astronomer would have said at the time: "In the days of such-and-such an observer, the spring equinox was in such-and-such a sign of the zodiac, at such-and-such a star; since then it has traveled two degrees; now two degrees are here equivalent to two hundred years; therefore that observer lived two hundred years before me." It is certain that an astronomer reasoning in this way would be wrong by exactly fifty-four years. That is why the ancients, doubly in error, invented their Great Year of a complete revolution of the heavens, taking about thirty-six thousand years. But the moderns know that that imaginary revolution of the heaven belonging to the stars is nothing else than the revolution of the poles of the earth, which is completed in twenty-five thousand nine hundred years. It should be said here, in passing, that Newton, in determining the figure of the earth, explained the reason for that revolution most happily.

Once all this is laid down, in order to establish chronlogy it remains to find at what star the colure of the equinox cuts the ecliptic in the spring nowadays, and whether some ancient cannot be found who has told us at what point the ecliptic was cut in his time by the same colure of the equinoxes.

Clement of Alexandria reports that Chiron, a member of the expedition of the Argonauts, observed the constellations during the course of that famous expedition, and fixed the spring equinox in the middle of Aries, the autumnal equinox in the middle of Libra, the summer solstice in the middle of Cancer, and the winter solstice in the middle of Capricorn.

Long after the expedition of the Argonauts, and a year

before the Peloponnesian War, Meton observed that the point of the summer solstice was on the eighth degree of Cancer.

Now there are thirty degrees in each sign of the zodiac. In the time of Chiron the solstice was at the halfway point of the sign—that is, at the fifteenth degree; a year before the Peloponnesian War it was at the eighth: thus it had retarded by seven degrees. A degree amounts to seventy-two years: thus, from the beginning of the Peloponnesian War back to the Argonauts' enterprise, there is only a matter of seven times seventy-two, making five hundred and four years, and not seven hundred as the Greeks said. And so in comparing the state of the heavens today with what it was then, we see that the expedition of the Argonauts must be set about nine hundred years before Christ, and not some fourteen hundred years; and consequently the world is less old than we thought by about five hundred years.

In this way all periods are brought closer together, and everything takes place later than it is said to. I do not know whether this system will have much success, or whether people are going to resolve, on the basis of these ideas, to reform the chronology of the world. Perhaps it will strike the scholars as excessive to grant to one man the honor of having perfected physics, geometry, and history, all at once. That would be a sort of universal monarchy difficult for self-conceit to be comfortable in. Naturally, then, at the same time that very great philosophers attacked him on the subject of attraction, others fought his system of chronology. Time, which ought to show to whom the victory belongs, may only leave the dispute more doubtful.

LETTER EIGHTEEN

ON TRAGEDY

THE English, as well as the Spaniards, already had a theater while the French still had nothing but fair-booths.
Shakespeare, who was reputed the Corneille[1] of the English,
flourished about the time of Lope de Vega. He it was who
created the English theater. His was a fecund genius, full
of vigor, ranging from simple naturalness to the sublime,
without the least glimmer of taste or the slightest knowledge
of the rules. I am going to tell you something rash, but true:
the greatness of Shakespeare has been the ruin of the
English stage. There are such beautiful scenes, such grand
and terrible passages scattered throughout those monstrous
farces of his called tragedies, that these plays have always
been put on with great success. Time, which alone makes
the reputation of men, in the end makes their faults respectable. Most of the crude whimsy and the enormous
extravagance of this author has, after two hundred years,[2]
acquired the right to pass for sublimity. Almost all the
modern authors have copied him; but what succeeded in
Shakespeare is hissed in them, and you can imagine that the
veneration people have for this ancient increases with their
contempt for the moderns. It doesn't occur to them that he
ought not to be imitated, and the poor success of his copy-
ists only makes people think him inimitable.

You know that in the tragedy of the Moor of Venice, a

[1]In another edition: "whom the English take for a Sophocles."
[2]Voltaire's hasty arithmetic.

most moving play, a husband strangles his wife on the stage, and that when the deed is done she cries out that her murder is most unjust. You know also that in *Hamlet* some gravediggers drink and sing comic songs while digging a grave, and joke about the skulls they come upon in a style fitting to their profession. You will be surprised, however, to hear that this boorishness was imitated in the reign of Charles II, the reign of manners, the golden age of the fine arts.

Otway, in his *Venice Preserved,* introduces his senator, Antonio and Nacky, the courtesan into the midst of the horrors of the Marquis of Bedamar's conspiracy. The Senator plays with his courtesan all the monkey tricks of an old lecher, impotent and out of his head. He pretends to be a bull and then a dog; he bites the legs of his mistress, who kicks him and strikes him with a whip. This buffoonery, written for the vilest riffraff, has been cut out of Otway's play, but they have left in Shakespeare's *Julius Caesar* the jokes of the Roman shoemakers and cobblers who are brought on to the scene with Brutus and Cassius. The reason is that the stupidity of Otway is modern and that of Shakespeare is old.

No doubt you are objecting that up to now those who have said anything to you about the English theater, and especially about this famous Shakespeare, have shown you nothing but his faults, and that no one has translated any of those striking passages for whose beauties all faults must be forgiven. I reply that it is easy enough to recount in prose the errors of a poet, but extremely difficult to translate his fine verses. The scribblers who set themselves up as critics of celebrated writers all compile volumes; give me rather two pages that will acquaint us with a few beauties. For I shall always maintain with people of taste that there is more profit in a dozen lines of Homer and of Virgil than in all the critiques ever made on these two great men.

I have ventured to translate a few passages from the best English poets. Here is one from Shakespeare. Pardon the imitation for the sake of the original, and remember always when you see a translation that it is only a feeble print of a fine painting.

I have chosen the soliloquy from the tragedy of *Hamlet* that everybody knows and that begins with this verse:

"To be or not to be, that is the question."

Hamlet, Prince of Denmark, is speaking.

Demeure; il faut choisir et passer à l'instant
De la vie à la mort, ou de l'être au néant:
Dieux cruels! s'il en est, éclairez mon courage.
Faut-il vieillir courbé sous la main qui m'outrage,
Supporter ou finir mon malheur et mon sort?
Qui suis-je? qui m'arrête? et qu'est-ce que la mort?
C'est la fin de nos maux, c'est mon unique asile;
Après de longs transports c'est un sommeil tranquille;
On s'endort et tout meurt; mais un affreux réveil
Doit succéder peut-être aux douceurs du sommeil.
On nous menace, on dit que cette courte vie,
De tourments éternels est aussitôt suivie.
O mort! moment fatal! affreuse éternité,
Tout coeur à ton seul nom se glace épouvanté.
Eh! qui pourrait sans toi supporter cette vie,
De nos Prêtres menteurs bénir l'hypocrisie;[3]
D'une indigne maîtresse encenser les erreurs,
Ramper sous un Ministre, adorer ses hauteurs,
Et montrer les langueurs de son, âme abattue,
A des amis ingrats qui détournent la vue?
La mort serait trop douce en ces extrémités;
Mais le scrupule parle et nous crie, "Arrêtez."

---

[3]It seems that "to bless the hypocrisy of our lying priests" is not in Shakespeare.

Il défend à nos mains cet heureux homicide,
Et d'un héros guerrier fait un chrétien timide . . .

Don't think that I have rendered the English word for word here. Woe to the makers of literal translations, who, in proceeding word by word, enfeeble the sense. This is where one can truly say that the letter killeth but the spirit giveth life.

Here is a passage from another famous English tragic poet, Dryden, who wrote in the time of Charles II. He was a more fertile than judicious author, who would have had an unblemished reputation if he had written only a tenth as much as he did. His great fault is to have wanted to be a universal genius.

The piece begins thus:

"When I consider life, 'tis all a cheat.
Yet fool'd by hope, men favour the deceit."

De desseins en regrets, et d'erreurs en désirs,
Les mortels insensés promènent leur folie.
Dans des malheurs présents, dans l'espoir des plaisirs,
Nous ne vivons jamais, nous attendons la vie.
Demain, demain dit-on, va combler tous nos voeux;
Demain vient, et nous laisse encore plus malheureux.
Quelle est l'erreur, hélas! du soin qui nous dévore?
Nul de nous ne voudrait recommencer son cours:
De nos premiers moments nous maudissons l'aurore,
Et de la nuit qui vient nous attendons encore
Ce qu'ont en vain promis les plus beaux de nos jours . . .[4]

---

[4]"When I consider life, 'tis all a cheat;
   Yet, fooled with hope, men favour the deceit;
   Trust on, and think to-morrow will repay:
   To-morrow's falser than the former day;
   Lies worse, and, while it says, we shall be blest
   With some new joys, cuts off what we possest.
   Strange cozenage! None would live past years again,

It is in such detached passages that the English tragic poets have so far excelled. Their plays are almost all barbarous, devoid of decorum, of order, and of probability, but there are dazzling flashes in the middle of their night. The style is too bombastic, too unnatural, too much influenced by the Hebrew writers in all their Asiatic inflation. And yet one must admit that in hoisting the English language up to teeter on the stilts of the figurative style, they have raised the mind pretty high as well, though it goes at an awkward gait.

The first Englishman to have made a reasonable play, and one written with elegance from beginning to end, is the illustrious Mr. Addison. His *Cato of Utica* is a masterpiece in its diction and in the beauty of its verse. The role of Cato is to my mind far superior to that of Cornélie in the *Pompée* of Corneille, for Cato is great without pomposity, and Cornélie—besides not even being a necessary character—has a propensity for gibberish. Mr. Addison's Cato seems to me the finest character on any stage, but the other roles in the play are out of keeping with this one. And the work as a whole, well written as it is, suffers from a spiritless love intrigue, which spreads over all a languor that kills it.

The custom of introducing love into dramatic works at random passed over from Paris to London about the year 1660, along with our ribbons and perukes. The ladies, who there as well as here adorn the theaters, will no longer tolerate on the stage any subject matter but love. The canny Addison was so weakly obliging as to bend the natural austerity of his character to suit the manners of his time, and spoiled a masterpiece to please the public.

Yet all hope pleasure in what yet remain:
And, from the dregs of life, think to receive,
What the first sprightly running could not give.
I'm tired with waiting for this chemic gold,
Which fools us young, and beggars us when old."
            —*Aureng-Zebe*, Act IV, Scene I

Since Addison, plays have been more according to rule, audiences more particular, and authors more correct and less daring. I have seen some new plays that are very well behaved, but dull. It seems as if the English used to be born for the production of irregular beauties. The brilliant freaks of Shakespeare are a thousand times more delightful than modern sobriety. The poetic genius of the English until now has resembled a thick-spreading tree planted by nature, lifting its thousand branches as it pleases, and growing irregularly and with vigor. Prune it against its nature to the shape of a tree in the gardens of Marly,[5] and it will die.

LETTER NINETEEN

ON COMEDY

I do not know how the wise and ingenious M. de Muralt, from whose pen we have had the *Letters on the English and the French,* managed, in writing of comedy, to confine himself to critical remarks on a comic writer named Shadwell. That author was sufficiently scorned in his time; he was by no means the poet of respectable people. His plays, enjoyed by the vulgar for a few performances, were disdained by all people of taste, and resembled so many plays I have seen in France that attracted the crowd and repelled readers, and that, as has been said,

"All Paris condemns and all Paris attends."

[5]Reference is to a château, 10 kilometers from Versailles, built for Louis XIV by Mansart.

M. de Muralt ought, I think, to have spoken to us about an excellent author who was living then: Mr. Wycherley, who was long the declared lover of the most distinguished mistress[1] of Charles II. This man, who spent his life in the highest society, was perfectly acquainted with its vices and follies, and with the firmest of brushes painted them in their true colors.

He did a misanthrope, imitated from Molière. All the strokes of Wycherley are more bold and emphatic than those in our own misanthrope, but they are also less elegant and decorous.[2] The English author corrected the only fault in Molière's play, its lack of plot and interest. The English play is interesting and its plot is ingenious; it is no doubt too rude for our tastes. Here is a naval captain full of valor, frankness, and scorn for the human race. He has a wise and sincere friend whom he distrusts, and a mistress who loves him tenderly and on whom he does not deign to bestow a glance. On the other hand, he has put all his confidence in a false friend who is the most unworthy man alive, and has given his heart to the most perfidious coquette of her whole sex; he is positive that this woman is a Penelope, and this false friend a Cato. He goes away to fight against the Dutch, and leaves all his money, his jewelry, every last thing he owns, to this virtuous woman, and entrusts her to this faithful friend, on whom he counts so greatly. However, the true honest man, whom he so mightily distrusts, embarks with him; and the mistress he has not even deigned to look at disguises herself as a page[3] and makes the voyage without the captain's noticing her sex during the whole campaign.

[1]The Duchess of Cleveland.

[2]"Philosophy, liberty, and the climate lead to misanthropy. London, which has no Tartuffes, is full of Timons." Passage, in editions of 1756–84, within a larger passage substituted for our opening section of Letter XIX.

[3]In the play, Fidelia is called "little volunteer."

Having blown up his vessel in a sea fight, the captain returns to London without support, with no ship and no money, accompanied only by his page and his friend, and realizing neither the friendship of the one nor the love of the other. He goes straight to the pearl among women, whom he expects to recover along with his money box and her fidelity: he finds her married to the honest rascal in whom he has confided, and his deposit no more chastely preserved than the rest. Our man has the greatest imaginable difficulty in believing that a virtuous woman could play such tricks; whereupon, the better to convince him, that good lady falls in love with the page, whom she determines to take by storm. But since justice must be done and, in a play, vice must be punished and virtue rewarded, we find as it turns out that the captain puts himself in the page's place, goes to bed with his faithless beauty, cuckolds his traitorous friend, runs him through the body, retrieves his money box and marries his page. You will note that the play has even been larded with a Comtesse de Pimbesche,[4] an old litigant, kinswoman of the captain, who is quite the most amusing creature and the finest character on the stage.

Wycherley drew from Molière another play no less singular and no less audacious. It is a sort of *École des Femmes*.[5]

The main character in the piece is a rake, the terror of the husbands of London, who, to be more certain of success, decides to spread the word that in his latest illness the surgeons thought proper to make a eunuch of him. What with this fair name, all the husbands bring their wives to him, and the poor man has no longer any problem but choosing. He is particularly interested in a little country girl who is extremely innocent and amorous, and who cuckolds

[4]In Racine's *Les Plaideurs*. Voltaire refers here to Widow Blackacre.
[5]*The Country Wife.*

her husband with a simplicity worth more than the clever-
ness of the most expert of ladies. This play is not, if you
must, the school of good behavior, but it is truly the school
of wit and of good comedy.

A knight named Vanbrugh wrote some comedies that
are even more amusing but less skillful. He was a man of
pleasure, and a poet and architect into the bargain. It is held
that he wrote as he built, with a somewhat heavy hand. He
it was who built the famous Blenheim Palace, a weighty and
durable monument to our unhappy battle of Hochstedt. If
the apartments were only as wide as the walls are thick, this
palace would be tolerably commodious.

In Vanbrugh's epitaph[6] we find the hope that the earth
will not lie lightly on him, considering that he put such a
pitiless load on it during his lifetime.

This knight, who came over to tour France before the
war of 1701, was put in the Bastille, and stayed there some
time,[7] without ever managing to find out what had caused
our Ministry to honor him with that distinction. He wrote a
comedy in the Bastille; and, what seems to me very strange,
in the whole play not a word is aimed against the country in
which he suffered this outrage.

The Englishman who, of all his nation, has carried the
glory of the comic theater to the highest point is the late
Mr. Congreve. He wrote few plays, but all are excellent of
their kind. The rules of the drama are rigorously observed
in them; they are full of characters the subtleties of whose

[6]Under this stone, reader, survey
  Dead Sir John Vanbrugh's house of clay.
  Lie heavy on him, earth! for he
  Laid many heavy loads on thee.
  —Abel Evans (1679–1737),
  satiric poet and clergyman.

[7]1690-92. The pretext for arresting him was that he had no passport, but some
think that it was the vengeance of a woman.

modeling are done with an extreme delicacy of touch; you are not subjected to the slightest unpleasantness in the way of humor; you find, throughout, the language of gentlemen with the behavior of knaves: which proves that he knew the world well, and that he lived in the midst of what is called good company. He was infirm and almost a dying man when I knew him. He had one fault, and that was not sufficiently to esteem his original calling of authorship, which had made his reputation and his fortune. He spoke to me of his works as if of trifles beneath his dignity, and told me, in our very first conversation, to consider him only as a gentleman living a most quiet life. I replied that if he had had the misfortune of being only a gentleman like any other, I should never have come to see him; and I was very much shocked at such misplaced vanity.

His plays are the wittiest and the most scrupulously written, those of Vanbrugh the gayest, and those of Wycherley the most vigorous.

It should be noted that none of these wits spoke ill of Molière. It is only bad writers among the English who have slandered[8] this great man. It is the bad musicians of Italy who scorn Lully, but a Buononcini esteems him and does him justice, as a Mead[9] thinks highly of a Helvétius and a Silva.[10]

England has other good comic poets, such as Sir Richard Steele and Mr. Cibber, an excellent comedian and moreover poet laureate, a title that seems ridiculous but that nonetheless brings with it an income of a thousand *écus*[11]

[8]Referring to Thomas Shadwell.

[9]Physician to Newton and to Queen Caroline.

[10]The first was a physician, father of the philosopher; the second a Parisian doctor famous in Voltaire's time.

[11]The laureate received £100 a year.

and some handsome privileges. Our great Corneille did not have so much.

Don't ask, however, that I go into the least detail here about these English plays I am such a great admirer of, nor that I pass on to you a piece of wit or humor from the Wycherleys and Congreves. Laughter does not survive translation. If you want to know English comedy, there is nothing for it but to go to London, stay there three years, get a good grasp of English, and attend the theater every day. I find no great pleasure in reading Plautus and Aristophanes. Why? Because I am neither a Greek nor a Roman. The fineness in phrasing of witty remarks, allusions, the rightness or appositeness of things—all that is lost on a foreigner.

It is different in tragedy. There it is all a matter of great passions and of heroic foolishness consecrated by old errors of fable or of history. *Oedipus* and *Electra* belong to the Spaniards, to the English, and to ourselves, as well as to the Greeks. But good comedy is the speaking picture of the follies of a nation, and if you are not thoroughly acquainted with that nation you can hardly judge the painting.

LETTER TWENTY

ON PERSONS OF RANK WHO CULTIVATE LEARNING

THERE was a time in France when the arts were cultivated by persons of the first importance in the state. Courtiers particularly took them up, in spite of dissipation, of the taste for trifles, of the passion for intrigue—all deities of the nation.

It seems to me that today the vogue at Court is not for learning. Perhaps in a while the fashion of thinking will return. All that is necessary is for a king to wish it; you can do what you please with this nation. In England people have a habit of thinking, and learning there is more highly honored than in France. This fortunate condition is a necessary consequence of their form of government. In London there are about eight hundred persons who have the right to speak in public and to support the interests of the nation. About five or six thousand claim the same honor in their turn; all the rest set themselves up as judges of these latter, and each man may publish what he thinks about public affairs. Thus the whole nation is under the necessity of educating itself. You are always hearing them talk of the governments of Athens and of Rome; in spite of themselves they think they had better read the authors who have treated of those governments; this study leads naturally to belles-lettres.

In general, men have the kind of mind that corresponds with their calling. Why as a rule have our magistrates, our lawyers, our doctors, and many of the clergy more learning, taste, and wit than one finds in all the other professions? The answer is that it's really their calling to have a cultivated mind, as it is that of a business man to know business. Not long ago a very young English peer came to see me in Paris on his return from Italy; he had done a description of that country in verse as elegantly written as anything by Lord Rochester or by our Chaulieus, Sarrasins, and Chapelles.[1]

The translation I have made from it is so far from attaining to the energy and sprightly humor of the original that I am obliged seriously to beg pardon of the author and of those who understand English; however, since I have no other means of making known these verses of Lord————,[2] here they are in my own language:

> Qu'ai-je donc vu dans l'Italie?
> Orgueil, astuce et pauvreté,
> Grands compliments, peu de bonté,
> Et beaucoup de cérémonie;
> L'extravagante comédie
> Que souvent l'Inquisition[3]
> Veut qu'on nomme religion,
> Mais qu'ici nous nommons folie.
> La nature, en vain bienfaisante,
> Veut enrichir ces lieux charmants;
> Des Prêtres la main désolante
> Étouffe ses plus beaux présents.
> Les Monsignors, soi-disant grands,
> Seuls dans leurs palais magnifiques,
> Y sont d'illustres fainéants,
> Sans argent et sans domestiques.

[1]Men of the world and writers of polished light verse. Chaulieu, an abbé, lived on into the eighteenth century.

[2]John Lord Hervey (1696–1743).

[3]Voltaire's note: "He doubtless means the farces that certain preachers put on in the public squares."

Pour les petits, sans liberté,
Martyrs du joug qui les domine,
Ils ont fait voeu de pauvreté,
Priant Dieu par oisiveté,
Et toujours jeûnant par famine.
Ces beaux lieux, du Pape bénis,
Semblent habités par les diables,
Et les habitants misérables
Sont damnés dans le paradis.[4]

[4]Literally translated into English: "What then did I see in Italy? Pride, cunning, and poverty, elaborate compliments, little kindness, and a great deal of ceremony; the extravagant farce that the Inquisition often demands that we call religion, but that here we call madness. Nature, beneficent in vain, wishes to enrich this charming country; the desolating hand of priests smothers her loveliest gifts. The so-called great nobles, alone in their magnificent palaces, are illustrious idlers without money or servants. As for the little people, lacking liberty, martyrs of the yoke that masters them, they have made a vow of poverty, praying to God out of laziness, and always fasting for reasons of famine. These beautiful places, blessed by the Pope, seem haunted by devils, and the miserable inhabitants are damned in the midst of paradise."

Previous editors and translators of Voltaire have not known Hervey's original. The Earl of Ilchester, in *Lord Hervey and His Friends, 1726-38* (London, 1950), published for the first time, from among the Fox papers at Melbury, a verse letter written in 1729 by Hervey to his wife, part of which, as anyone can see, Voltaire imitated in this chapter of the *Lettres Philosophiques*. Here are the passages of Hervey that apply.

Throughout all Italy beside,
What does one find but want and pride?
Farces of superstitious folly,
Decay, distress, and melancholy,
The havoc of despotic pow'r,
A country rich, its owners poor,
Unpeopled towns, and lands untill'd.
The nobles miserably great,
In painted domes, and empty state,
Too proud to work, too poor to eat.
No arts the meaner sort employ,
They nought improve, nor ought enjoy.
Each clown from mis'ry grows a Saint,
He prays from idleness, and fasts from want.
• • •

Perhaps it will be said that these are the verses of a heretic; but every day people translate—and even quite badly—the verses of Horace and of Juvenal, who had the misfortune to be pagans. You are certainly aware that a translator is not answerable for the sentiments of his author; all he can do is to pray God for his conversion. And I don't fail to do that for the sake of his lordship.

Whilst Milan's sons, oppress'd by power,
Their fate in Paradise deplore,
Ah! what avail her fertile plains,
Her olives, vines, and swelling grains?
A foreign Prince her wealth demands,
Her vintage press'd by foreign hands,
A foreign hand her harvest spoils;
Vienna fattens on her toils."

The license taken by Voltaire in his version is characteristic and instructive.

LETTER TWENTY-ONE

ON THE EARL OF ROCHESTER AND MR. WALLER

EVERYONE knows Lord Rochester by reputation. M. de Saint-Évremond has said a good deal about him, but he has acquainted us only with Rochester the famous man of pleasure, the rake; I should like to make known the man of genius and the great poet. Among other works that shone with that flowing imagination that was his only, he did some satires on the same subjects as those chosen by our famous Boileau.[1] I know nothing more useful for the perfecting of taste than to compare great geniuses who have tried their skill on the same subject matter.

This is how Boileau argues against the human reason in his satire on man:

> Cependant, à le voir, plein de vapeurs légères,
> Soi-même se bercer de ses propres chimères,
> Lui seul de la nature est la base et l'appui,
> Et le dixième Ciel ne tourne que pour lui.
> De tous les animaux il est ici le maître;
> Qui pourrait le nier, poursuis-tu? Moi, peut-être:
> Ce maître prétendu qui leur donne des lois,
> Ce roi des animaux, combien a-t-il de Rois?

> Behold him of his boasted reason vain,
> Drunk with the fumes of his distemper'd brain;
> Of nature he the base and corner-stone;
> The Heav'n of Heav'ns revolves for him alone;

---

[1]Voltaire here calls him Despréaux.

Of all that breathes on earth the sov'reign lord,
And who will dare to doubt that sov'reign's word?
Why, faith, my friend, that doubt belongs to me,
This king of beasts, how many kings has he?[2]

Here, more or less, is how the Earl of Rochester expresses himself in his satire on mankind;[3] but the reader must continue to remind himself that these are free translations of English poets, and that the constraint of our versification and the delicate proprieties of our language do not allow of an equivalent for the impetuous license of English style.

Cet esprit que je hais, cet esprit plein d'erreur,
Ce n'est pas ma raison, c'est la tienne, Docteur;
C'est ta raison frivole, inquiète, orgueilleuse,
Des sages animaux rivale dédaigneuse,
Qui croit entre eux et l'Ange occuper le milieu,
Et pense être ici-bas l'image de son Dieu,
Vil atome importun, qui croit, doute, dispute,
Rampe, s'élève, tombe, et nie encor sa chute;
Qui nous dit: 'Je suis libre,' en nous montrant ses fers,
Et dont l'oeil trouble et faux croit percer l'Univers,
Allez, révérends fous, bienheureux fanatiques!
Compilez bien l'amas de vos riens scolastiques!
Pères de visions et d'énigmes sacrés,
Auteurs du labyrinthe où vous vous égarez,
Allez obscurément éclaircir vos mystères,
Et courez dans l'école adorer vos chimères!
Il est d'autres erreurs: il est de ces dévots,
Condamnés par eux-même à l'ennui du repos.
Ce mystique encloîtré, fier de son indolence,

[2]Satire VIII. I quote the version found in the Smollett edition of Voltaire. It is better than John Oldham's.

[3]"A Satire against Mankind" (1675).

Tranquille au sein de Dieu, qu'y peult-il faire? Il pense.
Non, tu ne penses point, misérable, tu dors,
Inutile à la terre et mis au rang des morts;
Ton esprit énervé croupit dans la mollesse;
Réveille-toi, sois homme, et sors de ton ivresse.
L'homme est né pour agir, et tu prétends penser!

And 'tis this very reason I despise,
This supernatural gift that makes a mite
Think he's the image of the infinite;
Comparing his short life, void of all rest,
To the eternal and the ever blest;
This busy puzzling stirrer up of doubt,
That frames deep mysteries, then finds 'em out,
Filling with frantic crowds of thinking fools,
The reverend bedlams, colleges, and schools;
Borne on whose wings, each heavy sot can pierce
The limits of the boundless universe. . . .
'Tis this exalted power whose business lies
In nonsense and impossibilities;
This made a whimsical philosopher,
Before the spacious world his tub prefer;
And we have many modern coxcombs who
Retire to think, 'cause they have nought to do.
But thoughts were given for action's government;
Where action ceases, thought's impertinent.
Our sphere of action is life's happiness,
And he that thinks beyond thinks like an ass.

Whether these ideas are true or false, it is certain that they
are expressed with that energy which makes a poet.

I shall take good care not to examine the thing like a
philosopher, or at this point to abandon the brush for the
compasses. My sole purpose, in this letter, is to make
known the genius of the English poets, and I am going to
go on in the same style.

A good deal has been heard about the celebrated Waller in France. MM. de La Fontaine, Saint-Évremond, and Bayle have praised him, but people know nothing of him but his name. He enjoyed in London just about the same repute as Voiture did in Paris, and I think he deserved it more. Voiture appeared at a moment when we were emerging from barbarism and were still ignorant. Men wanted to be witty, but as yet were incapable of wit. They looked for turns of phrase instead of thoughts: imitation diamonds are more easily found than genuine ones. Voiture, born with a frivolous and facile talent, was the first to shine in that dawn of French literature. If he had come after the men who made the glory of the century of Louis XIV, either he would have remained unknown, or no one would have mentioned him except with contempt, or he would have reformed his style. Boileau praises him, but in his first satires, when his taste was not yet formed; he was young, and at the age when one forms one's opinion of men by their reputation rather than by what they are themselves. Besides, Boileau was often quite wrong, when he praised and when he censured. He praised Segrais, whom no one reads; he insulted Quinault, whom everyone knows by heart; he says not a word about La Fontaine. Waller, better than Voiture, was still not quite perfect. His elegant works are full of grace, but his negligence makes them dull, and falseness of thought often disfigures them. The English had not yet come to write with a fine accuracy.[4] His serious works have a vigor that one would not expect from the softness of his other pieces. He wrote a funeral eulogy on Cromwell, which with all its faults is accepted as a masterpiece. To understand this work you must know that

---

[4] *"avec correction,"* or, as they said in those days, "correctly."

Cromwell died on the day of an extraordinarily violent storm.

The piece begins thus:

Il n'est plus; c'en est fait; soumettons-nous au sort:
Le ciel a signalé ce jour par des tempêtes,
Et la voix du tonnerre, éclatant sur nos têtes,
    Vient d'annoncer sa mort.
Par ses derniers soupirs il ébranle cette île,
Cette île que son bras fit trembler tant de fois,
    Quand, dans le cours de ses exploits,
    Il brisait la tête des rois
Et soumettait un peuple à son joug seul docile.
Mer, tu t'en es troublée. O mer! tes flots émus
Semblent dire en grondant aux plus lointains rivages
Que l'effroi de la terre, et ton maître, n'est plus.
Tel au Ciel autrefois s'envola Romulus,
Tel il quitta la terre au milieu des orages,
Tel d'un peuple guerrier il reçut les hommages:
Obéi dans sa vie, à sa mort adoré,
Son palais fut un temple, etc.

UPON THE LATE STORM, AND OF THE DEATH OF HIS HIGHNESS ENSUING THE SAME

We must resign! Heaven his great soul does claim
  In storms, as loud as his immortal fame;
  His dying groans, his last breath, shake our isle,
  And trees uncut fall for his funeral pile;
  About his palace their broad roots are tossed
  Into the air.—So Romulus was lost!
New Rome in such a tempest missed her King,
And from obeying fell to worshipping.
On Oeta's top thus Hercules lay dead,
With ruined oaks and pines about him spread;
The poplar, too, whose bough he wont to wear

On his victorious head, lay prostrate there;
Those his last fury from the mountain rent:
Our dying hero from the continent
Ravished whole towns; and forts from Spaniards reft,
As his last legacy to Britain left.
The ocean, which so long our hopes confined,
Could give no limits to his vaster mind;
Our bounds' enlargement was his latest toil,
Nor hath he left us prisoners to our isle;
Under the tropic is our language spoke,
And part of Flanders hath received our yoke.
From civil broils he did us disengage,
Found nobler objects for our martial rage;
And, with wise conduct, to his country showed
Their ancient way of conquering abroad.
Ungrateful then! if we no tears allow
To him, that gave us peace and empire too.
Princes, that feared him, grieve, concerned to see
No pitch of glory from the grave is free.
Nature herself took notice of his death,
And, sighing, swelled the sea with such a breath,
That, to remotest shores her billows rolled,
The approaching fate of her great ruler told.

It was in reference to this eulogy on Cromwell that Waller made to King Charles II the reply found in Bayle's dictionary. The King, to whom Waller had just presented, according to the custom of kings and poets, a poem stuffed with praise, reproached him with having done better for Cromwell. Waller replied: "Sir, we poets succeed better in fiction than in truth." That answer was not so sincere as the one made by the Dutch ambassador who, when the same king complained that people had less respect for him than for Cromwell, said, "Ah, sir, that Cromwell was something else again."

My purpose is not to comment on the character of Waller or of anyone else. I judge dead men by their works alone; for me all the rest has been wiped out. I will only say that Waller, born at court, with an income of three thousand pounds a year,[5] never had the fatuous pride or the indifference to abandon his talent. The Earls of Dorset and of Roscommon, the two Dukes of Buckingham, Lord Halifax, and how many others, have not thought it beneath them to become very great poets and illustrious writers. Their works do them more honor than their names. They have cultivated letters as if they expected to make their fortune at it; they have, in addition, rendered the arts respectable in the eyes of the people, who, in all things, need to be led by the great, and who, however, pattern themselves less on them in England than anywhere else in the world.

[5]Translating the roundness of "60,000 livres," though £2,500 would be a nearer equivalent.

LETTER TWENTY-TWO

ON MR. POPE AND SOME OTHER FAMOUS POETS

I wanted to speak to you of Mr. Prior, one of the most agreeable of the English poets, whom you saw in Paris as Envoy Extraordinary and Minister Plenipotentiary in 1712. I expected also to give you some idea of the poetry of Lord Roscommon, of Lord Dorset, and so on; but I realize that to do so I should have to write a big book, and that after a great deal of trouble I should only have given you a very imperfect idea of all those works. Poetry is a species of music: it must be heard before it can be judged. When I translate for you certain passages from these foreign poems, I take down for you, imperfectly, something of their music, but I cannot express the flavor of their song.

There is one English poem especially that I should despair of acquainting you with; it is called *Hudibras*. The subject is the civil war and the sect of Puritans held up to ridicule. It is *Don Quixote* and our own *Satire Ménippée* melted together; it is, of all the books I have ever read, the one in which I have found the most wit; but it is also the most untranslatable. Who would believe that a book that seizes upon all the absurdities of which the human race is capable, and that has more ideas in it than words, could not stand translation? The reason is that almost everything in it makes allusion to actual affairs: the brunt of the ridicule falls on the theologians, whom few people of fashion know much about; footnotes are necessary every moment of the way, and a joke explained is no longer a joke: every annotator of witticisms is a fool.

That is why the French will never understand very well the books of the ingenious Doctor Swift,[1] who is called the Rabelais of England. He has the honor to be a priest, like Rabelais, and, like him, to deride everything; but people do him great injury, in my humble opinion, to call him by that name. Rabelais, in his extravagant and unintelligible book, let loose an extreme jollity and an extreme impertinence; he poured out erudition, filth, and boredom; you will get a good story two pages long at the price of volumes of nonsense. Only a few persons of eccentric tastes pride themselves on understanding and esteeming this work as a whole; the rest of the nation laugh at the jokes of Rabelais and hold his book in contempt. He is regarded as chief among buffoons; we are annoyed that a man who had so much wit should have made such wretched use of it; he is a drunken philosopher who wrote only when he was drunk.[2]

Mr. Swift is Rabelais in his right mind and living in good company; it is true he has not the gaiety of the older man, but he has all the delicacy, the rationality, the selectivity, the good taste that are wanting in our Curé of Meudon. The style of his verses is unusual, almost inimitable; true wit and humor are his province in verse and in

[1] "You will find in the same pacquet the second volume of m^r. Gulliver, which by the by, I don't advise you to translate. Stick to the first, the other is over-strain'd. The reader's imagination is pleased and charmingly entertaind by the new prospects of the lands which Gulliver discovers to him, but that continued series of new fangled follies, of fairy tales, of wild inventions, palls at last upon our taste. Nothing unnatural may please long. T'is for this reason that commonly the second parts of romances are so insipid."—Voltaire to Thieriot, March 11, 1727 (Besterman 302).

[2] He changed his mind about Rabelais: "I repent of having in times past spoken too ill of him." Voltaire to Mme du Deffand, April 12, 1760 (Besterman 8108).

prose; but really to understand him you must travel a bit in his country.[3]

You can more easily get some idea of Mr. Pope; he is, I think, the most elegant, the most correct, and—which is in itself a great deal—the most harmonious poet England has had. He turned the harsh wheezings of the English trumpet into the sweet sounds of the flute. He may be translated, because he is remarkably clear, and because his subjects are for the most part general ones, within the province of all nations.

The French will soon know his *Essay on Criticism* through the verse translation the Abbé du Resnel is making.[4]

Here is a passage from the poem *The Rape of the Lock,* which I have just translated with my usual freedom; for, once again, I know nothing worse than to translate a poet word for word.

> Umbriel à l'instant, vieux Gnome rechigné,
> Va, d'une aile pesante et d'un air renfrogné,
> Chercher, en murmurant, la caverne profonde
> Où, loin des doux rayons que répand l'oeil du monde,
> La Déesse aux vapeurs a choisi son séjour.
> Les tristes Aquilons y sifflent à l'entour,
> Et le souffle malsain de leur aride haleine
> Y porte aux environs la fièvre et la migraine.
> Sur un riche sofa, derrière un paravent,
> Loin des flambeaux, du bruit, des parleurs et du vent,
> La quinteuse Déesse incessament repose,

---

[3]In an additional passage dating from 1756, Voltaire remarks of the *Tale of a Tub* that, though Swift was ridiculing Catholicism, Lutheranism, and Calvinism, "he said, for his own reasons, that he did not touch Christianity itself. He claims to have respected the Father, while giving a hundred lashes to the three children. Some difficult people have thought that the switch was so long it reached the Father."

[4]It was published in 1730.

Le coeur gros de chagrins, sans en savoir la cause,
N'ayant pensé jamais, l'esprit toujours troublé,
L'oeil chargé, le teint pâle et l'hypocondre enflé.
La médisante envie est assise auprès d'elle,
Vieux spectre féminin, décrépite pucelle,
Avec un air dévot déchirant son prochain,
Et chansonnant les gens l'Évangile à la main.
Sur un lit plein de fleurs négligemment penchée,
Une jeune beauté non loin d'elle est couchée:
C'est l'Affectation, qui grasseye en parlant,
Écoute sans entendre, et lorgne en regardant,
Qui rougit sans pudeur, et rit de tout sans joie,
De cent maux différents prétend qu'elle est la proie,
Et, pleine de santé sous le rouge et le fard,
Se plaint avec mollesse, et se pâme avec art.

Umbriel, a dusky, melancholy sprite
As ever sullied the fair face of light,
Down to the central earth, his proper scene,
Repair'd to search the gloomy cave of Spleen.
Swift on his sooty pinions flits the Gnome,
And in a vapour reach'd the dismal dome.
No cheerful breeze this sullen region knows,
The dreaded East is all the wind that blows.
Here in a grotto shelter'd close from air,
And screen'd in shades from day's detested glare,
She sighs for ever on her pensive bed,
Pain at her side, and Megrim at her head.
Two handmaids wait the throne; alike in place,
But diff'ring far in figure and in face.
Here stood Ill-nature, like an ancient maid,
Her wrinkled form in black and white array'd!
With store of prayers for mornings, nights, and noons,
Her hand is fill'd; her bosom with lampoons.
There Affectation, with a sickly mien,
Shows in her cheek the roses of eighteen,
Practis'd to lisp, and hang the head aside,
Faints into airs, and languishes with pride;

On the rich quilt sinks with becoming woe,
Wrapt in a gown for sickness and for show.

If you were to read the passage in the original, instead
of in this feeble translation, you would compare it with the
description of Mollesse in *le Lutrin*.[5]

And that's the best I can do here on the English poets.
I have touched a little on the subject of their philosophers.
As for good historians, I don't know that they have yet had
any; it took a Frenchman to write their history. Perhaps the
genius of the English, which is either cold or impetuous, has
not yet seized upon that artless eloquence which is History's, and that air it has that is both noble and simple.
Perhaps also the spirit of party, which blurs the vision, has
discredited all their historians: half the nation is always the
enemy of the other half. I have found people who assured
me that the Duke of Marlborough was a milksop, and that
Mr. Pope was a blockhead, as, in France, certain Jesuits see
in Pascal a small mind, and certain Jansenists say that
Father Bourdaloue was only a babbler. Mary Stuart is a
sainted heroine to the Jacobites; to the rest she is a
debauchee, an adulteress, and a murderess; so in England
they have scurrilous pamphlets and no history. It is true
that there is at present a Mr. Gordon, an excellent translator of Tacitus, who is quite capable of writing the history of
his country, but M. Rapin de Thoyras has forestalled him.
All in all, it seems to me that the English do not by any
means have such good historians as we, that they have no
true tragedies at all, that they have charming comedies,
admirable passages of poetry, and philosophers who ought
to be the preceptors of the human race.

The English have greatly profited from literary works in

[5] See Appendix.

our language; we ought in our turn to borrow from them, having lent to them before; the English and we did not come till after the Italians, who have been our masters in all things, and whom we have surpassed in some. I don't know which of the three nations deserves the preference; but happy the man who is able to savor their different excellences!

LETTER TWENTY-THREE

ON THE CONSIDERATION OWED TO MEN OF LETTERS

NEITHER in England nor in any other country in the world does one find such establishments for the sake of the fine arts as there are in France. Almost everywhere there are universities, but only in France are there such serviceable encouragements for astronomy, for all aspects of mathematics, for medicine, for research into antiquity, for painting, for sculpture, and for architecture. Louis XIV immortalized himself by founding these institutions, and that immortality did not cost him two hundred thousand francs a year.

I confess that it astonishes me that the parliament of England, which went so far as to promise twenty thousand guineas to whoever should make the impossible discovery of the longitude, should never have thought of imitating Louis XIV in munificence toward the arts.

To be sure, merit finds in England other rewards more reputable in the eyes of the nation. Such is the respect that this people has for talent, that a man of merit there always makes his fortune. In France, Mr. Addison would have belonged to some academy, and would have been able to obtain, through the influence of some woman, a pension of twelve hundred livres; or rather, somebody would have done his business for him on the pretext that in his tragedy of *Cato* certain strokes had evidently been made against the porter of a man of position. In England, he was secretary of state. Mr. Newton was master of the Mint; Mr. Congreve held an important office; Mr. Prior was a plenipotentiary. Doctor Swift is a Dean in Ireland and is more highly esteemed there than the Primate. If the religion of Mr. Pope does not permit him to hold a place, it at least has not prevented his translation of Homer from bringing him two hundred thousand francs. For a long time in France I saw the author[1] of *Rhadamiste* on the verge of dying of hunger; and the son of one of the greatest men France has had, who was beginning to follow in his father's footsteps, would have been reduced to misery had it not been for M. Fagon.[2] What encourages the arts most in England is the prestige they enjoy: the portrait of the prime minister hangs above the fireplace in his office; but I have seen that of Mr. Pope in twenty houses.

Mr. Newton was honored during his lifetime and after his death as he should have been. The leaders of the nation disputed the honor of being his pallbearers. Go into Westminster Abbey. It is not the tombs of kings that one admires there, but the monuments erected by the gratitude of the nation to the greatest of the men who have contributed to its glory. You will see their statues, as one saw at Athens those of such men as Sophocles and Plato; and I am convinced that the mere sight of these glorious monuments

[1]Crébillon, whose masterpiece *Rhadamiste et Zénobie* was published in 1711. In old age he was given a pension by Mme de Pompadour.

[2]Louis Racine was granted certain offices through the help of Fagon (d. 1718), who was chief physician to the king.

has roused more than one mind and been the making of more than one great man.

People have even reproached the English with having gone too far in honoring simple merit; they have taken exception to their having buried the famous actress Mrs. Oldfield[3] in Westminster Abbey with nearly the same honors accorded Mr. Newton. Some have asserted that they made a show of honoring the memory of that actress to such a degree in order to make us feel more strongly the barbarity and cowardly injustice they reproach us with for having thrown out like rubbish the body of Mlle. Lecouvreur.[4]

But I can assure you that the English, in the funeral ceremonies of Mrs. Oldfield, whom they buried in their own Saint-Denis, consulted none but their own tastes. They are far from attaching any infamy to the art of Sophocles and Euripides, or from cutting off from the rest of society those who devote their lives to reciting before them works that are the boast of the nation.

In the days of Charles I, and early in those civil wars begun by fanatical rigorists, who themselves were in the end their victims, a great deal was written against the theater, all the more because Charles I and his wife, the daughter of our Henry the Great, were extremely fond of it.

A certain Dr. Prynne, scrupulous to a fault, a man who would have thought himself damned if he had worn a cassock instead of a short coat, and who would have liked one half of mankind to have massacred the other for the glory of God and the propagation of the faith, took upon himself the writing of a very bad book against some rather good comedies that were put on quite innocently every day in the

[3]Anne Oldfield (1683-1730).

[4]Adrienne Lecouvreur (1692–1730). Voltaire's poem against the clergy's refusal to give her proper burial obliged him to leave Paris.

presence of the King and Queen. He cited Rabbinical authority and some passages from St. Bonaventura to prove that the
Oedipus of Sophocles was the work of the Evil One, and that
Terence was *ipso facto* excommunicate; and he added that
Brutus, who was a very severe Jansenist, had doubtless assassinated Caesar only because Caesar, who was High Priest,
had himself composed an *Oedipus;* finally he said that all
who attended a play were excommunicates who abjured their
chrism and their baptism. This was an outrage on the King
and the whole royal family. The English then respected
Charles I; they had no intention of allowing anyone to talk of
excommunicating that King whose head they later cut off.
Mr. Prynne was summoned before the Star Chamber and
condemned to see his fine book burned by the hangman, and
also to lose his ears. His trial appears in the public registers.

In Italy one takes good care not to cast any slurs on the
Opera or to excommunicate Signor Senesino or Signora
Cuzzoni. For my part, I should venture to hope that any
number of bad books that have been published against the
theater in France might be suppressed; for when the Italians and the English learn that we brand with the greatest
infamy an art in which we excel, that we condemn as impious a play that is acted among the religious and in convents,
that we dishonor plays in which Louis XIV and Louis XV
have been actors, that we give Satan the authorship of works
that have been reviewed by the strictest magistrates and
acted before a virtuous queen; when, I say, foreigners hear
about this insolence, this want of respect for royal authority,
this Gothic barbarity that people dare to call Christian
severity, what do you expect them to think of our country?
And how can they conceive, either that our laws authorize
an art that has been declared to be so vile, or that anyone
should dare to brand with such vileness an art authorized

by the laws, rewarded by sovereigns, cultivated by great men, and admired by nations; and that in the same book-shop Père Le Brun's declamation against our theater is to be found side by side with the immortal works of Racine, Corneille, Molière, and so on?

LETTER TWENTY-FOUR

ON ACADEMIES

THE English had, long before us, an Academy of Science;[1] but it is not so well regulated as ours, and that perhaps only because it is older. For if it had been established after the Academy of Paris, it would have adopted some of its wise rules and perfected the others.

The Royal Society of London lacks the two things most necessary to man, rewards and rules. A seat in the Academy in Paris means to a geometrician, to a chemist, a small, secure fortune; on the contrary, in London it costs money to belong to the Royal Society. Whoever says, in England, "I love the arts," and desires to belong to the Society, belongs to it instantly. But in France, to be a member and pensioner of the Academy, it is not enough to be an amateur; one must be a scholar and contest the seat with rivals all the more formidable in that they are incited by fame, by interest, by difficulty itself, and by that inflexibility of mind that

[1]The Royal Society received its patent in 1660; the Académie des Sciences was founded in 1666.

ordinarily comes of the persistent study of the calculative sciences.

The Academy of Science is wisely limited to the study of nature, and in truth it is a field broad enough to occupy fifty or sixty persons. The London Society indifferently mixes literature with physics. It seems to me that it is better to have a special academy for literature, so that nothing may be confused, and that one may not be confronted with a dissertation on Roman coiffures alongside a hundred new kinds of curves.

Since the London Society requires little order and offers no encouragement, and that of Paris is on another footing altogether, it is not surprising that the transactions of our academy are superior to theirs: well-disciplined and well-paid soldiers must in the end prevail over volunteers. It is true that the Royal Society has had a Newton, but it did not produce him; few of his colleagues even understood him. A genius like Mr. Newton belonged to all the academies of Europe, for all had much to learn of him.

The famous Dr. Swift formed the plan, in the last years of the reign of Queen Anne, of establishing an academy for the language, after the example of the Académie Française. This project was supported by the Earl of Oxford, Lord Treasurer, and even more strongly by Viscount Bolingbroke, Secretary of State, who had the gift of speaking extempore in parliament with as much purity as Swift writing in his study, and who would have been the patron and the ornament of that academy. The members of whom it was to be composed were men whose works will last as long as the English language: there were Dr. Swift, Mr. Prior, whom we have seen here as a diplomat, and who in England has the same reputation as La Fontaine has among us; there were Mr. Pope, the Boileau of England, Mr. Congreve, who can be called their Molière; several others, whose names just now escape me, would all have made that company flourish from its birth. But suddenly the Queen died; the Whigs took it into their heads to hang the patrons of the academy, and that, as you can well imagine, was a mortal blow to literature. The members of this body would have had a great advantage over those who first composed the French Academy; for Swift, Prior, Congreve, Dryden, Pope, Addison, etc., had fixed the English language by their writings, whereas Chapelain, Colletet, Cassaigne, Faret, Perrin, Cotin, your first Academicians, were the disgrace of your nation, and their very names became so ridiculous that, if some tolerably good writer had the misfortune to be born Chapelain or Cotin, he was obliged to change his name. It would especially have been necessary for the English Academy to propose for itself different pursuits from ours. One day a wit of that country asked me for the Transactions of the Académie Française. "It doesn't write up any," I replied, "but it has published sixty or eighty volumes of compliments." He ran through one or two of them; he could never comprehend that style, though he had a thorough understanding of all our good writers. "All I get from these fine discourses," he said to me, "is a faint idea that the Member Elect, having declared that his predecessor was a great man, that Cardinal Richelieu was a very great man, Chancellor Séguier a sufficiently great man, and Louis XIV a more than great man, the Director then replies in the same words, and adds that the Member Elect may very likely be some sort of great man himself, and that as for him, the Director, he will hang on to his share."

It is easy to see by what fatality almost all these discourses have done so little honor to this body: *vitium est temporis potius quam hominus.*[2] The custom was impercepti-

---

[2] "It is more the fault of the time than of the man." Lanson traces the substance of the quotation to Seneca.

bly established that each Academician should repeat these eulogies on his reception: it was a sort of law to bore the public. If one then tries to discover why the greatest geniuses who have become a part of this body have sometimes made the worst harangues, the reason once more turns out a simple one; it's that they wanted to shine, that they wanted to treat totally worn-out subject matter in some novel way. The necessity of speaking, the embarrassment of having nothing to say, and the desire to be witty are three things capable of making even the greatest man ridiculous. Unable to find any new thoughts, they looked for new turns of phrase, and spoke without thinking, like people chewing with empty mouths, trying to look as if they were eating, while perishing of starvation.

Instead of the rule of the Académie Française to publish all these speeches, by which, and by nothing else, it has become known, there should be a rule not to publish them at all.

The Academy of Belles-Lettres[3] has designed a wiser and more useful project, which is to present to the public a collection of Transactions full of research and scholarly critiques. These publications are already highly esteemed in foreign parts; one can only wish that they had gone rather deeper into some matters, and that others had not been treated at all. One could, for example. have done very well without some dissertation or other on the prerogatives of the right hand over the left, and various other studies which, under less ridiculous titles, are hardly less frivolous.

The Academy of Science in its researches, which are more difficult and of a more obvious utility, includes both the knowledge of nature and the perfecting of the arts. It is

[3]Académie des Inscriptions et Belles-Lettres.

to be believed that studies so profound and so continuous, calculations so exact, discoveries so ingenious, prospects so extensive, will at last produce something that will work for the good of the world.

Up to now, as we have all observed together, it is in the most barbarous centuries that the most useful discoveries are made; it seems that the role of the most enlightened periods and of the most learned gatherings is to ponder over what ignorant persons have invented. We know nowadays, after the long disputes of Mr. Huyghens and M. Renaud, how to determine the most advantageous angle made by the rudder of a vessel with the keel; but Christopher Columbus had discovered America without even suspecting the existence of that angle.

I certainly do not infer from this that we should confine ourselves to working in the dark; but it would be well that physicists and geometricians joined practice to theory as much as possible. Is it necessary that what does most honor to the human mind should often be that which is least useful? A man with the help of good sense and the four rules of arithmetic becomes a great merchant, a Jacques Coeur, a Delmet, a Bernard, whereas a poor algebraist spends his life looking into numbers for ratios and for properties astonishing but useless, which will not so much as teach him what the exchange is. All the arts are pretty much alike in this: there is a point beyond which research becomes a matter of mere curiosity. These truths ingeniously arrived at but without utility are like stars that, fixed too far from us, give us no light.

As for the Académie Française, what a service it would render to literature, the language, and the nation, if, instead of every year publishing compliments, it reprinted the good works of the century of Louis XIV, purified of all the errors in language that have slipped into them! Corneille and

Molière are full of them; La Fontaine is alive with them. Those that one could not correct would at least be noted. Europe, which reads these authors, would by their means gain a sure knowledge of our language. The purity of our language would be established forever; good French books, printed with such care at the expense of the Crown, would be one of the most glorious monuments of the nation. I have heard it said that M. Boileau once made the same suggestion, and that it was again put forth by a man whose wit, wisdom, and sound judgment are well known;[4] but this idea has had the fate of many another useful project, of being first approved and then ignored.

LETTER TWENTY-FIVE

ON THE PENSÉES OF M. PASCAL

I send you the critical observations I long ago made on the *Pensées* of M. Pascal. Please don't compare me here to Hezekiah, who wanted to burn all the books of Solomon. I respect the genius and the eloquence of Pascal; but the more I respect them, the more I am persuaded that he himself would have revised many of these *Pensées,* which he had jotted down on paper as they came to him, so as to scrutinize them later on; and it is as an admirer of his genius that I combat certain of his ideas.

---

[4]"L'Abbé de Rothelin of the French Academy"—note in the Lockman translation (1733). F. A. Taylor adds, "He was government Censor at the time of the publication of the *Lettres Philosophiques.*"

It seems to me that, on the whole, Pascal's motive in writing these *Pensées* was to show mankind in an odious light. He is dead set on painting us all wicked and miserable. He writes against human nature about as he wrote against the Jesuits. He attributes to the essence of our nature what pertains to certain men only. He eloquently insults the human race. I venture to take the side of humanity against this sublime misanthropist; I dare assert that we are neither so wicked nor so miserable as he says. Besides, I am quite convinced that if in the book he contemplated he had followed the plan that is manifest in his *Pensées,* he would have made a book full of eloquent paralogisms and of falsehoods admirably deduced. In fact, I think that all these books that people have been writing lately as proofs of the Christian religion are more likely to shock than to edify. Do these authors claim to know more about it than Jesus Christ and the Apostles? It's like trying to hold up an oak by setting reeds against it; you can take those useless reeds away without fear of doing any harm to the tree.

I have chosen with discretion certain thoughts of Pascal's; I put my replies below them. It is for you to decide whether I am wrong or right

I.[1]The greatness and the wretchedness of man are so plain to see that the true religion must necessarily teach us that there is in him some mighty principle of greatness, and at the same time some mighty principle of wretchedness. For the true religion must know our nature perfectly, in other words must know everything about our nature that is great and everything about it that is wretched, and the reason for both. It must also explain to us the rea-

---

[1]For the numbering of these items, see the Note on the Text, p. 273.

son for the astonishing contrarieties that meet within us.

This way of reasoning seems both false and dangerous, for the fable of Prometheus and of Pandora, the androgynes of Plato, and the dogmas of the Siamese would explain these apparent contrarieties just as well. The Christian religion would remain no less true even if nobody drew these ingenious conclusions, which can serve no purpose but to make the wit shine.

Christianity teaches nothing but simplicity, humanity, charity; to wish to reduce it to metaphysics is to make of it a source of errors.

> II. Let us examine all the religions of the world by this requirement and see if any besides the Christian satisfies it. Will it be that one taught by the philosophers who propose for the chief good a good that is within us? Is that the true good? Have they found the remedy for our ills? Is man cured of his presumption by being made equal to God? And those who have made us equal with the beasts, and who have given us earthly pleasures for the chief good— have they brought us the remedy for our lusts?

The philosophers taught no religion; it is not their philosophy that we are combatting. Never has a philosopher said he was inspired by God, for at that instant he would have ceased to be a philosopher and played the prophet. It is not a question of knowing whether Jesus Christ should carry the day against Aristotle; the point is to prove that the religion of Jesus Christ is the true one, and that those of Mahomet, the pagans, and all the rest are false.

> III. And yet without this mystery, the most incomprehensible of all, we are incomprehensible to

ourselves. The knot of our condition draws its twists and its turns from the abyss of original sin, so that man is more inconceivable without this mystery than this mystery is inconceivable to man.

Is this reasoning, to say, "Man is inconceivable without this inconceivable mystery"? Why wish to go further than Scripture? Is there not some temerity in supposing that Scripture needs support, and that these philosophical ideas can give it any?

What would M. Pascal have replied to a man who said to him: "I know that the mystery of original sin is the object of my faith and not of my reason. I understand very well, without any mystery, what man is. I see that he comes into the world like the other animals; that giving birth is more painful to mothers the more delicate they are; that sometimes women and female animals die in childbirth; that there are sometimes badly formed children who live deprived of one or two senses and of the faculty of reason; that those who are best formed are those who have the liveliest passions; that self-love is the same among all mankind, and that it is as necessary to them as the five senses; that this same self-love is given us by God for the preservation of our being, and that he has given us religion to regulate this self-love; that our ideas are just or inconsequent, obscure or luminous, according as our organs are more or less sound, more or less finely made, and according as we are more or less impassioned; that in all things we depend on the air around us, and on the food we eat, and that in all this there is nothing contradictory. Man is not an enigma, as you picture it to yourself in order to have the pleasure of guessing it. Man appears to be where he belongs in nature, superior to the animals, whom he is like in his organs, inferior to other beings, whom he resembles probably in thought. He is, like all we see, a mixture of good and evil, of pleasure and of pain. He is provided with passions in order that he may act, and with reason that he may govern his actions. If man were perfect, he would be God, and these so-called contrarieties, which you call *contradictions*, are the necessary ingredients that enter into the composition of man, who is what he must be.

IV. Let us follow our own movements, observe ourselves, and see if we do not find the living traits of these two natures.

Would so many contradictions be found in a simple subject?

This doubleness of man is so obvious that some have thought we had two souls, for a simple subject to them seemed incapable of such diversity, of such sudden changes, from an overweening pride to a horrible prostration of spirits.

Our varying wills are not contradictions in nature, and man is not a simple subject. He is composed of a countless number of parts: if a single one of these parts is altered a little, it follows necessarily that all the impressions on the brain are altered, and that the animal has new thoughts and new desires. It is very true that we are at one time prostrate with grief, at another swollen with self-conceit: and that must be when we find ourselves in opposite situations. An animal that its master pets and feeds, and another that is slaughtered gradually, and with style, for purposes of dissection, have quite contrary feelings. So do we. And the differences in us are so little contradictory that it would be contradictory if they did not exist.

The fools who have said we had two souls could by the same token have given us thirty or forty; for a man in a great passion has often thirty or forty different ideas about the same thing, and must necessarily have them, according as that thing appears to him under different aspects.

This so-called *doubleness* of man is an idea as absurd as it is metaphysical. I would just as soon say that the dog that bites and fawns is double; that the hell, who takes such care of her little ones, and who afterward abandons them to the point of failing to recognize them, is double; that the mirror, which represents different things at one time, is double; that the tree, which is sometimes burdened with leaves and sometimes stripped of them, is double. I admit that man is inconceivable; but so is all the rest of nature, and there are no more contradictions to be seen in man than in everything else.

V. Not to bet that God exists, is to bet that he does not. Which do you choose, then? Weigh the gain and the loss in deciding to believe that God exists. If you win, you win all; if you lose, you lose nothing. Bet that he exists, then, without hesitation.—"Yes, one must bet; but perhaps I am laying too much."— Look, since there is equal risk of winning and losing, if you had only two lives to gain for one, you might still bet.

It is plainly false to say, "Not to bet that God exists is to bet that he does not"; for he who doubts and asks to be informed is certainly not betting, either for or against.

Besides, that article seems a bit indecent and childish; that notion of gambling, of losses and winnings, does not suit the gravity of the subject.

In addition, the interest I have in believing a thing is not a proof of the existence of that thing. You tell me you will give me dominion over the world if I believe you are right. I hope then with all my heart that you are right;

but until you have proved it to me, I can not believe you.

Begin, one might say to M. Pascal, by convincing my reason. I have a stake, no doubt, in the existence of a God; but if, in your system, God has only come for so few persons; if the smallness of the number of the elect is so frightening; if I can do nothing at all by myself, tell me, if you please, what I have to gain in believing you. Have I not an obvious interest in being persuaded to the contrary? How can you have the effrontery to show me a limitless happiness, to which, out of a million men, hardly one has the right to aspire? If you want to convince me, set about it in another way, and don't go telling me about games of chance, about bets, about heads and tails; or, on the other hand, dismay me with the thorns you strew on the path that I not only wish to tread but must. Your reasoning would only serve to make atheists, if the voice of all nature did not cry out to us that there is a God, with a strength as notable as the weakness of these subtleties.

> VI. When I see the blindness and misery of man, and these astonishing contrarieties that reveal themselves in his nature, and when I observe the whole universe to be mute, and man without light, given up to himself, and as if lost in this obscure corner of the universe, not knowing who put him here, what he has come to do, what will become of him when he dies, I am terrified like a man who has been carried, sleeping, on to a horrid desert island, and who awakes without any knowledge of where he is, and without any means of escape; and thereupon I marvel that one does not fall into despair at so miserable a state.

While I was reading that reflection I received a letter

from a friend of mine,[2] who lives in a distant country. These are his words:

"I am here as you left me, neither gayer, nor sadder, nor richer, nor poorer, enjoying perfect health, with all that makes life agreeable, without love, without avarice, without ambition, and without envy; and so long as it all lasts, I shall boldly call myself a very happy man."

There are many men as happy as he. It is with men as with animals: a certain dog sleeps and eats with his mistress; another turns the spit and is every bit as contented; yet another runs mad, and we kill him. As for me, when I look at Paris or London I see no reason whatever for falling into this despair that M. Pascal is talking about; I see a town that in no way resembles a desert island, but is peopled, opulent, civilized, a place where men are as happy as human nature allows. Who is the wise man who will be ready to hang himself because he does not know how to see God face to face, and because his reason cannot unravel the mystery of the Trinity? One might as well despair over not having four feet and two wings.

Why make us hate our nature? Our existence is not so unhappy as they try to make us think. To look upon the universe as a dungeon, and all mankind as criminals who are going to be executed, is the idea of a fanatic. To believe that the world is a place of delight, where one should experience nothing but pleasure, is the dream of a Sybarite. To think that the earth, men, and animals are what they must be, according to the law of Providence, is, I believe, the part of a wise man.

[2]Everard Fawkener (1684–1758), apparently from England, and in December, it may be, of 1728. He was to be knighted in 1735 and sent as ambassador to Constantinople, where he had been more than once before. In England Voltaire had lived for some time at Fawkener's house at Wandsworth.

VII. [The Jews think] that God will not leave the other peoples in darkness for ever; that a liberator of all will come; that they are here in this world in order to announce him; that they were expressly created to be the heralds of this great event, and to call upon all peoples to unite with them in expectation of the liberator.

The Jews have always been waiting for a liberator; but their liberator is for them and not for us. They await a Messiah who will give the Jews mastery over the Christians; and we hope that the Messiah will one day unite the Jews with the Christians. On this matter they think precisely the contrary of what we do.

VIII. The law by which this people is governed is altogether the most ancient law in the world, the most perfect, and the only one in any State that has been preserved without interruption. Philo Judaeus proves this in different places, and Josephus, admirably, in writing against Apion, where he shows that it is so old that the very word *law* was unknown to the most ancient authors until more than a thousand years later, so that Homer, who spoke of so many peoples, never used it. And it is easy to judge of the perfection of that law by simply reading it, when one will see that everything has been provided for with such wisdom, equity, and discrimination that the most ancient Greek and Roman legislators, having some knowledge of it, borrowed from it their main laws: which is evident from those they call the Twelve Tables, and from the other proofs Josephus gives.

It is quite false that the law of the Jews is the most ancient, since before Moses, their legislator, they lived in

Egypt, in the whole world the country most renowned for its wise laws.

It is quite false that the word *law* was not known till after Homer. He speaks of the laws of Minos. The word for law is in Hesiod. And if it were to be found neither in Hesiod nor in Homer, that would prove nothing. There were kings and judges; so there were laws.

It is also quite false that the Greeks and Romans took laws from the Jews. They could not have done so in the early days of their republics, for at that time they could not have known the Jews; they could not have done so in the days of their greatness, for then they had for those barbarians a contempt known to all the world.

IX. This people is still admirable in its sincerity. They preserve, with love and faithfulness, the book in which Moses declares that they have always been ungrateful to God, and that he knows that they will be even more so after his death: but that he calls heaven and earth to witness against them that he has told them so often enough; that one day God, in anger against them, will disperse them among, all the peoples of the earth; that, since they have angered him by adoring Gods that were not their Gods, he will answer them by taking to himself a people that was not his people. Nevertheless, at the risk of their lives they preserve this book which dishonors them in so many ways. There is a sincerity without example in the world, nor with its roots in nature.

That sincerity has its examples everywhere, and its roots in nature only. The pride of every Jew finds reason to believe that it is not his detestable politics, his ignorance of the arts, his grossness that has been his undoing, but the wrath of God inflicted upon him. He thinks with satisfaction that it has taken miracles to down him, and that his nation is still the darling of the God who punishes it.

Let a preacher mount the pulpit and say to the French, "You are villains, heartless and ill-behaved; you were beaten at Hochstedt and at Ramillies because you could not defend yourselves"—he would be stoned. But if he says, "You are Catholics cherished by God; your infamous sins angered the Eternal, who delivered you into the hands of the Heretics at Hochstedt and at Ramillies, but when you returned to the Lord he blessed your courage at Denain"—these words will make the audience love him.

> X. If there is a God, we must love only him and not the beings he has made.

We must love the beings he has made, and very tenderly; we must love our country, our wives, our fathers, our children; and it is so necessary to love them that God makes us love them in spite of ourselves. The contrary principles are fit only to produce barbarous dialecticians.

> XI. We are born unjust; for each of us tends toward himself. That is against all order. We must tend toward the whole; and the slope down to the self is the beginning of all disorder in war, in government, in economy, etc.

That is according to all order. It is as impossible for a society to be founded and to survive without self-love as it would be to produce children without concupiscence, to imagine keeping alive without an appetite, etc. It is the love of ourselves that helps the love of others; it is through our mutual needs that we are useful to the human race; it is the foundation of all commerce; it is the eternal bond of men. Without it not an art would have been invented, not a society of ten persons formed. It is this self-love, which every animal has received from nature, that warns us to respect the self-love of others. Law regulates self-love, and religion perfects it. It is certainly true that God could have made creatures that were solely attentive to the good of others. In that case, merchants would have gone to the Indies out of charity, and the mason would have sawn stone to give pleasure to his neighbor. But God has established things otherwise. Let us not denounce the instinct he gives us, and let us make what use of it he bids us to.

XII. [The hidden meaning of the prophecies] could not lead into error, and there was only one people so carnally-minded as that which could mistake it. For when goods are promised in abundance, what prevented them from understanding true goods but their cupidity, which limited the meaning to goods of this earth?

In good faith, would the most spiritual people on earth have understood it otherwise? They were slaves of the Romans; they awaited a liberator who would lead them to victory and would make Jerusalem respected throughout the world. How, by the light of their reason, could they see this conqueror, this monarch in the poor and crucified Jesus? How could they understand, by the name of their capital, a celestial Jerusalem, they to whom the Decalogue had not so much as mentioned the immortality of the soul? How could a people so attached to its law, without superior insight, recognize in the prophecies, which were not their law, a God concealed in the form of a circumcised Jew, who by his new religion destroyed and made abominations of Circumcision and the Sabbath, sacred foundations of the Judaic law? Once more, let us adore God without trying to pierce the obscurity of his mysteries.

> XIII. The time of the first coming of Jesus Christ is foretold. The time of the second is not, because the first had to be hidden, whereas the second must be resplendent and so evident that even his enemies will acknowledge him.

The time of the second coming of Jesus Christ was foretold even more clearly than the first. M. Pascal had apparently forgotten that Jesus Christ, in the twenty-first chapter of St. Luke, says expressly: "And when ye shall see Jerusalem compassed with armies, then know that the desolation thereof is nigh. . . . Jerusalem shall be trodden down. . . . And there shall be signs in the sun, and in the moon, and in the stars . . . the sea and the waves roaring . . . for the powers of heaven shall be shaken. And then they shall see the Son of man coming in a cloud with power and great glory."

Haven't we here the second coming distinctly foretold? But if it has not yet happened, it is not for us to be so bold as to question Providence.

> XIV. The Messiah, according to carnal Jews, is to be a great temporal prince. According to carnal Christians, he came to dispense us from loving God, and to give us sacraments which will do everything without our help. Neither the one nor the other is the Christian religion or the Jewish.

This article is really a stroke of satire rather than a Christian reflection. One can see that it's the Jesuits he is aiming at here. But, truly, has any Jesuit ever said that Jesus Christ came to dispense us from loving God? The dispute over the love of God is purely a dispute over words, like most of the other learned quarrels that have caused such intense hatreds and such frightful woes.

Still another fault appears in this article. That is the supposition that awaiting a Messiah was a point of religion among the Jews. It was only a consoling idea spread among that nation. The Jews hoped for a Liberator. But they were not required to believe in one as an article of faith. Their whole religion was contained in the books of the law. The prophets have never been regarded by the Jews as legislators.

> XV. To examine the prophecies we must understand them. For if one believes that they have only one meaning it is certain that the Messiah has not come; but if they have two meanings, it is certain that he has come in Jesus Christ.

The Christian religion is so true that it has no need of dubious proofs. Now if anything could shake the foundations of that holy and reasonable religion, it is this opinion of M. Pascal. If you believe him, everything in Scripture has two meanings; but a man who had the misfortune to be incredulous might say to him: "He who gives two meanings to his words intends to deceive the world, and such duplicity is punishable by law. How can you unblushingly attribute to God what is punished and detested in men? In fact, only consider with what scorn and indignation you treat the oracles of the pagans, because they had two meanings! Couldn't one say rather that the prophecies directly concerned with Jesus Christ have only one meaning, as those of Daniel, Micah, and others? Couldn't one even say that if we knew nothing at all about the prophecies, religion would be none the less confirmed?"

XVI. The infinite distance between body and mind shadows forth the infinitely more infinite distance between mind and charity; for charity is supernatural.

One assumes that M. Pascal would not have let this galimatias stand in his work, if he had had the time to write it.

XVII. The most evident weaknesses are strength to those who understand these things. For example, the two genealogies in St. Matthew and St. Luke. It is clear that that was not the result of collaboration.

Ought the editors of Pascal's *Pensées* to have printed this thought, the mere exposure of which is perhaps capable of doing harm to religion? What is the good of saying that these genealogies, matters fundamental to the Christian religion, contradict each other, without also saying what it is they may agree on? The antidote should have been presented along with the poison. What would be thought of a lawyer who should say, "My client contradicts himself, but that weakness is a strength to those who understand these things"?

XVIII. May we then no longer be reproached for lack of clarity, since we profess it; but may the truth of religion be recognized in the very obscurity of religion, in the little light we have on it, and in our indifference toward knowing it.

Strange tokens of truth, these that Pascal brings forward!

What other tokens has falsehood? So in order to be believed all we have to say is, "I am obscure, I am unintelligible"! It would be a good deal more sensible to bring to our eyes only the light of faith, rather than this darkness of erudition.

XIX. If there were only one religion, God would be too manifest.

What! You say that if there were only one religion, God would be too manifest! Well! Are you forgetting that you say on every page that one day there will be only one religion? According to you, God will then be too manifest.

XX. I say that the Jewish religion consisted in none of those things, but only in the love of God, and that God condemned all the other things.

What! God condemned all that he himself had laid down to the Jews, with so much care and in such prodigious detail! Isn't it truer to say that the law of Moses consisted in both love and ritual? To reduce it all to the love of God smacks less of the love of God, perhaps, than of the hatred every Jansenist has for his Molinist neighbor.

XXI. There is nothing more important to life than the choice of a calling; chance decides it. Custom makes masons, soldiers, roofers.

What, after all, can lead to soldiers, masons, and all the kinds of manual laborers, except what we call chance and custom? Only in the arts of genius is the decision made by oneself. But in the kinds of work that everyone can do, it is most natural and most reasonable that custom should decide.

XXII. Let everyone examine his thoughts; he will find them always occupied with the past and the future. We hardly ever think of the present; and if we do, it is only to arrange the future by its light. The present is never our end; past and present are our means; the future alone is our object.

Far from complaining, we ought to thank the author of nature for giving us this instinct that ceaselessly carries us toward the future. The most precious treasure of man is that *hope* which allays our afflictions, and which paints future pleasures for us in our possession of present ones. If man were so unhappy as to be completely taken up with the present, we would not sow, we would not build, we would not plant, we would provide for nothing: we would lack everything in the midst of that false satisfaction. Could an intelligence like Pascal's espouse a commonplace as false as that one? Nature has settled it that every man enjoys the present in eating, producing children, listening to agreeable sounds, keeping busy his faculties of thinking and feeling; and that in coming out of these states—often in the middle of them, even—he thinks of tomorrow, for otherwise he would die of want today.

XXIII. But when I have looked closer, I have found that that aversion men have for repose, and to living with themselves, comes from a truly effective cause—that is, from the natural unhappiness of our weak and mortal condition, a condition so miserable that nothing can console us when nothing prevents us from thinking of it, and when we see only ourselves.

This phrase "see only ourselves" makes no sense. What sort of thing is a man who doesn't act and yet supposedly contemplates himself? I say not only that such a man would be an imbecile, useless to society, but that such a man cannot exist: for what would he contemplate? His body, his feet, his hands, his five senses? Either he would be an idiot or he would make some use of all that. Would he stop at contemplating his faculty for thought? But he can contemplate that faculty only by exercising it. Either he will think of nothing at all, or he will think of the ideas he has already had, or else he will compose new ones. Now he cannot get ideas except from the outside. So there he is, necessarily occupied either with his senses or with his ideas; there he is, outside himself—or an imbecile.

Once more, it is impossible for human nature to stay in that imaginary torpor; it is absurd to think it can; it is lunatic to maintain that it can. Man is born for action as the sparks fly upward and as stone is earthbound. Not to be doing anything is the same for man as not to exist. All the differences are between gentle and turbulent occupations, dangerous and beneficial ones.

> XXIV. Men have a secret instinct which impels them to seek for amusement and occupation outside themselves, an instinct that comes from their sense of endless misery; and they have another secret instinct, a remnant of the greatness of their original nature, which tells them that happiness is to be found only in quietude.

That secret instinct, being the first principle and the necessary foundation of society, comes rather from the goodness of God, and it is more the instrument of our happiness than a sense of our misery. I don't know what our first fathers did in the terrestrial paradise; but if each of them thought only of himself, the survival of the human race was certainly in peril. Isn't it absurd to think that they had perfect senses—that is, perfect instruments of action, for the unique purpose of contemplation? And isn't it amusing that thinking heads should imagine that indolence is a title of greatness, and action a lowering of our nature?

> XXV. That is why, when Cineas[3] said to Pyrrhus, who proposed to take his ease with his friends once he had conquered a large part of the world, that he would do better to bring his happiness closer by taking that ease now rather than taking so much trouble to get to it, he gave a sort of advice that ran into great difficulties, and was hardly more reasonable than the plan of the young man of ambition. Both of them supposed that man can be content with himself and his present goods, without filling the emptiness of his heart with imaginary hopes—which is false. Pyrrhus could not have been content either before or after conquering the world.

The example of Cineas is good enough in the satires of Boileau, but not in a book of philosophy. A wise king can be happy at home; and if Pyrrhus is presented to us as a fool, that means nothing where the rest of mankind are concerned.

> XXVI. We must realise that man is so wretched that he would grow bored even without the remotest cause of boredom, from the peculiar nature of his condition.

On the contrary, man is most happy in this regard, and we are most obliged to the author of nature for having

[3]See Boileau, *"Epitre au Roi"* and Plutarch "Pyrrhus."

attached boredom to inaction, so as to force us to be useful to our neighbor and to ourselves.

XXVII. How does it happen that this man who recently lost his only son and who, crushed with lawsuits and quarrels, was so full of trouble this morning, has now forgotten it all? Don't be surprised: he is busy guessing where a stag will pass, that his dogs have been ardently pursuing for six hours. That is all man needs, however full of grief he may be. If one can persuade him to take part in some sort of diversion, he will be happy for as long as he does so.

That man is doing wonderfully well. Dissipation is a surer remedy for pain than quinine for fever. Let's not blame nature, which is always ready to come to our aid.

XXVIII. Imagine a number of men in chains, and all condemned to death, where some of them being every day slaughtered in the sight of the others, those who remain see their own state in that of their fellows, and looking upon one another sorrowfully and without hope, wait their turn. This is a picture of the condition of man.

This comparison is surely not a just one. Chained wretches who are butchered one after the other are wretched not only because they suffer, but because they undergo what other men are spared. It is not naturally a man's lot to be either chained or butchered; but all men are made, like animals and plants, to grow, to live a certain length of time, to reproduce their kind, and to die. In a satire you can emphasize the bad side of man as much as you please, but the moment you look at the thing reasonably you must admit that of all the animals man is the most perfect, the most happy, and the one that lives longest. Instead, then, of being surprised and grieved at the unhappiness and brevity of our life, we ought to be surprised and pleased at our happiness and how long we live. To argue merely as a philosopher, I dare say there is a good deal of pride and temerity in maintaining that we ought by nature to be better off than we are.

> XXIX. Among the pagans, the wise men who said there was only one God were persecuted, the Jews hated, and the Christians even more so.

They were sometimes persecuted, just as a man would be today who came to teach us to worship a God independently of the accepted cult. Socrates was not condemned for having said, "There is only one God," but for having set himself against the country's outward forms of worship, and for having most inopportunely made some powerful enemies. As for the Jews, they were hated not because they believed in only one God but because they had a ridiculous hatred of other nations, because they were barbarians who pitilessly massacred their conquered enemies, because this base people, superstitious, ignorant, cut off from the arts, cut off from commerce, despised the peoples that were most civilized. As for the Christians, they were hated by the pagans because they tended to overthrow both religion and empire—which they finally succeeded in doing, as the Protestants made themselves masters of the same countries wherein they had long been hated, persecuted, and massacred.

> XXX. The faults of Montaigne are great. He is full of dirt and impropriety. That kind of thing is

worthless. His opinions on self-destruction and on death are horrible.

Montaigne speaks as a philosopher, not as a Christian: he gives the pros and cons of self-destruction. Speaking philosophically, what harm does a man do to society who departs from it when he can no longer serve it? An old man has the stone and suffers intolerable pain. He is told, "If you don't have yourself cut, you are going to die; if you are cut, you will be able to continue your dotage, to dribble, and shuffle along for a year, a burden to yourself and to others." I suppose the old fellow would choose to be no longer a burden to anybody. This is pretty much the kind of circumstance Montaigne is talking about.

XXXI. How many stars have telescopes revealed to us that did not exist for our philosophers of old! We used to boldly attack the Scriptures on what is said there in so many passages about the great number of stars. "There are only a thousand and twenty-two," we said. "We know it."

It is certain that Holy Scripture, in questions of natural philosophy, always adjusted itself to the prevailing opinion; thus it assumes that the earth is immobile, that the sun moves, etc. It is by no means from any astronomical subtlety that it says the stars are innumerable, but to be in agreement with the ideas of ordinary people. As a matter of fact, though our eyes can discern only about a thousand and twenty-two stars, nevertheless when we stare fixedly at the sky, dazzled, we think we see an infinity of them. Scripture, then, speaks in accordance with this vulgar prejudice, for Scripture has not been given us in order to make physicists of us; and there is every indication that God did not reveal either to Habakkuk or to Baruch or to Micah that one day an Englishman named Flamsteed would put in his catalogue more than seven thousand stars seen through the telescope.

> XXXII. Is it courage in a dying man, in all his weakness and agony, to affront an all-powerful and eternal God?

That has never happened; and only in a violent fit of delirium could a man say, "I believe in a God, and I defy him."

> XXXIII. I willingly believe the histories whose witnesses get themselves killed.

The difficulty is not only to know whether one is to believe witnesses who die to support their testimony, as so many fanatics have done, but whether these witnesses have in actual fact died for that reason; whether their testimonies have been preserved; whether they lived in the countries where it is said they died. Why did Josephus, born at the time of the death of Christ; Josephus, enemy of Herod; Josephus, not much attached to Judaism—why did he not say a word about all that? There is something that M. Pascal would have successfully unraveled, as so many eloquent writers have done since.

> XXXIV. The sciences have two extremes which meet. The first is the pure natural ignorance that all men are born in; the other extreme is that which great souls arrive at, who, having run through all that men can know, find that they know nothing, and meet in that ignorance from which they first set forth.

This thought is a pure sophism, and its falseness consists in the word *ignorance* which he uses in two different senses. One who can neither read nor write is an ignorant person; but a mathematician, because he is ignorant of the principles hidden in nature, is not at the same point of ignorance from which he departed when he began to learn to read. Mr. Newton did not know why a man's arm moves when he wants it to, but he was not for that reason less learned about other things. One who does not know Hebrew, and who does know Latin, is learned in comparison with one who only knows French.

> XXXV. It is not happiness to be able to find delight in diversion, for the latter comes from elsewhere and from outside; and thus it is dependent, and consequently subject to be disturbed by a thousand accidents that bring inevitable sorrows.

That man is at present happy who is experiencing pleasure, and that pleasure can only come from outside. We cannot have either sensations or ideas except through external objects, as we cannot nourish our body except by introducing into it foreign substances that change into our own.

> XXXVI. Extreme intelligence is accused of madness, like the extreme want of it. Nothing is thought good but mediocrity.

It is not extreme intelligence but extreme vivacity and copiousness of mind that is accused of madness. Extreme intelligence is extreme exactness, extreme subtlety, extreme scope—diametrically opposed to madness.

Extreme *want of intelligence* is a deficiency in apprehension, an emptiness of ideas; this is not madness, it is stupidity. Madness is a derangement of the organs, which shows a number of objects too fast, or which holds the imagination on a single one with too much concentration and violence.

Nor is it mediocrity that is thought good, but the keeping away from the two opposite vices; it is what is called *the happy medium,* and not *mediocrity.*

XXXVII. If our condition were truly a happy one, it would not be necessary to divert ourselves from the thought of it.

Our condition is precisely to think about external objects, with which we have a necessary connection. It is false that one can divert a man from thinking about the human condition; for, to whatever he applies his mind, he applies it to something necessarily bound up with the human condition. And once again, to think about oneself abstracted from natural objects is to think of nothing whatever. One had best consider that carefully.

Far from preventing a man from thinking of his condition, one never converses with him about anything but the delights of that condition. One talks to a learned man about fame and learning; to a prince, about what is related to his greatness; to every man one talks of pleasure.

XXXVIII. The great and the humble have the same troubles, the same quarrels, and the same passions. But one group are at the top of the wheel, and the other close to the center—and thus less disturbed by the same movements.

It is false that the humble are less disturbed than the great; on the contrary, their despair is more acute because they have fewer resources. Of a hundred Londoners who kill themselves, there are ninety-nine from the lower classes, and scarcely one of high station. The comparison of the wheel is ingenious and false.

XXXIX. Men are not taught to be upright men, and are taught everything else; yet they pride themselves on nothing so much as that. So they pride themselves only on knowing the one thing they have not learned.

Men are taught to be upright men, and, if they were not, few would manage to be. Let your son, in his childhood, take everything he finds within his grasp, and at fifteen he will be a highwayman. Praise him for having told a lie, and he will become a false witness. Pamper his concupiscence, and he will surely be a libertine. Everything is taught to men—virtue, religion.

XL. What a stupid project Montaigne had of painting his own portrait! And this not in passing, and against his maxims, since everyone makes mistakes, but by means of his maxims themselves, and by his first and main purpose. For to say silly things by chance and through weakness is an ordinary failing, but to say them by design—and the kinds of things he says—it's that that is intolerable.

What a charming project Montaigne had of painting his portrait, artlessly, as he has done! For he has painted a picture of human nature. And what a paltry project, that of Nicole, of Malebranche, of Pascal, to decry Montaigne!

XLI. When I have considered how it is that one puts so much faith in so many impostors who say they have remedies, to the point that one often puts one's life in their hands, it has seemed to me that the true reason is that there are real remedies. For it could hardly be possible there should be so many false ones, and that so much faith should be placed in them, if there were no real ones. If there never had been any, and all evils had been incurable, it is impossible that men should have imagined they could give remedies, and even more so that so many others could have put faith in those who boasted they had such remedies. Just as if a man boasted he could keep people from dying, nobody would believe him, because there is no example of such a thing. But, since there have been numbers of remedies that have been verified by the actual knowledge of the greatest men, men's belief has been won over, for since the thing cannot be denied in general (there being particular results which are true), the people, unable to distinguish which among these particular effects are the same ones, believe them all. In the same way, the reason why people believe in so many lunar influences that are untrue is that there are true ones, like the ebb and flow of the sea.

So it also seems clear to me that there are so many false miracles, false revelations, sorceries, only because there are true ones.

It strikes me that human nature can stumble into falsity without the help of truth. A thousand false influences were imputed to the moon before anyone imagined the slightest veritable relationship between it and the tides of the sea. The first man who was ever ill believed, without any difficulty, in the first charlatan. Nobody has seen any werewolves or wizards, and many people have believed in them. Nobody has seen any transmutation of metals, and a number have been ruined by believing in the philosopher's stone. Did the Romans, the Greeks, all the pagans believe in the false miracles with which they were inundated only because they had seen true ones?

XLII. The harbor guides those who are in a ship, but where shall we find this fixed point in morality?

In that single maxim accepted by all nations: "Do not do to others what you would not like to have done to you."

XLIII. *Ferox gens nullam esse vitam sine armis putat.*[4] They prefer death to peace; the others prefer death to war. Any opinion can be preferred to life, the love of which seems so strong and so natural.

It was of the Catalans that Tacitus said that; but there is no nation of whom it has been said, or could be said, "It prefers death to war."

XLIV. The more intellect one has, the more original men one finds. Ordinary people see no difference between men.

There are very few truly original men. Almost all behave, think, and feel according to the influence of custom and education. Nothing is so rare as a mind that strikes out on a new path. But of that crowd of men who walk together, each has little differences in bearing that fine eyes can perceive.

XLV. There are then two kinds of mind: the one

---

[4] *Rati* rather than *putat.* "A savage nation who count life worthless without arms." —Livy, XXXIV, xvii.

penetrates acutely and profoundly into the conclusions from premises, and that is the exact mind; the other comprehends a great number of premises without confusing them, and that is the geometrical mind.

Present usage, I believe, calls the methodical and logical mind the geometrical one.

XLVI. Death is easier to bear without thinking of it than the thought of death without danger.

One cannot say that a man bears death easily or uneasily, if he does not think of it at all. Whoever feels nothing bears nothing.

XLVII. We suppose that all men conceive the objects they meet, and are sensible of them, in the same way; but we suppose this quite gratuitously, for we have no proof of it. I do see that we apply the same words to the same occasions, and that every time two men see snow, for example, they both express their sight of this same object by means of the same words, both saying that it is white; and from this conformity of application we draw a powerful conjecture of conformity of idea. But it is not absolutely convincing, though there are grounds for betting on the affirmative.

It was not the color white that should have been brought forth as proof. White, which is a combination of all rays, appears bright to everybody, dazzles a bit in the long run, has the same effect on all eyes. But one might say that perhaps the other colors are not perceived by all eyes in the same way.

XLVIII. All our reasoning reduces to this: the surrender to feeling.

Our reasoning reduces to the surrender to feeling in matters of taste, not in matters of science.

XLIX. Those who judge a work by rule are to the rest as those who have a watch are to those who have not. The one says, "We have been here for two hours"; the other says, "Only three quarters of an hour." I look at my watch; I say to the one, "You are bored," and to the other, "Time flies for you."

In works of taste, in music, in poetry, in painting, taste takes the place of the watch, and he who judges them only by rules, judges badly.

L. Caesar was too old, I think, to set out to amuse himself by conquering the world. Such an amusement was good enough for Alexander; he was a young man difficult to stop. But Caesar should have been more mature.

People generally suppose that Alexander and Caesar left home with the purpose of conquering the world. That isn't the way it was. Alexander succeeded Philip in the generalship of Greece, and was charged with the just undertaking of avenging the injuries inflicted on the Greeks by the king of Persia. He beat the common enemy and pushed his conquests as far as India because the realm of Darius extended to India—just as the Duke of Marlborough would have come as far as Lyons, if it had not been for Marshal de Villars.

As for Caesar, he was one of the leaders of the republic.

He quarreled with Pompey, as the Jansenists with the Molinists; and then it was a question of which one would exterminate himself. A single battle, in which not ten thousand men were killed, decided the whole thing.

For the rest, M. Pascal's *pensée is* perhaps false in every sense. It took maturity in Caesar to disentangle himself from so many plots; and it is astonishing that Alexander, at his age, should have renounced pleasure to pursue so painful a war.

> LI. It is an amusing thing to consider that there are people in the world who, after renouncing all the laws of God and nature, have made new ones for themselves which they obey to the letter, as, for example, thieves, etc.

That is even more useful than amusing to consider, for it proves that no society of men can subsist for a single day without rules.

> LII. Man is neither an angel nor a beast; and as ill-luck will have it, whoever tries to play the angel plays the beast.

Whoever tries to destroy the passions, instead of regulating them, tries to play the angel.

> LIII. A horse does not try to be admired by its companions. One sees among them some sort of rivalry in running, but it is of no consequence; for, once in the stable, the one who is heaviest and least well set up does not because of this give up his oats to another. It is different among men. Their virtue seems to them not enough in itself, and they are not satisfied if it gives them no advantage over others.

Neither does the least well set up man give up his bread to his betters, but the strongest takes it away from the weakest; and among animals and men the big ones eat up the little ones.

LIV. If man began by studying himself, he would see how incapable he is of going beyond himself. How could a part comprehend the whole? He will hope perhaps to know at least the parts to which he bears some proportion. But the parts of the world are all so closely connected and linked one with another that I believe it impossible to know one without the other and without the whole.

Man should not be turned aside from his search for what is useful to him through any consideration that he is unable to know everything.

Non possis oculo quantum contendere Lynceus, Non tamen idcirco contemnas lippus inungi.[5]

We know many truths; we have made many useful inventions. Let us console ourselves for not knowing the possible connections between a spider and the rings of Saturn, and continue to examine what is within our reach.

LV. If lightning fell on low places, the poets and those who only know how to reason about things of that sort would lack proofs.

A comparison is not a proof either in poetry or in prose: in poetry it serves as embellishment, and in prose it

---

[5]"Though your eyes may not be as far-seeing as those of Lynceus, you do not scorn to anoint them when they are sore." Horace, *Epistles* I. 1, 28.

serves to clarify things and make them more palpable. The poets who have compared the misfortunes of the great with lightning striking mountains, would make comparisons to the contrary if the contrary happened.

> LVI. It is that compound of body and of spirit which has caused almost all philosophers to mix up the ideas of things, and attribute to body what belongs only to the spirit, and to spirit what is only consonant with body.

If we knew what spirit is, we could complain that philosophers have attributed to it what does not belong to it. But we do not know what either spirit or body is. We haven't the slightest conception of the one, and we have only very imperfect ideas of the other. Thus we cannot know the limits of either.

> LVII. As we say *poetical beauty,* so we ought also to say *geometrical beauty* and *medical beauty.* But we do not; and the reason is that we know very well what the purpose of geometry is, and what the purpose of medicine, but we do not know in what consists the pleasure which is the purpose of poetry. We do not know what that natural model is that we are to imitate; and, lacking that knowledge, we have invented certain bizarre terms: *golden age, marvel of our day, fatal laurel, fair luminary,* etc.; and we call this jargon poetical beauty. But whoever can imagine a woman dressed after this model, will see a pretty maiden covered with mirrors and chains of brass.

This is all wrong. We should not speak of *geometrical* or *medical beauty* because a theorem and a purge do not affect the senses agreeably, and because we give the name of *beauty* only to the things that charm the senses, like music, painting, eloquence, poetry, fine architecture, etc.

The reason M. Pascal adduces is just as false. We know very well in what the object of poetry consists: it consists in depicting with force, clarity, delicacy, and harmony. Poetry is harmonious eloquence. M. Pascal must have had very little taste to be able to say that *fatal laurel, fair luminary,* and other such nonsense are poetical beauties; and the editors of these *Pensées* must have been persons very little versed in literature to have printed a reflection so unworthy of its illustrious author.

I do not send you my other remarks on the *Pensées* of M. Pascal; they would drag out the discussion too long. It is enough to have thought to find certain errors of inattention in this great genius. It is consoling to so limited an intelligence as mine to be convinced that the greatest men can be wrong like the common herd.

NOTE ON THE TEXT

The text used as the basis for this translation is that of Jore (Rouen, 1734), as established by Gustave Lanson in his critical edition of the *Lettres Philosophiques* (Paris, 1909). The translator has also consulted with great profit the editions of Raymond Naves (in the *Classiques Garnier*), Henri Labroue (Paris, 1910) and F. A. Taylor (Oxford: Blackwell, 1958). The footnotes, without exception, are those of the translator and for this reason have not been bracketed.

Because the text which Voltaire used for his references in the letter on the *Pensées* of Pascal is very different from the text which is consulted today, we reprint, for convenience of reference, the table included in Naves' notes to Letter XXV, "On the *Pensées* of M. Pascal."

Pensée I: Brunschvicg, fragment 430.

II:	430	XV:	642	XXVIII:	199
III:	434	XVI:	793	XXIX:	556
IV:	430 and 47	XVII:	578	XXX:	63
V:	233	XVIII:	565	XXXI:	266
VI:	646[1]	XIX:	585	XXXII:	209
VII:	619	XX:	610	XXXIII:	593
VIII:	620	XXI:	97	XXXIV:	327
IX:	631 and 630	XXII:	172	XXXV:	170
X:	479	XXIII:	139	XXXVI:	378
XI:	477	XXIV:	139	XXXVII:	165
XII:	571	XXV:	139	XXXVIII:	180
XIII:	757	XXVI:	139	XXXIX:	68
XIV:	607	XXVII:	139	XL:	62

[1] I have not been able to verify or correct Brunschvicg references 646 and 209.

XLI:	817	XLVII:	392	LIII:	401
XLII:	383	XLVIII:	274	LIV:	72
XLIII:	156	XLIX:	5	LV:	39
XLIV:	7	L:	132	LVI:	72
XLV:	2	LI:	393	LVII:	33
XLVI:	166	LII:	358		

SELECTED BIBLIOGRAPHY

EDITIONS OF VOLTAIRE'S WORKS

Oeuvres complètes de Voltaire. Edited by A. Beuchot. 72 vols. Paris, 1828.

Oeuvres complètes de Voltaire. Edited by Louis Emile Dieudonné Moland. 52 vols. Paris: French and European Publications, Inc., 1877–85.

Oeuvres complètes de Voltaire/Complete Works of Voltaire. Edited by Theodore Besterman. Geneva: Institut et Musée Voltaire; Toronto: University of Toronto Press, 1968.

Candide. A critical edition by André Morize. Paris: Institut de Literature Française, 1957.

Candide: Ou L'optimisme. Vol. 48 of *The Complete Works of Voltaire/Ouevres complètes de Voltaire*, a critical edition by René Pomeau; revised edition, Paris: Nizet, 1980.

Candide: Ou, L'optimisme. Edition by André Magnan. Paris: PUF, 1987.

Lettres Philosophiques. Edited by Gustave Lanson. 2 vols. Paris: Hachette, 1930.

Lettres Philosophiques. Edited by F. A. Taylor. Oxford: Blackwell, 1943; rev. ed. 1953.

Lettres Philosophiques. Edited by Raymond Naves. Paris: Garnier, 1962.

COLLATERAL READING

Ayer, A. J. *Voltaire*. New York: Random House, 1986.

Ballantyne, Archibald. *Voltaire's Visit to England (1726–1729)*, Geneva: Slatkine Reprints, 1970. Reprint of London edition, 1893.

de Beer, Gavin. "Voltaire's British Visitors," in *Studies on Voltaire and the Eighteenth Century IV* (1957), 7–136.

Besterman, Theodore (ed.). *Voltaire's Correspondence*. 107 vols. Geneva: Institut et Musée Voltaire, 1953–1965.

―――. *Voltaire's Notebooks*. 2 vols. Geneva: Institut et Musée Voltaire, 1952.

―――. *Correspondence and Related Documents*. Volumes 85–135 of *Oeuvres complètes/Complete Works*, 1968–1977.

―――. *Notebooks*. Volumes 81–82 of *Oeuvres complètes/Complete Works*, 1968.

―――. *Voltaire*. New York: Harcourt, Brace and World, Inc., 1969. 3rd rev. ed., Oxford: Basil Blackwell, 1976.

Brailsford, Henri N. *Voltaire*. London: Oxford University Press, 1963.

Cassirer, Ernst. *The Philosophy of the Enlightenment*. Princeton: Princeton University Press, 1951.

Cherpack, Clifton. "Positivism, Piety, and the Study of Voltaire's Philosophical Tales." *The Eighteenth Century: Theory and Interpretation*, 24 (1983), 23–27.

Collins, J. Churton. *Voltaire, Montesquieu and Rousseau in England*. London, 1908.

Dahany, Michael. "The Nature of Narrative Forms in Candide." *Studies on Voltaire and the Eighteenth Century*, 114 (1973), 113–140.

Dalnekoff, Donna Isaacs. "The Meaning of Eldorado:

Utopia and Satire in Candide." *Studies on Voltaire and the Eighteenth Century*, 123 (1974), 41–59.

Fletcher, Dennis. "Candide and the Philosophy of the Garden." *Trivium*, 13 (May 1978), 18–30.

———. "Candide and the Theme of the Happy Husbandman." *Studies on Voltaire and the Eighteenth Century*, 161 (1976), 137–147.

Havens, George R. "Voltaire's Marginal Comments upon Pope's *Essay on Man*." *Modern Language Notes*, XLIII (1928), 429–439.

———. "Voltaire and Alexander Pope," *Essays on Voltaire and the Enlightenment in Honor of Otis Fellows*. Geneva: Droz, 1974, 124–150.

Henry, Patrick. "Sacred and Profane Gardens in Candide." *Studies on Voltaire and the Eighteenth Century*, 176 (1979), 133–152.

Ilie, Paul. "The Voices in Candide's Garden." *Studies on Voltaire and the Eighteenth Century*, 148 (1975), 37–113.

Langdon, David J. "Modesty and Pretension in Candide." Dalhousie French Studies, 14 (1988), 15–31.

Lanson, Gustave. *Voltaire*. 2 vols. Paris: Hachette, 1964; English translation by Robert A. Waggoner. New York: Wiley, 1966.

Lounsbury, Thomas R. *Shakespeare and Voltaire*. New York: B. Blom, 1968.

Murray, Geoffrey. "Voltaire's Candide: The Protean Gardener, 1755–62. Special issue of *Studies on Voltaire and the Eighteenth Century*, 69 (1970), 1–386.

Schilling, Bernard N. *Conservative England and the Case Against Voltaire.* (1950). Hippocrene Books, Inc., 1972.

Stephen, Leslie. *History of English Thought in the Eighteenth Century.* 2 vols. London: 3rd ed., 1902.

———. *English Literature and Society in the Eighteenth Century.* Reprint Services Corporation, 1992. Reprint of the 1931 edition.

Strachey, Lytton. "Voltaire and England," in *Books and Characters.* New York: Harcourt Brace, 1922, 107–135.

Torrey, Norman L. "Bolingbroke and Voltaire, a Fictitious Influence," *P.M.L.A.,* XLII (1927), 788–797.

———. "Voltaire's English Notebook," *Modern Philology,* XXVI (1928), 307–325

———. *Voltaire and the English Deists.* New Haven: Yale University Press, 1930. Reprinted by Archon Books, 1967.

———. *The Spirit of Voltaire.* New York: Columbia University Press, 1938.

Vartanian, Aram. *Diderot and Descartes: A Study of Scientific Naturalism in the Enlightenment.* Westport, Conn.: Greenwood Press, 1975.

Wade, Ira O. *Voltaire and Candide: A Study in the Fusion of History, Art and Philosophy.* Princeton: Princeton University Press, 1959.

Waldinger, Renee (ed.). *Approaches to Teaching Voltaire's Candide.* New York: Modern Language Association of America, 1987.

APPENDIX

It is particularly interesting to know what the author of *Candide* (1759) thought of Pope's *Essay on Man* (1733-34), which came out too late to be mentioned in the *Philosophical Letters* as originally written. With an admiration of Pope which, however qualified, he never forswears, he writes on February 12, 1736, to Pierre Joseph Thoulier d'Olivet:

> Have you a translation of Pope's *Essay on Man*? It is a beautiful poem in English—though with ideas running through it that are quite false—on happiness.[1]

For the 1756 edition of his works, Voltaire changed the end of Letter XXII, after "Mollesse in *le Lutrin*," to read as follows.

> The *Essay on Man* of Pope seems to me the most beautiful, most useful, most sublime didactic poem ever written in any language. It is true that the whole groundwork of it is to be found in Lord Shaftesbury's *Characteristics*, and I do not know why Mr. Pope gives the honor solely to Lord Bolingbroke, without saying a word about Shaftesbury, the pupil of Locke.
>
> Everything related to metaphysics has been thought in all periods and among all peoples who cultivate the mind, and this system much resembles that of Leibniz, which maintains that, of all possible worlds, God must have chosen the best, and that in this best it was necessary that the irregularities of our globe and the stupidities of its inhabitants should have their place. It also resembles that idea of Plato's that in the infinite chain of beings, our earth, our body, our soul are among the necessary links. But neither Leibniz nor Pope allows of the changes that Plato imagines to have happened to

[1]Number 978 of Besterman's edition of the letters.

these links, to our souls and our bodies. Plato spoke as a poet in his not very intelligible prose, and Pope speaks as a philosopher in his admirable verses. He says that everything has been from the beginning as it has had to be, and as it is.

I have been flattered, I confess, to see that he agrees with me in something I said some years ago: "You are surprised that God should have made man so limited, so ignorant, so unhappy. Why are you not surprised that he didn't make him more limited, more ignorant, and more unhappy?"[2] When a Frenchman and an Englishman think the same, they must certainly be right.

The son of the famous Racine has printed a letter from Pope, addressed to him, in which Pope recants. That letter is written in the tone and style of M. de Fénelon. It was brought to him, he says, by Ramsay,[3] the editor of Télémaque; Ramsay the imitator of Télémaque, as Boyer[4] was of Corneille; Ramsay the Scot, who wanted to belong to the Académie Française; Ramsay, who regretted not being a doctor of the Sorbonne. But one thing I know, along with all the men of letters in England, is that Pope, with whom I have spent much time, could hardly read French; that he didn't speak a word of our language; that he never wrote a letter in French; that he was incapable of it: and that, if he did write this letter to the son of our Racine, it must have been that toward the end of his life God suddenly gave him the gift of tongues, as recompense for so admirable a work as his *Essay on Man*.[5]

[2]See section XXVIII, Letter XXV.

[3]Andrew Michael Ramsay (1686–1743), "the Chevalier de Ramsay," knight of the order of St. Lazarus. His imitation of his friend Fénelon's *Télémaque* is *Les Voyages de Cyrus, avec un Discours sur la Mythologie des Payens* (Paris, 1727). It was translated into English and reprinted with additions for nearly a century.

[4]Abbé Claude Boyer (1618–98), author of many plays and member of the academy.

[5]The original MS of the letter, written in English, was found in our own time, by Professor Emile Audra, in the Bibliothèque Nationale.

Pope, he says in the "Poem on Natural Law" (c. 1751; pub. 1756), "carried the torch into the abyss of being, and man with his aid alone began to know himself." In the preface to his poem (published at the same time) on the Lisbon Disaster, the earthquake that on the first of November, 1755, had caused the death of some thirty thousand persons, Voltaire assures us that the theological objections made against the *Essay on Man* have not harmed it in the least; then he says,

> The author of the poem on the "Lisbon Disaster" does not combat the illustrious Pope, whom he has always admired and loved: he thinks like him on almost all points; but, profoundly conscious of the woes of mankind, he rises up against the abuse that is currently made of the ancient axiom *All is well*. He adopts that sad and more ancient truth, recognized by all men, that *there is evil on the earth*; he avows that the phrase *All is well*, taken in an absolute sense and without hope of a future, is nothing but an insult to the sorrows of our life.

When you announce that "All is well," he tells us in this poem on the earthquake, the universe gives you the lie, and your heart refutes your mind a hundred times over. All things are at war, and the innocent, as well as the guilty, undergo inevitable evil in this universe of eternal disorder. God is either a father indiscriminately punishing his children, all of whom are born guilty of original sin, or else he is a serenely indifferent First Cause. The truth of the matter can come to us only through revelation—and certainty about revelation is a cause of persecution and war. Though his poem is alive with pity and indignation at the condition of man, Voltaire says at the end that he does not rise up against Providence: he knows how to suffer but not how to complain. He also knows he had better be careful what he says.

He is still full of the subject in a letter written to Elie Bertrand on February 18, 1756:

> Evil is on the earth, and I should be mocking myself to say that a thousand unhappy people make for happiness. Yes, there is evil, and few men would care to begin their careers over again, perhaps not one in a hundred thousand. And when I am told that it all couldn't be otherwise, reason is outraged and so are my own afflictions. A workman with bad materials and bad instruments can quite understandably explain that he "couldn't do it any other way." But my poor Pope, my poor hunchback, whom I have known, whom I have loved—who told you that God could not have made you without a hump? You smile at the apple story. Yet humanly speaking, and putting the sacred aside, it is more reasonable than the optimism of Leibniz: it explains why you are a hunchback, ill, and a little malicious.
>
> We need a god who speaks to the human race. Optimism leads to despair. It is a cruel philosophy under a consoling name. Alas! if all is well when all is in pain, we shall be able to go on to a thousand worlds, where we shall suffer, and where all will be well. We shall go from misfortune to misfortune, looking for a better state. And if *all is well*, how do the Leibnizians make room for something better? This *better*—isn't it a proof that all is not well? And then—who doesn't know that Leibniz had no expectation of anything better. Just between us, my dear sir, all of them—Leibniz and Shaftesbury and Bolingbroke and Pope—were only trying to be clever. As for me, I suffer and I say so.[6]

On November 4, 1758, he writes in English to George Keith, the tenth Earl Marischal,

[6]Besterman 6066.

This present war is the most hellish that was ever fought. Y^r lordship saw formerly one battle a year at the most. But nowadays the earth is cover'd with blood and mangled carcasses, almost every month. Let the happy madmen who say that all what is, is well, be confounded. T'is not so indeed with twenty provinces exhausted and with three hundred thousand men murdered.[7]

Then comes *Candide,* and after it his long fever of rage against philosophical optimism subsides, for as Charles Philip Theodore of Sulzbach, the Elector Palatine, remarks to Voltaire on February 23, 1759,

Optimism has long since been banished from our globe, and if Pope were still living I doubt that he would maintain, seeing all that has happened in the last few years, that "all what is, is right."[8]

[7]Besterman 7220.

[8]Besterman 7422. The quotation marks are mine: these words are in English.

A NOTE ON THE TYPE

The principal text of this Modern Library edition
was composed in a digitized version of
Horley Old Style, a typeface issued by
the English type foundry Monotype in 1925.
It has such distinctive features
as lightly cupped serifs and an oblique horizontal bar
on the lowercase "e."